Varieties of English

By the same author

Selected Readings in English Literature and Thought
Literary Appreciation

Varieties of English

Practice in advanced uses of English

What I do is me: for that I came
G. M. HOPKINS

H. L. B. MOODY

LONGMAN

LONGMAN GROUP LIMITED
London

*Associated companies, branches and representatives
throughout the world*

*First Published *1970
New impression *1971; *1972; *1973; *1974; *1975*

ISBN 0 582 52601 9

*Photoset in Malta by St Paul's Press Ltd
Printed in Hong Kong by
Yu Luen Offset Printing Factory Ltd*

Contents

Foreword

The purpose of this book is to provide a collection of material for the study and practice of the English language in educational establishments of many kinds but all at the stage somewhere between the end of 'secondary' and the beginning of 'tertiary' or 'higher' education.

As this book appears at the beginning of the eighth decade of the twentieth century, all who use it will be aware that many developments have been taking place both in the understanding of language as a characteristic product of human culture and in the processes involved in language learning. We have attempted to take full note of all significant recent developments without sacrificing the values and merits of some earlier techniques of study. Much of the ferment in the field of language teaching in recent years has been centred upon the earlier stages; but it was for example significantly recorded at a conference of teachers of English Language held in London at the end of 1967: 'Perhaps we were in danger of not giving enough training for the higher levels of language learning'.

This book, which was planned some time before the conference expressed that opinion, is an attempt to provide for that very need, and may be useful not only in the sixth forms of secondary schools, but in teacher training colleges, and in various types of introductory language courses in universities.

Acknowledgements

We are grateful to the following for permission to reproduce copyright material.

George Allen & Unwin Ltd and Harcourt, Brace & World Inc. for an extract from *Language in Thought and Action* by S. I. Hayakawa (second edition), © 1964 by Harcourt, Brace & World Inc.; Edward Arnold (Publishers) Ltd and Harcourt, Brace & World Inc. for an extract from *A Passage to India* by E. M. Forster, Copyright 1924 by Harcourt, Brace & World, Copyright 1954 by E. M. Forster, and an extract from *The Hill of Devi* by E. M. Forster, Copyright 1953 by E. M. Forster; The Athlone Press of the University of London for an extract from *Rethinking Anthropology* by E. R. Leach; Beaverbrook Newspapers Ltd for an extract from 'Siamese Twins' from the *Daily Express* issue dated 17 August 1968; Mr Quentin Bell, and Chatto & Windus Ltd for an extract from *Civilization* by Clive Bell; Blackie & Son Ltd for an extract 'Solids' from *A Structural Introduction to Chemistry* by E. T. Harris; The Bodley Head and Random House Inc. for an extract from *Ulysses* by James Joyce, Copyright 1914, 1918 by Margaret Caroline Anderson and renewed 1942, 1946 by Nora Joseph Joyce; Jonathan Cape Ltd and Charles Scribner's Sons for an extract from *Cry, the Beloved Country* by Alan Paton, Copyright 1948 by Alan Paton; Jonathan Cape Ltd, The Society of Authors as the literary representative of the Estate of James Joyce, and The Viking Press Inc. for an extract from *A Portrait of the Artist as a Young Man* by James Joyce, Copyright 1916 by B. W. Huebsch, renewed 1944 by Nora Joyce; Cassell & Co. Ltd and Houghton Mifflin Co. Inc. for an extract from *The Second World War* by Sir Winston Churchill; Chatto & Windus Ltd for an extract from *Four Guineas* by Elspeth Huxley; The Clarendon Press, Oxford for extracts from *The Renaissance* by Edith Sichel 1914, *English History 1914–45* by A. J. P. Taylor 1965, and *Doubt and Certainty in Science* by J. Z.

& World Inc. for an extract from *To The Lighthouse* by Virginia Woolf, Copyright 1927 by Harcourt, Brace & World Inc., renewed 1955 by Leonard Woolf; the World Publishing Company for an extract from an essay on 'The English Language' by Harold Whitehall as it appears in *Webster's New World Dictionary*, College Edition, and an extract from *Primitive Art* by Paul S. Wingert, A Meridian Book, Copyright © 1962 by Paul S. Wingert.

We have been unable to trace the copyright holders of the following items and would appreciate any information that would enable us to do so. An extract from *Africa Treasury* by Langston Hughes, an extract from *Amharic Love Song* (Black Orpheus), and an extract from the *Nigerian Report on Secondary Education*.

We would also like to thank the following for permission to reproduce the illustrations:

Abbey Life Assurance Company Limited and Hambros Bank Limited for page 179; Air India for page 177; The British Van Heusen Company Limited for page 176; Esso Petroleum Company Limited for page 26; Robert Ireson for page 153, first reproduced in *The Penguin Car Handbook*; The National Trust for page 41, photograph by Charles Woolf; Nigeria Magazine for page 42; William Papas for page 99, first reproduced in *The Guardian*; *The Sunday Times* for page 26.

Introduction

A SURVEY OF BASIC PRINCIPLES

What *is* English? There may at first seem little need to ask this question. All students will have experience of 'English', as a subject in the curriculum, as a series of appointments in the timetable, with either more or less happy associations. If we face the question more rigorously – What is *English?* – we can only answer that 'English' is a language. An adjective serving as a noun, it refers to the English language, that language which over some 500 years has been evolved by the inhabitants of part of that small island off the west coast of Europe known as England, working in unplanned collaboration with those who have come to it from elsewhere, and with those who have gone out from it to other parts of the world taking the language along with them. Now in fact the inhabitants of England, even including other groups which constitute the United Kingdom, are only a minority of those peoples throughout the world who depend on 'English' as their principal, or at least a very important second language.

'English', therefore, is a *language*. What do we mean by that? It is no part of the plan of this book to be theoretical, abstract, or purely analytical. We shall hope, as Wordsworth said in 1798, 'to keep our readers at all times in the company of flesh and blood'. There is no doubt an important place for the detailed study of language as such at various levels and to various depths, but this book makes no claim to compete in this field. The following brief survey, however, is necessary to indicate how all the work offered and suggested in this book does spring from, and relate to, a fundamental appreciation of the nature of language.

All human beings have developed techniques of communication by means of language: and different communities have developed their own particular species (Urdu, Arabic, Hopi, Greek, French, Chinese, English, etc.). A language fundamentally is the system of possibilities available to its users of employing

1

significant noises and patterns of noises produced by the organs of speech (the lungs, vocal chords, hard and soft palate, tongue, teeth, lips, nose and so on). Derived from the spoken forms of language, in many cases there are more permanent systems of written or printed signs which to varying extents record, and are based upon, the spoken forms. These sounds or signs, and the combinations of them, by a long process of tradition and learning, are used to refer to the objects, persons, ideas, and their relationships, which concern all human beings in the processes of conducting their lives both individual and collective. More generally, the use of language, we say, is to facilitate communications, to promote understanding between language-originator and language-recipient, and to enable useful, appropriate, and efficient action to take place.

We all know how long it takes to learn any language well – whether our own native language or that of another community. This is not because human beings are naturally 'slow of study' so much as because every language is an instrument of considerable intricacy and precision; indeed, in view of this, it is almost miraculous that, by the time an average child is about six years old, he has to a certain extent perfected the use of an extremely complicated system of communication symbols. A language, we see on further examination, is not just a haphazard stream of symbols; it is essentially systematic: that is to say, it operates according to series of recognisable laws and customs; beyond that, even, it can be seen as a system of systems, and those can conveniently be described at the following levels:

1 The sounds used in speaking   (phonology)
2 The individual 'words'   (lexis)
3 Significant variations in the form of words (e.g. cat/cats, die/died)   (morphology)
4 The combination of words into significant patterns   (syntax)
5 The combination of patterns (e.g. sentences) into longer utterance   (cohesion)
6 The association of words and word patterns with 'meaning' (semantics)

These constitute the basic elements of a language. But even when we have learned to operate the 'central core' we realise that this is by no means all that is necessary to be in full 'possession' of a language. Every language has developed means for the differentiation of distinct functions and occasions, and our knowledge of a language is incomplete until we can recognise, interpret and *originate* all the more subtle and complex signals it permits, in relation to the varying needs of our personal, social, political and professional involvements. In this connection, students of language now recognise such language variations, or 'sub-languages', as:

Dialect: specialised selections of words and forms of expression, distinctive of social or geographical groups

Register: 'dialects' associated with particular functions or professions (e.g. journalism, science, religion)

Collocation: the tendency of words to occur in regular and consistent associations (e.g. 'happy' with 'event' in relation to the birth of a child: 'satisfaction' with 'customers', in relation to shop-keeping, etc.)

Style: the possibility of variations upon the normal forms of language for special purposes of emphasis, persuasion, emotional effect, etc.

A further essential stage in the learning of a language is to discover how to use it as a method of building up sequences of organised and logical thought. To perform these activities efficiently, learners need to be aware also of how processes of 'thinking' can be perverted or destroyed by various kinds of abuse and misuse of language, as for example attaching greater precision to particular words than they normally bear, allowing the meaning of words to change imperceptibly in the course of an argument (e.g. in how many different senses has the word 'we' been employed in this introduction up to this point?), or permitting the contrastive nature of language (black, white: good, bad) to oversimplify complex problems.

A certain proportion of our language usage is, and ought to be, spontaneous and unconscious, involving rapid automatic responses to familiar kinds of stimuli; and, while this is particularly true in the case of a 'mother tongue', it is the aim of second- or foreign-language teaching to assist the development of the same facility in any other language that is being learned. On the other hand, there is also a very important additional stage in the mastery of a language, especially for people who occupy the roles in a community associated with the idea of being 'educated': that is, the deliberate and thoughtful use of the language in the pursuit of certain public aims and purposes. On these occasions, the user of the language is concerned with such things as the precise formulation of objectives, the selection of material and forms of expression, all the skills of explanation and persuasion, which have been studied since the time of the ancient Greeks under the title of rhetoric. Language at this stage is no longer a set of conditioned reflexes, of behavioural responses to 'stimuli': it partakes rather of the nature of 'art', the skilful manipulation and adaptation of a means of expression to particular and highly specific ends.

We can now define the purpose of this book as being to facilitate the systematic study and employment of the English language in some of its principal varieties, and for some of the principal purposes for which it is liable to be used by any educated person. It is, of course, perfectly feasible to plan a book concentrating on any of the single, separable 'styles' of English (e.g. commercial, scientific, legal, even military), and a number of books have in fact been produced on such lines. In an institution of higher education, however, we suppose that the aim should be to give not just one, or a few, kinds of specialised training, but, in the best traditions of 'liberal education', a training of the 'general powers' of the mind, an insight into the connections and relations between various forms of specialised knowledge, and a facility in recognising and employing the full range of expression which language permits.

HOW TO USE THIS BOOK

The book is divided into two parts:
Part I   *Passages for interpretation and analysis.*
Part II   *Passages for comparison.*
On the whole students should work through Part I, before going on to a Part II.

PART I
This consists of twelve sections of five passages each. The general nature of each section is indicated by its title and briefly discussed in a short introductory note. No assumption should be made that all the five passages in a section are closely comparable. While there are means available nowadays for making a more logical, systematic analysis of language, it would be unrealistic to suppose that all language falls clearly into distinct and separate categories. Almost any extended utterance which is produced in response to the exigencies of particular situations will tend to shift from one type of language activity to another quite unpredictably. Nevertheless, while embodying incidental differences, each of the sections of Part I seeks to illustrate one of the principle functions or varieties of language. Sections 1–6 are more concerned with 'functions', Section 7–12 with 'varieties'.

Each passage is provided with study questions, divided into two groups, A and B. Group A ('Interpretation') in each case is concerned with the 'message', and helps to draw attention to all aspects of what the writer has sought to communicate. This will at the most basic level be 'factual', but must also concern relationships, qualifications, arguments, attitudes, allusions, and so on. Group B ('Analysis') is more concerned with recognition and appreciation of the *means used* to convey the message, and will invite consideration of language in accordance with modern methods of analysis, while drawing upon earlier methods of appreciation where these are appropriate. The kind of analysis we aim to develop is one which is comprehensive and flexible enough to deal with *any form of language utterance*, including of course any piece of literature, but embracing also such things as daily journalism, advertisement copy-writing, government

5

decrees, political speeches, ordinary conversation, and scientific papers.

It seems logical that Group A questions should be considered before Group B. It was one of the old vices of literary studies to encourage 'appreciation' of texts which had not always been clearly, or in detail, understood; and oddly this tendency may seem to be condoned by some modern schools of language analysis which, at certain levels, give prime place to 'structure' and seem to imply that 'meaning' is of less consequence. This of course would be inappropriate in a work which is intended to be above all educational.

A point of incidental interest is that, while all the passages in Part I have been selected primarily to illustrate various aspects of language, many of them are quite notable pieces of writing in their own right and will give access to a wide range of topics, problems and authors of general interest.

At the end of each of the twelve sections will be found a further set of questions, suggestions and exercises, Group C, concerned with 'Production'. Study of a language in any meaningful sense, must surely imply not only *recognition* of various features, but the ability to *use* the language oneself. *Using a language* has the twofold commitment of being able [a] to receive any messages it may be used to transmit, accurately and in whatever degree of complexity they may involve, and [b] to transmit messages of any degree of complexity and in such forms of language as are socially acceptable. Group C has been devised so that students may have plenty of opportunities for active writing of many kinds, linked quite closely with the various topics of Part I.

PART II

Whereas Part I is organised according to systems, Part II is more empirical. In the early stages of any study it is helpful to be shown the principal elements, the main outlines, the chief possibilities. If the study is one which is to have any relevance to the encounters of actual life, it must at a certain stage allow the student to fare forward without props or guide-lines, taking on and evaluating whatever comes his way. Although Part II contains a number of passages of poetry as well as prose, all these exercises can be satisfactorily attempted with the help of a knowledge of the resources of language examined in Part I.

6

FURTHER CONSIDERATION
OF INTERPRETATION, ANALYSIS
AND PRACTICAL PRODUCTION

INTERPRETATION

Advanced students will be inclined to suppose that they know well enough 'how to read', but there is plenty of evidence to show that even advanced students often fail to 'read' with adequate efficiency, whether with regard to 'comprehension' or to 'speed'.

Words At the word level it is of great importance to ascertain the meaning referred to by particular words, in relation to the particular context. Most words in a language, as any good dictionary makes clear, are capable of being used in many different senses, and it is essential to recognise the appropriate one as soon as possible. It is well to remember the saying 'There are no synonyms', as each writer in the course of an extended discourse tends to invest even familiar words with additional layers of meaning from his own personal thoughts and interests. Consider for example what happens to the word 'style' in the following extract:

Finally, there should grow the most austere of all mental qualities; I mean the sense for style. It is an aesthetic sense, based on administration for the direct attainment of a foreseen end, simply and without waste. Style in art, style in literature, style in science, style in logic, style in practical execution have fundamentally the same aesthetic qualities, namely, attainment and restraint. . . . Style, in its finest sense, is the last acquirement of the educated mind; it is also the most useful. It pervades the whole being. The administrator with a sense of style hates waste; the engineer with a sense for style economises his material; the artisan with a sense for style prefers good work. Style is the ultimate morality of mind.

from *The Aims of Education*, A. N. WHITEHEAD

Starting out with the idea that 'style' is in the first place something to do with the senses, a matter of aesthetics, the author develops a train of thought which leaves us with the perception of 'style' connected with a great diversity of activities ending up as a concept of 'morality'.

Grammar Beyond the recognition of words individually, it is equally important to follow up faithfully the syntactic or

7

grammatical structure which the writer has employed to embody his 'thought'. When reading 'easy' material, we are hardly conscious of its 'grammar' as it seems entirely natural. However, if a passage is difficult, or not immediately comprehensible, it is essential to trace out the grammatical structure which alone can guide us towards the intended meaning. For example, in any difficult sentence, it is essential to discover the Subject-Predicate nucleus, which helps us to distinguish firstly the topic under consideration and secondly what is being said about it. When we are sure of the basic aim of a sentence, we can then go on to observe the kind of relationship among the subordinate parts, whether in phrase groups

(e.g. 'The President of the World Bank's new leather briefcase')

or in the clause structure

(e.g. 'If these conditions are fulfilled, and provided that financial resources prove to be adequate, some progress may be expected').

While taking note of the structure of complex sentences, it is also important to give due weight to the many significant qualifications which may be introduced by other aspects of the language. In the previous example, we would note the difference of meaning between 'some progress' and 'progress', and between '*may* be expected' and '*is* expected' or '*can* be expected'. Some of the most fundamental distinctions in language are of course registered by some of the most apparently commonplace words, such as can/could, ought/must, is/seems, thinks/knows, etc. We have probably all seen examples of the way in which brief quotations, e.g. in newspaper headlines, by suppressing the full grammatical structure of a thought, can often entirely misrepresent it.

Cohesion Apart from correctly interpreting the signals of meaning in individual sentences, it is important to observe the way in which sentences are organised into connected discourses. We need to detect for example what kind of relationship exists among the sentences, e.g. whether they illustrate a general statement, whether they follow a line of narrative or demonstration, whether they are discussing the 'pros and cons' of a topic, whether they set out to prove a particular conclusion. We have to pay particular attention to the various kinds of 'connective words', such as *next, also, but, nevertheless, or, whereas, provided that, unless,* and so on, but we shall also remember that many connective features do not appear at the beginnings of sentences or clauses. Furthermore we must be aware that the relationship between sentences in a paragraph is not always expressed in an actual word, but is implied in the statements made and their juxtaposition with each other. In this connection we need to keep in mind the fundamental types of logical thinking, whether Inductive (from the particular to the general) or Deductive (from the general to the particular).

Above all, we need to keep with us a degree of scepticism, and avoid the assumption that everything we hear, or even everything we read, is necessarily 'the truth, the whole truth, and nothing but the truth'. While the honourable function of language is to promote communication, we must remember that another of its historic functions, sometimes deliberate, sometimes accidental, is in 'concealing and confusing' thought.

APPRECIATION
This involves judging any particular piece of language against the 'total resources' of the language. The scheme upon which this book is based falls into the four sections of:

1 *Structure*,   the fundamental elements of the language in its normal, standard forms:

    i.e.   1.1 Word sounds   (phonology)
              1.2 Word meaning   (lexis)
              1.3 Phrase meaning   ⎫
              1.4 Clause meaning   ⎬ (syntax)
              1.5 Sentence meaning ⎭
              1.6 Sentence organisation   (cohesion)

2 *Function*,   the principal kinds of purpose for which language can be employed:

              2.1 Subjective, or personal
              2.2 Informative, or 'objective'
              2.3 Evocative
              2.4 Persuasive
              2.5 Logical
              2.6 Artistic

3 *Selection*,   The particular selection made in areas of the language where choice of alternatives is possible:

              3.1 Collocation
              3.2 Dialect
              3.3 Register
              3.4 Style

4 *Modes*,   While function is concerned with the ultimate aim or purpose of language, here we consider some of the principal ways in which language operates:

              4.1 Statement (including negative)

9

4.2 Question
4.3 Exclamation
4.4 Dialectic (logical sequences)
4.5 Rhythmic
4.6 Comparative (analogy, metaphor, etc.)
4.7 Indirect (Irony, ellipsis, etc.)

A scheme such as the above, must of course be employed with discretion. Not all of the 'resources' of language will be evident in any particular piece.

PRODUCTION

How do we best set about the business of practical writing? Many well-known authors have recorded their own particular methods and each student in an institution of higher education will presumably be capable of devising methods which best suit his own temperament and capacity. The following general stages should probably appear in every case:

1 Formulation of objective or aim.
2 Decisions on social 'context'. For what kind of readers is the writer writing? Through what *channels* will his work be communicated (e.g. radio, popular press, learned journal)? In what role is he writing (as 'personal friend', 'populariser', 'expert', etc.)?
3 Plan. Selection of material. Sequence.
4 Draft. Trial and error. 'Try-out'.
5 Revision.

The following account, given by a great writer of English, may be of interest:

. . . I have as much difficulty as ever in expressing myself clearly and concisely; and this difficulty has caused me a very great loss of time; but it has had the compensating advantage of forcing me to think long and intently about every sentence, and then I have been led to see errors in reasoning and in my own observations or those of others.

There seems to be a sort of fatality in my mind leading me to put at first my statement or proposition in a wrong or awkward form. Formerly I used to think about my sentences before writing them down; but for several years I have found that it saves time to scribble in a vile hand whole pages as quickly as I possibly can, contracting half the words; and then correct deliberately. . . .

Having said this much about my manner of writing, I will add that with my large books I spend a good deal of time over the general arrangements of the matter. I first make the rudest outline in two or three pages, and then a larger one in several pages, a few words or one word standing for a whole discussion or series of facts. Each one of these headings is again enlarged and often transferred before I begin to write *in extenso*. . . .

Extract from *Autobiography*, by CHARLES DARWIN, 1881.

PART I

Passages for Interpretation
and analysis

Section 1

LANGUAGE FOR INFORMATION

While we shall not argue which use of language 'came first', there is no doubt that a principal function of language is the transmission of information. 'Information' itself is a wide term, and implies chiefly data of an objective, utilitarian kind. In most situations, basic data of course will include reasons, origins, relations, and distinctions, as well as plain facts. It is also important to observe that what seems to be objective information may at times be subtly coloured by other factors.

1.1

Career Guidance

The National Institute of Industrial Psychology is a scientific association engaged in research into the satisfaction and efficiency of people in their working lives. It has carried out work in the field of vocational guidance since 1922, and its reasons for doing so are primarily to continue the development of effective methods to assist people to choose a career which will give them satisfaction and enable them to use their natural abilities to the best possible effect.

For this reason, applicants are accepted on the under-
10 standing that they will reply to reasonable requests for brief information about their careers in later life. This is necessary in order to check the accuracy of the advice offered by the Institute, and to improve techniques for the assessment of abilities and inclinations. The Institute's present procedures have been developed as a result of over 30 years' research of this kind and through the researches carried out in universities and other establishments. Finance for research has been generously provided in the past from the Carnegie Trust

and at present is being assisted from funds provided jointly
20 by the Institute's members and the Ministry of Technology.
The Institute is not a profit-making organisation, and fees
for vocational guidance are used solely to cover the cost of
giving advice.

There are a number of problems in determining the value
and accuracy of the Institute's vocational guidance work,
which make it difficult to give concise evidence of the useful-
ness of its procedures. For example, it is always difficult to
decide whether a person, who is successful and happy in an
occupation suggested by the Institute, would have been any
30 more or less suited in a different line of work. Again, in a
proportion of cases, the Institute's advice may confirm a
choice which turns out well, but which would have been made
had the consultation not taken place. Then, too, there are
some people who, by reason of physical or psychological
handicap, are unlikely to achieve complete success or happiness in any occupation and whose cases have to be judged
on the basis of reasonably good adjustment as against serious
failure.

Despite these issues, the follow-up of cases has shown that
40 the Institute's procedures provide sound results in the sub-
stantial majority of cases, and comparisons of the careers
of those receiving advice based on the Institute's methods
with those receiving less systematic forms of guidance, show
a substantially higher degree of success for the Institute's
methods. Reviews of evidence obtained from follow-up work
are published from time to time in the Institute's journal
'Occupational Psychology'.

The Institute does not act as an employment agency and
can make no attempt to find employment for those who
50 seek vocational advice; nor does the psychologist attempt
to decide an individual's career for him. His function is to
bring out a clear picture of the applicant's vocational assets
in relation to appropriate occupations or groups of occupations.

In some cases this does no more than confirm the choice of
the applicant or of parents. This, however, may be of considerable value in showing that a youngster has the intellectual
and other abilities needed for success in a career which
demands long training.

60   In other cases the consultation may be effective mainly by
ruling out certain lines which had been considered – thus
avoiding the eventual disappointment and frustration which

16

would result from embarking on a training which cannot be finally completed.

from *The Choice of a Career*, published by the National Institute of Industrial Psychology

A: 1 From paragraph 1, explain what you understand by 'vocational guidance'?
2 What is the relation of 'vocational guidance' to other work done by the National Institute of Industrial Psychology?
3 On what conditions are applications for advice accepted?
4 What features of the Institute's work would entitle it to be called a 'scientific' association?
5 Show how the claims for the success of the Institute's work in 'vocational guidance' are carefully qualified.
6 How is the value of the Institute's work in 'vocational guidance' in fact demonstrated?
7 What are the limitations to the advice given by the Institute?

B: 1 Consider this extract as regards lucidity of expression.
2 How far does this extract consist of a logically developed sequence, and how far is it a series of unconnected items?
3 Observe the devices used to give 'cohesion'.
4 List the expressions used in this extract which are typical of scientific writing.
5 Which is the word used to express the Institute's sense of gratitude to the Carnegie Trust?
6 Discuss the justification for the commas used in the sentence in lines 28–29.
7 Point out any words or expressions which show that while this extract is intended to convey the scientific nature of the Institute's work, it is also addressed to members of the general public.
8 What is the relevance of the information contained in the sentence in lines 45–47?

1.2

The Textile Industry

During the Middle Ages the manufacture of cloth was divided amongst a number of guilds. One set of workers combed and carded wool, then it was spun on the spindle from the distaff by others, who turned their product over to the weavers, whose finished cloth was then fulled, finished, and dyed by other craftsmen. As mechanisation of several of these operations took place during the Middle Ages and complicated apparatus became necessary for economic production, the banker began to play his part in this picture. Most guilds

17

10 were seriously hampered by the lack of capital; the banker stepped in to finance the industrialisation of the various operations in the textile industry and began to assume the role of the employer and middleman. This was one of the reasons why this industry flourished in such rich countries as Flanders, Italy, and Britain.

One of the first operations to be mechanised was fulling, which had always been carried out by beating or treading the cloth in water with fuller's earth in order to make it shrink and 'felt', thus filling the gaps in the weave, and to scour and
20 clean it. The introduction of the waterwheel provided the opportunity to mechanise this heavy task of the fuller, the water being used to move lift hammers by means of a revolving drum attached to the shaft of the waterwheel, which thus did the work of several men.

The second operation to be mechanised was weaving. In the first century A.D. the Chinese knew the drawloom and the horizontal loom with four or more heddles, both of which allowed the manufacture of the more complicated fancy weaves like twills and satins or damasks. Similar types of
30 looms were used in third-century Syria, but we have no evidence that their heddles were moved by pedals or treadles. This substitution of hand operations by the foot-controlled heddles took place during the late twelfth and early thirteenth centuries and considerably speeded up the production of complicated fancy weaves.

The third operation to be mechanised was spinning. The whorl or wharve of the spindle was grooved and moved by a band connecting it with a large wheel turned by the left hand. This mechanised the twisting and winding of the yarn, but the
40 twist was still controlled by the spinner's left hand. This primitive 'bobbing wheel', which remained in use for coarse yarns up to the nineteenth century, is one of the early examples of the application of the crank in machinery. The crank, which permits the translation of reciprocal motion into rotary and vice versa, was seldom or never used in Antiquity. It is depicted in the Utrecht Psalter (A.D. 850) as moving a grinding-stone and it appears in hand querns. This principle was applied to the bobbing wheel and to the lathe (operating with a treadle) in the thirteenth century. The
50 further evolution of the bobbing wheel is obvious. In the course of the sixteenth century it was no longer moved by hand, but by foot by means of a treadle, thus leaving the spinner's hand free. During the fifteenth century the twisting

18

and winding operations were enabled to proceed simultaneously by the introduction of the flyer to the spinning-wheel making the so-called Saxony wheel.

from *A History of Science*, R. J. FORBES and E. J. DIJKSTERHUIS

A: 1 Explain [*a*] the general theme
      [*b*] the historical limits
      [*c*] the range of information – in this passage.
   2 Why did the cloth-making industry flourish during that period particularly in Flanders, Italy, and Britain?
   3 What is the meaning of the word 'mechanised' as used here. First draw your own conclusions; then check from the dictionary.
   4 From evidence in the passage itself, explain the processes of *spinning*, *weaving*, and *fulling*, and indicate how each first became mechanised.
   5 What is the use of the *crank* as a mechanical device? Give other examples, taken from your own observations. Compare the description of the *crank* given here with that in your dictionary. Are there any other, non-literal, uses of the word *crank*?

B: 1 Explain the general structure of ideas and material in this passage, referring as little as possible to 'content'.
   2 What can be observed about the following aspects of the passage:
      [*a*] the length of sentences?
      [*b*] the types of sentences?
      [*c*] the form of the main verbs, as regards (i) tense, (ii) voice – active or passive?
      [*d*] the frequency of (i) personal pronouns, (ii) abstract nouns, (iii) noun modifiers, (iv) verb modifiers?
      [*e*] words conveying subjective valuation?
      [*f*] figurative expressions?
   3 List words in the passage which are particulary associated with the following topics: economics and business; mechanics; cloth-making.
   4 Give your impression of
      [*a*] the type of writer
      [*b*] the type of reader
      [*c*] the type of publication, which this passage seems to imply.

1.3

Dictionaries in the Eighteenth Century

The first word book to embody the ideals of the age was Nathaniel Bailey's *Universal Etymological Dictionary of the English Language*, originally published in 1721, and then, in a beauti-

ful folio volume with illustrations by Flaxman, in 1731. This, one of the most revolutionary dictionaries ever to appear, was the first to pay proper attention to current usage, the first to feature etymology, the first to give aid in syllabification, the first to give illustrative quotations (chiefly from proverbs), the first to include illustrations, and the first to indicate pronun-
10 ciation. An interleaved copy of the 1731 folio edition was the basis of Samuel Johnson's *Dictionary* of 1755; through Johnson, it influenced all subsequent lexicographical practice. The position of dictionary pioneer, commonly granted to Johnson or to Noah Webster, belongs in reality to one of the few geniuses lexicography ever produced: Nathaniel Bailey.

Johnson's *Dictionary* (1755) enormously extends the techniques developed by Bailey. Johnson was able to revise Bailey's crude etymologies on the basis of Francis Junius' *Etymologicon Anglicanum* (first published in 1743), to make a systematic use
20 of illustrative quotations, to fix the spelling of many disputed words, to develop a really discriminating system of definition, and to exhibit the vocabulary of English much more fully than had ever been attempted before. In his two-volume work, the age and following ages found their ideal word book. Indeed, a good deal of the importance of the book lies in its later influence. It dominated English letters for a full century after its appearance and, after various revisions, continued in common use until 1900. As late as the '90s, most Englishmen used the word *dictionary* as a mere synonym for Johnson's
30 *Dictionary*; in 1880 a Bill was actually thrown out of Parliament because a word in it was not in 'the Dictionary'.

One of the tasks taken upon himself by Johnson was to remove 'improprieties and absurdities' from the language. In short, he became a linguistic legislator attempting to perform for English those offices performed for French by the French Academy. From this facet of his activities we get the notion, still held by many dictionary users, and fostered by many dictionary publishers, that the dictionary is a 'supreme authority' by which to arbitrate questions of 'correctness' and
40 'incorrectness'. The dictionaries of the second half of the eighteenth century extended this notion particularly to the field of pronunciation. By 1750, the increasing wealth of the middle classes was making itself felt in the social and political worlds. Those who possessed it, speakers, for the most part, of a middle-class dialect, earnestly desired a key to the pronunciations accepted in polite society. To provide for their needs, various pronunciation experts – usually of Scottish or

Irish extraction – edited a series of pronunciation dictionaries.
Of these, the most important are James Buchanan's *New*
50 *English Dictionary* (1769), William Kenrick's *New Dictionary of*
the English Language (1773), Thomas Sheridan's *General Dic-*
tionary of the English Language (1780), and, above all, John
Walker's *Critical Pronouncing Dictionary and Expositor of the*
English Language (1791). In such works, pronunciation was
indicated by small superscript numbers referring to the
'powers' of the various vowel sounds. Despite the legislative
function exercised by the authors of almost all of these works,
we must admit that they did indicate contemporary pronunciation with great accuracy, and when Walker's pronunciations
60 were combined with Johnson's definitions the result was a
dictionary which dominated the word-book field, both in
England and the United States, until well after 1850.

from Essays on Language and Usage, H. WHITEHALL

A: 1 In what respects was Bailey's Dictionary a pioneer work?
  2 What appears to be the weakness of illustrating the meaning of
    words, as Bailey did, by quotation of proverbs?
  3 In what ways did Johnson's Dictionary improve upon Bailey's?
  4 What explains the popularity of pronouncing dictionaries at that
    time?
  5 What is meant by the 'legislative function' of the dictionaries of that
    period. What other kind of function can be envisaged for dictiona-
    ries?
  6 What general thesis, embodying the notion of 'ideals', seems to be
    under consideration in the whole essay from which this excerpt is
    taken?

B: 1 Distinguish between the main development of this passage and
    the use of subordinate illustration.
  2 Illustrate the author's concern to base his exposition on precise
    facts.
  3 Point out the sentences employed in paragraphs 1 and 2 to convey
    concise information compactly.
  4 List the words from this passage which belong particularly to the
    discussion of language, and give a precise definition of each.
  5 Point out any evaluative words used in the passage, and estimate
    how far their use seems justified.
  6 Discuss the aptness of the metaphor 'foster' in its context (line 37).
  7 Point out other uses of metaphor in this passage, and explain the
    effect in each case.

1.4
Kano

Most of the imports into Kano from the north came down the Aïr road, and the rest through Kawar and Bornu. Apart from salt, they were a coarse silk from Tripoli and a wide range of European trade goods. The latter included Manchester cottons, French silks, glass beads from Venice and Trieste, paper, mirrors and needles from Styria, besides quantities of spices, sugar, and tea. Kano was also an important market for natron from Lake Chad, and kola nuts.

10 The valuable trade in kola nuts, most of which came from Gwanja in the hinterland of the Gold Coast, was largely controlled by the people of Kano. This nut, the *goro* of the natives and the early Arab travellers, had been in use in the Western Sudan since very early times. The twin interlocking kernels were regarded as a symbol of friendship, and no present was complete without kolas. The nut consequently acquired a ceremonial importance, and it became customary to swear oaths on a kola. Its bitter flavour appeals strongly to the African, it is undoubtedly very sustaining and it is widely regarded as a cure for impotency. Although the heavy cost of 20 transport always kept the price high and for long it was a luxury only the rich could afford, it became, and still remains, a necessity to a large part of the population.

The kola nut was one of the three articles of trade which used to traverse the whole of north-western Africa, from the Guinea coast to the shores of the Mediterranean. The others were Venetian glass beads and unwrought silk from Tripoli, both of which found their way to Gwanja for bartering for kolas, and to Badagry on the Slave Coast, which had become the chief centre of the European slave-trade.

30 Between Kano and Badagry there was no single, well-defined trade route. The two were separated by belts of thick bush and rain forest, inhabited by Yorubas and lesser pagans who were constantly at war with each other. The crossing of these belts was therefore hazardous, and trade tended to trickle unobtrusively and furtively along ill-defined tracks. It is small wonder that a zone which the Sudanese found so difficult to traverse had for so many centuries proved impenetrable by Europeans trading on the Guinea coast.

The Niger was crossed at various ferries, of which the most 40 important were at Rabba, near the modern Jebba, and Komie

(Wonjerque), just below Busa. There was a less important one farther upstream at Illo. From Komie a road ran north-east through Birnin Gwari and Zaria to Kano, and another followed the bank of the river through Yauri to north-west Hausa, where it joined the main kola route from Gwanja to Kano. These two roads, together with a third coming in from Wagadugu and Fadan Gurma, were the chief trade routes leading into Hausa from the west; they converged and met at or near Jega.

from *The Golden Trade of the Moors*, E. W. BOVILL

A: 1 Suggest the topic which gives a unity to this passage.
   2 In the absence of any dates, survey the evidence in the passage for believing it to refer to any particular period. What is the conclusion you reach?
   3 Set out the information given in this passage in the form of a map or diagram (use an atlas, if necessary).
   4 How far is it possible to see an Import-Export pattern in the trade described here?
   5 For what reasons has the kola nut been particularly valued? Was it more valued in the past than at the present?
   6 Consider the implications of the contrasted words *difficult* and *impenetrable* as associated here with 'Sudanese' and 'Europeans'.

B: 1 Examine the sequence of information given in this passage. How systematic do you consider it to be?
   2 Can you find any sentence pattern which seems typical of the whole passage?
   3 In contrast to B:2 what do you observe about the sentence concluding paragraph 2, 'Although .... population'?
   4 Point out any expressions which indicate that the writer is investing 'trade' with personal attributes (Personification).
   5 Would you classify this as a piece of scientific or literary writing?
   6 Consider the means used to distinguish between the 'general' and the 'particular'.
   7 Observe the means used to maintain cohesion between sentences. Does this seem to you to be done neatly or clumsily?

1.5

DDT

DDT (short for dichloro-diphenyl-trichloro-ethane) was first synthesised by a German chemist in 1874, but its properties as an insecticide were not discovered until 1939. Almost immediately DDT was hailed as a means of stamping out insect-borne disease and winning the farmers' war against crop destroyers overnight. The discoverer, Paul Muller of Switzerland, won the Nobel Prize.

DDT is now so universally used that in most minds the product takes on the harmless aspect of the familiar. Perhaps
10 the myth of the harmlessness of DDT rests on the fact that one of its first uses was the wartime dusting of many thousands of soldiers, refugees, and prisoners, to combat lice. It is widely believed that since so many people came into extremely intimate contact with DDT and suffered no immediate ill effects the chemical must certainly be innocent of harm.

This understandable misconception arises from the fact that – unlike other chlorinated hydrocarbons – DDT *in powder form* is not readily absorbed through the skin. Dissolved in oil, as it usually is, DDT is definitely toxic. If swallowed, it is
20 absorbed slowly through the digestive tract; it may also be absorbed through the lungs. Once it has entered the body it is stored largely in organs rich in fatty substances (because DDT itself is fat-soluble) such as the adrenals, testes, or thyroid. Relatively large amounts are deposited in the liver, kidneys, and the fat of the large, protective mesenteries that enfold the intestines.

This storage of DDT begins with the smallest conceivable intake of the chemical (which is present as residues on most foodstuffs) and continues until quite high levels are reached.
30 The fatty storage depots act as biological magnifiers, so that an intake of as little as $\frac{1}{10}$ of 1 part per million in the diet results in storage of about 10 to 15 parts per million, an increase of one hundredfold or more. These terms of reference, so commonplace to the chemist or the pharmacologist, are unfamiliar to most of us. One part in a million sounds like a very small amount – and so it is. But such substances are so potent that a minute quantity can bring about vast changes in the body. In animal experiments, 3 parts per million has been found to inhibit an essential enzyme in heart muscle; only 5
40 parts per million has brought about necrosis or disintegration of liver cells; only 2.5 parts per million of the closely related chemicals dieldrin and chlordane did the same.

This is really not surprising. In the normal chemistry of the human body there is just such a disparity between cause and effect. For example, a quantity of iodine as small as two ten-thousandths of a gram spells the difference between health and disease. Because these small amounts of pesticides are cumu-

latively stored and only slowly excreted, the threat of chronic
poisoning and degenerative changes of the liver and other
50 organs is very real.

from *Silent Spring*, RACHEL CARSON

A: 1 What is the implication in the statement that DDT was 'first
synthesised' in 1874?
2 What might account for the large gap between 1874 and 1939?
3 For what purposes has DDT been regarded as particularly beneficial?
4 Why was DDT so easily regarded as harmless?
5 What is the critical difference between DDT in powder form and
when dissolved in oil?
6 How do minute quantities of DDT gain entrance to the human
body?
7 Explain the effect of introducing small quantities of DDT into
animals.
8 What point is illustrated by the example of iodine?

B: 1 Why has this chemical substance been referred to as 'DDT'?
2 How does the writer emphasize the sudden and widespread discovery of the use of DDT?
3 List the words used in this passage which are normally encountered
in the discussion of:
[a]chemistry   [b]anatomy
4 What other information would you require before the explanation
of 'biological magnifiers' (line 30) becomes completely clear?
5 Point out any words, or longer expressions, which add a 'dramatic',
possibly a 'journalistic' quality to the passage at certain points. Can
this employment of language be justified in the present context?

Section 1 PRACTICAL

C: 1 Choose any branch of knowledge which to your understanding
illustrates a historical development by distinct stages, and write a
concise account as if for an encyclopedia article.
2 Suppose that your own town or locality is eager to attract new
industrial development. Write a leaflet, such as might be sent to
potential developers, presenting systematically everything that is
likely to be of interest (e.g. geography, history, communications,
population, etc. etc.).
3 Think of a skilled operation (whether in the field of arts, crafts,
sports, science or technology) and write an exact account of how it
is performed, imagining yourself as an instructor teaching the skill
to a group of learners.

4 In January 1967, Donald Campbell was killed in a specially constructed motor boat in which he was attempting to break the world's
water speed record, at somewhere in the region of 315 m.p.h. Study
the diagram and the brief explanation below; then write an account
of how the accident probably occurred, and how it might have been
prevented.

From the Sunday Times, 8 January 1967.

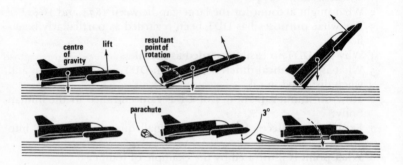

Top sequence: aerodynamic lift of floats throws Bluebird
into air. Below: how an emergency parachute could have
averted disaster by slowing down Bluebird when the bows
'take off'.

5 Write a complete account of the information conveyed in the
following map.

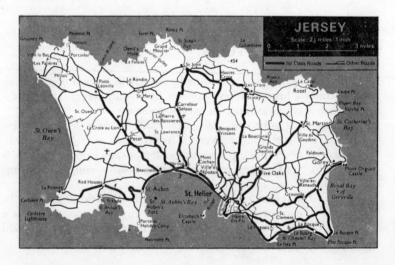

6 Write out a clear and orderly account of the information contained in the diagram below describing first the structure and then the enrolment.

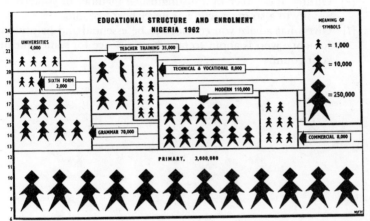

EDUCATIONAL STRUCTURE AND ENROLMENT
NIGERIA 1962

MEANING OF SYMBOLS

👤 = 1,000

👤 = 10,000

👤 = 250,000

UNIVERSITIES 4,000
TEACHER TRAINING 35,000
TECHNICAL & VOCATIONAL 8,000
SIXTH FORM 2,000
MODERN 110,000
GRAMMAR 70,000
COMMERCIAL 8,000
PRIMARY, 3,000,000

Notes : (i) Vertical axis indicates normal age of students, but in many cases ages are considerably higher.
(ii) Post primary enrolment is less than 10% of primary enrolment.

7 Imagine *one* of the following of which you would enjoy the opportunity of being Principal or Manager:

     an educational institution
     a place of sport or entertainment
     a business house
     an industrial concern.

Draw up a report or prospectus introducing it to the general public.

8 The following situations may be used for written or oral practice:

[a] Your account of a road accident of which you were a witness.

[b] You live in a very inaccessible place. Explain how to get there.

[c] You have suffered from a sequence of physical and psychological complaints. Describe your symptoms.

[d] You wish to apply for an appointment for which your qualifications are not entirely appropriate.

[e] You have prepared accommodation and entertainment for a group of visitors from a different community. Give your introductory explanation.

[f] Explain to a stranger what will happen and how he should behave at a ceremony to which you intend to take him.

[g] You have been asked to conduct an important visitor on a tour of an institution to which you belong. Outline your commentary.

[h] You have been commissioned to write a leaflet, instructing farmers, or craftsmen, on the advantages and operation of a new process or technique.

[i] You have suffered an injustice. Prepare, for your lawyer, a concise account of the situation.

[j] As a teacher, you propose to introduce a new type of work to your students. Prepare your introductory talk.

[k] Outline the career of a distinguished member of your community to a stranger who has never heard of him.

[l] Give what advice you consider to be essential and helpful to someone who is about to take up residence for some time in your country.

Section 2

LANGUAGE FOR OBSERVATION

One of the notable functions of language is to record observation – of men, places, incidents and processes; indeed accuracy and refinement of observation depend directly on the flexibility and resourcefulness of the language available to the observer. Some kinds of exact observation are best recorded, of course, in mathematical terms, but there is an enormous extent of human experience for which there is no better medium than language for the 'attempt to render the highest kind of justice to the visible universe' (as the author of 2.2 wrote).

2.1
Spring Funeral

They decided to bury him in our churchyard at Greymede under the beeches; the widow would have it so, and nothing might be denied her in her state.

It was a magnificent morning in early spring when I watched among the trees to see the procession come down the hill-side. The upper air was woven with the music of the larks, and my whole world thrilled with the conception of summer. The young pale wind-flowers had arisen by the wood-gale, and under the hazels, when perchance the hot sun pushed his
10 way, new little suns dawned, and blazed with the real light. There was a certain thrill and quickening everywhere, as a woman must feel when she has conceived. A sallow-tree in a favoured spot looked like a pale gold cloud of summer dawn; nearer it had poised a golden, fairy busby on every twig, and was voiced with a hum of bees, like any sacred golden bush, uttering its gladness in the thrilling murmur of bees, and in warm scent. Birds called and flashed on every hand; they made off exultant with streaming strands of grass, or wisps of fleece,

29

plunging into the dark spaces of the wood, and out again into
the blue.

A lad moved across the field from the farm below with a dog
trotting behind him – a dog, no, a fussy, black-legged lamb
trotting along on its toes, with its tail swinging behind. They
were going to the mothers on the common, who moved like
little grey clouds among the dark gorse.

I cannot help forgetting, and sharing the spink's triumph,
when he flashes past with a fleece from a bramble bush. It will
cover the bedded moss, it will weave among the soft red cow-
hair beautifully. It is a prize, it is an ecstasy to have captured
it at the right moment, and the nest is nearly ready.

Ah, but the thrush is scornful, ringing out his voice from
the hedge! He sets his breast against the mud, and models it
warm for the turquoise eggs – blue, blue, bluest of eggs, which
cluster so close and round against the breast, which round up
beneath the breast, nestling content. You should see the bright
ecstasy in the eyes of a nesting thrush, because of the rounded
caress of the eggs against her breast!

What a hurry the jenny wren makes – hoping I shall not see
her dart into the low bush. I have a delight in watching them
against their shy little wills. But they have all risen with
a rush of wings, and are gone, the birds. The air is brushed
with agitation. There is no lark in the sky, not one; the heaven
is clear of wings or twinkling dot –

Till the heralds come – till the heralds wave like shadows in
the bright air, crying, lamenting, fretting for ever. Rising and
falling and circling round and round, the slow-waving pewits
cry and complain, and lift their broad wings in sorrow. They
stoop suddenly to the ground, the lapwings, then in another
throb of anguish and protest, they swing up again, offering a
glistening white breast to the sunlight, to deny it in black
shadow, then a glisten of green, and all the time crying and
crying in despair.

The pheasants are frightened into cover, they run and dart
through the hedge. The old cock must fly in his haste, spread
himself on his streaming plumes, and sail into the wood's
security.

There is a cry in answer to the pewits, echoing louder and
stronger the lamentation of the lapwings, a wail which hushes
the birds. The men come over the brow of the hill, slowly,
with the old squire walking tall and straight in front; six
bowed men bearing the coffin on their shoulders, treading
heavily and cautiously, under the great weight of the glistening

white coffin, six men following behind, ill at ease, waiting their turn for the burden. You can see the red handkerchiefs knotted round their throats, and their shirt-fronts blue and white between the open waistcoats. The coffin is of new unpolished wood, gleaming and glistening in the sunlight; the men who carry it remember all their lives after the smell of new, warm elm-wood.

from *The White Peacock*, D. H. LAWRENCE

A: 1 Explain the physical relationship of the narrator, the funeral procession, and the general setting.
2 What seems to have been predominant in the mind of the narrator during this episode?
3 By means of what symbols is the spirit of the season presented?
4 Test the precision of the description by listing the principal characteristics of the various birds mentioned.
5 In what sense are the lapwings 'heralds'?
6 Why were there *twelve* coffin-bearers?
7 To what extent might this passage be acceptable to a reader who is not a native of England?

B: 1 How might the discrepancy between the occasion (i.e. a funeral) and the feeling developed in the passage be explained?
2 What effect is conveyed by 'woven' (line 6)?
3 How appropriate is the metaphor of 'conception' (lines 11–12)?
4 Explain the nature and the effect of the tense change which begins at line 27.
5 Select some examples of words chosen to record especial vividness of perception.
6 What is the effect of the broken sentence (line 22)?
7 What is the effect of the four clauses all beginning with 'it' in paragraph 4?
8 What special effects does the author succeed in producing in paragraph 5?
9 What special effect is gained by the sentence structure in lines 44–52?

2.2

A Storm

The thirty-second day out of Bombay began inauspiciously. In the morning a sea smashed one of the galley doors. We dashed in through lots of steam and found the cook very wet and indignant with the ship: 'She's getting worse every day. She's trying to drown me in front of my own stove!' He was very angry. We pacified him, and the carpenter, though washed away twice from there, managed to repair the door. Through that accident our dinner was not ready till late, but it didn't matter in the end because Knowles, who went to fetch it, got knocked down by a sea and the dinner went over the side. Captain Allistoun, looking more hard and thin-lipped than ever, hung on to full topsails and foresail, and would not notice that the ship, asked to do too much, appeared to lose heart altogether for the first time since we knew her. She refused to rise, and bored her way sullenly through the seas. Twice running, as though she had been blind or weary of life, she put her nose deliberately into a big wave and swept the decks from end to end. As the boatswain observed with marked annoyance, while we were splashing about in a body to try and save a worthless wash-tub: 'Every blooming thing in the ship is going overboard this afternoon.' Venerable Singleton broke his habitual silence and said with a glance aloft: 'The old man's in a temper with the weather, but it's no good bein' angry with the winds of heaven.' . . .

There was no leisure for idle probing of hearts. Sails blew adrift. Things broke loose. Cold and wet, we were washed about the deck while trying to repair damages. The ship tossed about, shaken furiously, like a toy in the hand of a lunatic. Just at sunset there was a rush to shorten sail before the menace of a sombre hail cloud. The hard gust of wind came brutal like the blow of a fist. The ship relieved of her canvas in time received it pluckily: she yielded reluctantly to the violent onset; then, coming up with a stately and irresistible motion, brought her spars to windward in the teeth of the screeching squall. Out of the abysmal darkness of the black cloud overhead white hail streamed on her, rattled on the rigging, leaped in handfuls off the yards, rebounded on the deck – round and gleaming in the murky turmoil like a shower of pearls. It passed away. For a moment a livid sun shot horizontally the last rays of sinister light between the hills of steep, rolling waves. Then a wild night rushed in – stamped out in a great howl that dismal remnant of a stormy day.

There was no sleep on board that night. Most seamen remember in their life one or two such nights of a culminating gale. Nothing seems left of the whole universe but darkness, clamour, fury – and the ship. And like the last vestige of a shattered creation she drifts, bearing an anguished remnant of sinful mankind, through the distress, tumult, and pain of an avenging terror. No one slept in the forecastle. The tin

50 oil-lamp suspended on a long string, smoking, described
wide circles; wet clothing made dark heaps on the glistening
floor; a thin layer of water rushed to and fro. In the bed-places
men lay booted, resting on elbows and with open eyes. Hung-
up suits of oil-skin swung out and in, lively and disquieting
like reckless ghosts of decapitated seamen dancing in a tempest.
No one spoke and all listened. Outside the night moaned and
sobbed to the accompaniment of a continuous loud tremor as
of innumerable drums beating far off. Shrieks passed through
the air. Tremendous dull blows made the ship tremble while
60 she rolled under the weight of the seas toppling on her deck.
At times she soared up swiftly as if to leave this earth for
ever, then during interminable moments fell through a void
with all the hearts on board of her standing still, till a frightful
shock, expected and sudden, started them off again with a
big thump. After every dislocating jerk of the ship, Wamibo,
stretched full length, his face on the pillow, groaned slightly
with the pain of his tormented universe. Now and then, for the
fraction of an intolerable second, the ship, in the fiercer burst
of a terrible uproar, remained on her side, vibrating and
70 still, with a stillness more appalling than the wildest motion.
Then upon all those prone bodies a stir would pass, a shiver of
suspense. A man would protrude his anxious head and a
pair of eyes glistened in the sway of light glaring wildly. Some
moved their legs a little as if making ready to jump out. But
several, motionless on their backs and with one hand grip-
ping hard the edge of the bunk, smoked nervously with quick
puffs, staring upwards; immobilised in a great craving for
peace.

from *The Nigger of the Narcissus*, JOSEPH CONRAD

A: 1 Explain factually the situation in which the events depicted occur.
   What time-span is involved?
 2 Why does Captain Allistoun 'hang on' to 'full topsails and foresail'
   so long?
 3 What shows that this was an exceptional storm?
 4 What precautions were taken at the approach of night?
 5 Why was there 'no sleep on board that night' (line 43)?
 6 How essential do you judge the author's attempt to present the
   ship as a symbol (lines 46–49)?
 7 What do you consider to be the author's predominant aim in this
   passage?

B: 1 In what way is 'a sea' used in a rather specialised sense in this
   passage (e.g. line 2)?

2 List the expressions belonging to the nautical register, and ascertain their meanings. How critical are they in the appreciation of the passage as a whole?

3 With what effect does the author combine details about the ship with details about the sailors?

4 How would you describe the basic style of the passage, e.g. formal, technical, colloquial?

5 Select and comment on some notable instances of metaphor or simile in this passage.

6 Comment on the success of the very short sentences which occur at various points in this narrative.

7 Comment on any sentences which have been constructed to produce particularly significant rhythmical effects.

2.3
Lagos

Lagos assaults you with its squalor and vitality. The narrow streets, the houses – hovels, mainly – made of mud or old tin and packed as close as playing-cards, the stinking open drains, the noise, the traffic, the jostling throngs – Lagos is Eastern in its feeling that sheer naked human life, mere existence, bubbles and pullulates with the frightening fecundity of bacteria. The town is on an island surrounded by a lagoon into which all the drains empty, and a sour and sulphurous smell frequently envelops the Marina, Lagos' nearest ap-
10 proach to a Chelsea Embankment or Riverside Drive.

Most Lagosians are in origin Yoruba, although every one of the multitudinous races of West Africa must be represented here. Yoruba women wear big, gay head-ties done in a knot at the back with the ends protruding, like brilliant giant butterflies. These women would sell their mothers' milk at a profit. In Lagos market they are packed as close as hens in a battery, each with her pile of wares. I was drawn to the herbalists' and witch-doctors' stalls, loaded with all sorts of leaves, pods and lumps of clay or chalk having medicinal
20 properties and with juju objects of many kinds, most of which defy recognition, though you can identify the tiny skulls of monkeys, the wings of bats and small crows, the antlers of baby deer, dogs' paws, bundles of feathers, all exactly like the witches' brew in *Macbeth*. Odd, how all the world over 'eye of newt and toe of frog, wool of bat and tongue of dog, adder's

fork and blindworm's sting' are the stock-in-trade of magicians.

I tried to ascertain the use of some of these remedies. A wizen-faced elder explained that if you burnt a bunch of
30 feathers and mixed the ash with scrapings off a monkey's skull and some dried bats-wing, and swallowed the resulting powder, you would vomit out a sickness of the stomach. Several were remedies for syphilis. Those – the majority, I expect – used for curses and charms were not explained. Cursing and poisoning are popular pastimes; a man was caught the other day putting pus from smallpox sores into an enemy's food. Probably he was a follower of Shopono, the Yoruba god of smallpox, whose priests by custom inherit the property of victims of the disease. Little wonder that, in by-
40 gone days, smallpox outbreaks were many and devastating.

The town is growing fast and sprawls across more and more of the island. But there are still unspoilt beaches, with long Atlantic rollers breaking on the hot white sand. Nothing is pleasanter than to walk there in the evening, away from the heat and noise of the town. The sea is quiet and colourless and the sun sinks flatly into it, without effulgence, red as a Dutch cheese. Outlines are not exactly blurred, but lack sharpness, because of the harmattan that blows over the desert a thousand miles away and yet dims this bright Atlantic air.

from *Four Guineas*, ELSPETH HUXLEY

A: 1 State objectively the principal facts enumerated in this passage.
   2 What principal aim seems to govern the selection and presentation of detail?
   3 Do you find the comment that 'Yoruba women would sell their mothers' milk at a profit' to be ambiguous?
   4 Point out some phrases which seem to betray the writer's 'jumping to conclusions'.
   5 What seems to be the writer's principal concern here? Is it entirely 'one-sided'?

B: 1 What is the effect of such words as 'assaults' (line 1), 'sprawls' (line 41)? Can you find any others which produce a similar effect?
   2 'Lagos is Eastern' (line 4). Consider the implications of 'Eastern' in relation to the context here.
   3 What is intended in the comparisons to Chelsea Embankment and Riverside Drive?
   4 What conclusions can you draw from the allusion to lines from *Macbeth*?
   5 What effects of contrast can be seen in this passage?

Music at Night

Moonless, this June night is all the more alive with stars. Its darkness is perfumed with faint gusts from the blossoming lime trees, with the smell of wetted earth and the invisible greenness of the vines. There is silence; but a silence that breathes with the soft breathing of the sea and, in the thin shrill noise of a cricket, insistently, incessantly harps on the fact of its own deep perfection. Far away, the passage of a train is like a long caress, moving gently, with an inexorable gentleness, across the warm living body of the night.

10   Music, you say; it would be a good night for music. But I have music here in a box, shut up like one of those bottled djinns in the *Arabian Nights*, and ready at a touch to break out of its prison. I make the necessary mechanical magic, and suddenly, by some miraculously appropriate coincidence (for I had selected the record in the dark, without knowing what music the machine would play), suddenly the introduction to the *Benedictus* in Beethoven's *Missa Solemnis* begins to trace its patterns on the moonless sky.

The Benedictus. Blessed and blessing, this music is in some sort the equivalent of the night, of the deep and living dark-
20   ness, into which, now in a single jet, now in a fine interweaving of melodies, now in pulsing and almost solid clots of harmonious sound, it pours itself, stanchlessly pours itself, like time, like the rising and falling, falling trajectories of a life. It is the equivalent of the night in another mode of being, as an essence is the equivalent of the flowers, from which it is distilled.

There is, at least there sometimes seems to be, a certain blessedness lying at the heart of things, a mysterious blessedness, of whose existence occasional accidents or providences
30   (for me, this night is one of them) make us obscurely, or it may be intensely, but always fleetingly, alas, always only for a few brief moments, aware. In the *Benedictus* Beethoven gives expression to this awareness of blessedness. His music is the equivalent of this Mediterranean night, or rather of the blessedness at the heart of the night, of the blessedness as it would be if it could be sifted clear of irrelevance and accident, refined and separated out into its quintessential purity.

'*Benedictus, benedictus . . .* ' One after another the voices take up the theme propounded by the orchestra and lovingly

40 meditated through a long and exquisite solo (for the blessedness reveals itself most often to the solitary spirit) by a single
violin. *'Benedictus, benedictus . . .'* And then, suddenly
the music dies; the flying djinn has been rebottled. With a
stuppid insect-like insistence, a steel point rasps and rasps the
silence.

from *Music at Night*, ALDOUS HUXLEY

A: 1 What factors seem to contribute to the perfection of the setting for
these paragraphs?
2 What exactly is the 'mechanical magic' (lines 13–14) the writer
makes, and what detail later in the passage indicates the period in
which it must have been written?
3 What does the writer use the music to symbolise?
4 What do the words 'trace its patterns' tell us about the music that
is heard?
5 What usually prevents us from perceiving the 'blessedness' that
the writer speaks of?

B: 1 'all the more' (line 1). – In what way "all the more"?
2 How does the writer emphasise the idea of 'silence'?
3 Explain how the writer treats the noise of the train in the far
distance.
4 What is the dramatic effect of 'Music, you say' (line 10)?
5 How appropriate is the reference to the djinns and the *Arabian
Nights*?
6 With what object is the long sentence, lines 18–24, constructed as
it is?
7 Why does the writer retreat from the word 'is' (line 27)?
8 What is the effect of the *'Benedictus, benedictus . . .'*, repeated later
in the final paragraph?
9 What is the effect of the word 'rasps' (line 44)?

2.5
Rejected

Then they were gone: the final feet, the final door. Then he
heard the car drown the noise of the insects, riding above,
sinking to the level, sinking below the level so that he heard
only the insects. He lay there beneath the light. He could not
move yet, as he could look without actually seeing, hear without actually knowing; the two wireends not yet knit as he

lay peacefully, licking his lips now and then as a child does. Then the wireends knit and made connection. He did not know the exact instant, save that suddenly he was aware of his
10 ringing head, and he sat up slowly, discovering himself again, getting to his feet. He was dizzy; the room went round him, slowly and smoothly as thinking, so that thinking said *Not yet* But he still felt no pain, not even when, propped before the bureau, he examined in the glass his swollen and bloody face and touched his face. 'Sweet Jesus,' he said. 'They sure beat me up.' He was not thinking yet; it had not yet risen that far *I reckon I better get out of here I reckon I better get out of here* He went toward the door, his hands out before him like a blind man or a sleepwalker. He was in the hall without having
20 remembered passing through the door, and he found himself in another bedroom while he still hoped perhaps not believed that he was moving toward the front door. It was small too. Yet it still seemed to be filled with the presence of the blonde woman, its very cramped harsh walls bulged outward with that militant and diamond-surfaced respectability. On the bare bureau sat a pint bottle almost full of whisky. He drank it, slowly, not feeling the fire at all, holding himself upright by holding to the bureau. The whisky went down his throat cold as molasses, without taste. He set the empty bottle
30 down and leaned on the bureau, his head lowered, not thinking, waiting perhaps without knowing it, perhaps not even waiting. Then the whisky began to burn in him and he began to shake his head slowly from side to side, while thinking became one with the slow, hot coiling and recoiling of his entrails: 'I got to get out of here.' He re-entered the hall. Now it was his head that was clear and his body that would not behave. He had to coax it along the hall, sliding it along one wall toward the front, thinking. 'Come on, now; pull yourself together. I got to get out.' Thinking *If I can just get it*
40 *outside, into the air, the cool air, the cool dark* He watched his hands fumbling at the door, trying to help them, to coax and control them. 'Anyway, they didn't lock it on me,' he thought. 'Sweet Jesus, I could not have got out until morning then. I never would have opened a window and climbed through it.' He opened the door at last and passed out and closed the door behind him, arguing again with his body which did not want to bother to close the door, having to be forced to close it upon the empty house where the two lights burned with their dead and unwavering glare, not knowing that the house
50 was empty and not caring, not caring anymore for silence

38

and desolation than they had cared for the cheap and brutal nights of stale oftused glasses and stale oftused beds. His body was acquiescing better, becoming docile. He stepped from the dark porch, into the moonlight, and with his bloody head and his empty stomach hot, savage, and courageous with whisky, he entered the street which was to run for fifteen years.

The whisky died away in time and was renewed and died again, but the street ran on. From that night the thousand streets ran as one street, with imperceptible corners and changes of scene, broken by intervals of begged and stolen rides, on trains and trucks, and on country wagons with he at twenty and twenty-five and thirty sitting on the seat with his still, hard face and the clothes (even when soiled and worn) of a city man and the driver of the wagon not knowing who or what the passenger was and not daring to ask. The street ran into Oklahoma and Missouri and as far south as Mexico and then back north to Chicago and Detroit and then back south again and at last to Mississippi. It was fifteen years long: it ran between the savage and spurious board fronts of oil towns where, his inevitable serge clothing and light shoes black with bottomless mud, he ate crude food from tin dishes that cost him ten and fifteen dollars a meal and paid for them with a roll of banknotes the size of a bull-frog and stained too with the rich mud that seemed as bottomless as the gold which it excreted. It ran through yellow wheat fields waving beneath the fierce yellow days of labour and hard sleep in haystacks beneath the cold mad moon of September, and the brittle stars: he was in turn labourer, miner, prospector, gambling tout; he enlisted in the army, served four months and deserted and was never caught. And always, sooner or later, the street ran through cities, through an identical and well-nigh inter-changeable section of cities without remembered names, where beneath the dark and equivocal and symbolical arch-ways of midnight he bedded with the women and paid them when he had the money, and when he did not have it he bedded anyway and then told them that he was a negro. For a while it worked; that was while he was still in the south. It was quite simple, quite easy. Usually all he risked was a curs-ing from the woman and the matron of the house, though now and then he was beaten unconscious by other patrons, to waken later in the street or in the jail.

from *Light in August*, WILLIAM FAULKNER

NOTE *Joe Christmas, the central character of this novel, is dogged by un-certainty as to whether he has an element of negro blood, which makes it very difficult for him to adjust to American society.*

A: 1 What can you infer has just happened to Joe?
2 What characteristics of 'thinking' are implied here in lines 12 and 30–31?
3 How does the author indicate that this experience constitutes a turning point in Joe's life?
4 What were the features of Joe's life for the fifteen years following?
5 What exactly was the 'gold' (line 75)?
6 What general attitude towards Joe is expressed by the author in this passage?

B: 1 What is the effect of the rhythm of the first sentence?
2 Explain the metaphor of the 'wireends' (lines 6 and 8). Why does this word seem puzzling at first sight?
3 'Sweet Jesus' (line 15). Would you condemn the author for blas-phemy here, or how would you justify the use of this expression?
4 What is the effect of the light bulbs in this passage?
5 Demonstrate the effect produced by the use of short and long sentences in relation to the context.
6 How does the author convey the effect of Joe's reduced conscious-ness here, especially in lines 11–42.
7 Discuss the symbol of the 'street' (line 56).

Section 2 PRACTICAL

c: 1 Describe the scene at a railway station or airport as an important person arrives.

2 Describe the growth of any plant you have had the opportunity of watching, through all the stages of its growth, development, maturity, and decline.

3 Suppose that you have had some reason to get up an hour before dawn. Describe the signs and stages by which the rest of the world 'wakes up'.

4 Describe in detail a local festival or ceremony from your own area, aiming to convey as much of the spirit of the events and the feelings of those participating as possible.

5 Describe the stages of your acquaintance with a new person who 'comes into your life' – a friend, teacher, priest, neighbour, etc. etc.

6 Give an eye-witness account of characteristic scenes from the same town as you may have introduced in Section 1 *C* 2.

7 Give your picture in words of a great storm sweeping over a locality with which you are familiar.

8 Arrange a visit to a factory, printing press, power station, etc., and give your detailed impressions of what you saw and how it impressed you.

9 Give your detailed impression of what is represented in the picture below.

From *National Trust Properties, 1963*; Godreavy, Cornwall

41

10 Convey what you 'see' in the artistic work below, i.e. not only specific objects which you can identify, but the character and effect of the whole.

Lino Bronze Relief 1966—BEAUTY AND **WILD** LIFE *by Onobrakpeya*

Section 3

LANGUAGE FOR THOUGHT

'Thought' is the principal means by which men recognise, classify and organise their experience, and make plans for further action. The precise connections between 'language' and 'thought' is still a matter of absorbing experiment and speculation by psychologists and philosophers, but we are all aware of how our ability to 'think things out' depends on our command of language. Conversely, we often become aware of how the processes of thought can miscarry if language is inadequately controlled.

3.1

Erosion

Erosion in Nature is a beneficent process without which the world would have died long ago. The same process, accelerated by human mismanagement, has become one of the most vicious and destructive forces that had ever been released by man. What is usually known as 'geological erosion' or 'denudation' is a universal phenomenon which through thousands of years has carved the earth into its present shape. Denudation is an early and important process in soil formation, whereby the original rock material is continuously
10 broken down and sorted out by wind and water until it becomes suitable for colonisation by plants. Plants, by the binding effects of their roots, by the protection they afford against rain and wind and by the fertility they impart to the soil, bring denudation almost to a standstill. Everybody must have compared the rugged and irregular shape of bare mountain peaks where denudation is still active with the smooth and harmonious curves of slopes that have long been protected by a mantle of vegetation. Nevertheless, some slight

denudation is always occurring. As each superficial film of
20 plant-covered soil becomes exhausted it is removed by rain
or wind, to be deposited mainly in the rivers and sea, and
a corresponding thin layer of new soil forms by slow weather-
ing of the underlying rock. The earth is continuously discard-
ing its old, worn-out skin and renewing its living sheath of
soil from the dead rock beneath. In this way an equilibrium
is reached between denudation and soil formation so that,
unless the equilibrium is disturbed, a mature soil preserves
a more or less constant depth and character indefinitely. The
depth is sometimes only a few inches, occasionally several
30 feet, but within it lies the whole capacity of the earth to produce life. Below that thin layer comprising the delicate organism known as soil is a planet as lifeless as the moon.

The equilibrium between denudation and soil formation is
easily disturbed by the activities of man. Cultivation, de-
forestation or the destruction of natural vegetation by graz-
ing or other means, unless carried out according to certain
immutable conditions imposed by each region, may so accelerate denudation that the soil, which would normally be
washed or blown away in a century, disappears within a year
40 or even within a day. But no human ingenuity can accelerate
the soil-renewing process from lifeless rock to an extent at all
comparable to the acceleration of denudation.

This man-accelerated denudation is what is now known as
soil erosion. It is the almost inevitable result of reducing
below a certain limit the natural fertility of the soil – of man
betraying his most sacred trust when he assumes dominion
over the land. . . .

That the ultimate consequence of unchecked soil erosion,
when it sweeps over whole countries as it is doing today, must
50 be national extinction is obvious, for whatever other essential
raw material a nation may dispense with, it cannot exist without fertile soil. Nor is extinction of a nation by erosion merely
a hypothetical occurrence that may occur at some future date;
it has occurred several times in the past. Erosion has, indeed,
been one of the most potent factors causing the downfall of
former civilisations and empires whose ruined cities now lie
amid barren wastes that once were the world's most fertile
lands. The deserts of North China, Persia, Mesopotamia, and
North Africa tell the same story of the gradual exhaustion of
60 the soil as the increasing demands made upon it by expanding
civilisation exceeded its recuperative powers. Soil erosion,
then as now, followed soil exhaustion. . . .

44

For erosion is the modern symptom of maladjustment between human society and its environment. It is a warning that
Nature is in full revolt against the sudden incursion of an exotic
civilisation into her ordered domains. Men are permitted to
dominate Nature on precisely the same condition as trees and
plants, namely on condition that they improve the soil and
leave it a little better for their posterity than they found
70 it. Agriculture in Europe, whatever its other weaknesses,
has been, and perhaps still is, a practice tending on the whole
to increase soil fertility. When adopted and adapted elsewhere
it has resulted, almost invariably, in a catastrophic decrease
in fertility. The illusion that fertility can always be restored
by applying some of the huge amounts of artificial fertilisers
now available has been shattered by the recognition that
fertility is not merely a matter of plant-food supply (for even
exhausted soils usually contain ample reserves of plant food),
but is also closely connected with soil *stability*. An exhausted
80 soil is an unstable soil. Nature has no further use for it and
removes it bodily. The process is the same as denudation, but
whereas under normal conditions a fraction of an inch of soil
may become exhausted and be removed in a century, under
human control the entire depth of soil may become exhausted
and be eroded in a few years.

from *The Rape of the Earth*, G. V. JACKS AND R. O. WHYTE

A: 1 What is erosion, and what are its chief agents?
   2 How is 'erosion in Nature' a beneficent process, and yet in
     other circumstances a misfortune?
   3 How can soil be called an 'organism' (lines 31–32)?
   4 In what ways can human agency disturb the equilibrium between
     denudation and soil formation?
   5 Why is the possibility that soil erosion can lead to the extinction of
     nations not just a 'hypothetical occurrence' (line 53)?
   6 'Men are permitted . . .' (line 66) – by whom? What kind of
     philosophical framework to the passage does this imply?
   7 Why is the application of artificial fertilisers to the soil no solution
     to the problem of erosion?
   8 What might be the 'other weaknesses' (line 70) of European
     agriculture?

B: 1 Point out words which indicate that this passage is at a high level
     of generalisation.
   2 Discuss the precise meaning here, in relation to their other pos-
     sible meanings of:
     colonisation (line 11)

exotic (line 65)

3 What attitudes does the author seem to betray towards
 [a] the world of Nature
 [b] the activities of Man?
4 What evidence can you find to indicate that the writer aims to
 appeal to a wide range of unspecialised readers?
5 Consider the effect of the comparison of the earth's soil to a skin
 (line 24).
6 How is the reference to the moon (line 32) effective?
7 Consider the varieties of sentence structure in paragraph 2.
8 Discuss the idea of the 'sacred trust' (line 46) and man's 'assuming domination over the land' (line 47).

3.2
Heresy

It still remains to speak of one of the principal causes which
make diversity of opinion advantageous, and will continue to
do so until mankind shall have entered a stage of intellectual
advancement which at present seems at an incalculable distance. We have hitherto considered only two possibilities:
that the received opinion may be false, and some other opinion, consequently, true; or that, the received opinion being
true, a conflict with the opposite error is essential to a clear
apprehension and deep feeling of its truth. But there is a
10 commoner case than either of these: when the conflicting
doctrines, instead of being one true and the other false, share
the truth between them; and the nonconforming opinion is
needed to supply the remainder of the truth, of which the
received doctrine embodies only a part. Popular opinions, on
subjects not palpable to sense, are often true, but seldom
or never the whole truth. They are a part of the truth; sometimes a greater, sometimes a smaller part, but exaggerated,
distorted, and disjointed from the truths by which they ought
to be accompanied and limited. Heretical opinions, on the
20 other hand, are generally some of these suppressed and
neglected truths, bursting the bonds which kept them down,
and either seeking reconciliation with the truth contained in
the common opinion, or fronting it as enemies, and setting
themselves up, with similar exclusiveness, as the whole truth.
The latter case is hitherto the most frequent, as, in the human
mind, one-sidedness has always been the rule, and many-
sidedness the exception. Hence, even in revolutions of

opinion, one part of the truth usually sets while another rises. Even progress, which ought to superadd, for the most part only substitutes, one partial and incomplete truth for another; improvement consisting chiefly in this, that the new fragment of truth is more wanted, more adapted to the needs of the time, than that which it displaces. Such being the partial character of prevailing opinions, even when resting on a true foundation, every opinion which embodies somewhat of the portion of truth which the common opinion omits, ought to be considered precious, with whatever amount of error and confusion that truth may be blended. No sober judge of human affairs will feel bound to be indignant because those who force on our notice truths which we should otherwise have overlooked, overlook some of those which we see. Rather, he will think that so long as popular truth is one-sided, it is more desirable than otherwise that unpopular truth should have one-sided assertors too; such being usually the most energetic, and the most likely to compel reluctant attention to the fragment of wisdom which they proclaim as if it were the whole.

Thus, in the eighteenth century, when nearly all the instructed, and all those of the uninstructed who were led by them, were lost in admiration of what is called civilisation, and of the marvels of modern science, literature, and philosophy, and while greatly overrating the amount of unlikeness between the men of modern and those of ancient times, indulged the belief that the whole of the difference was in their own favour; with what a salutary shock did the paradoxes of Rousseau explode like bombshells in the midst, dislocating the compact mass of one-sided opinion, and forcing its elements to recombine in a better form and with additional ingredients. Not that the current opinions were on the whole farther from the truth than Rousseau's were; on the contrary, they were nearer to it; they contained more of positive truth, and very much less of error. Nevertheless there lay in Rousseau's doctrine, and has floated down the stream of opinion along with it, a considerable amount of exactly those truths which the popular opinion wanted; and these are the deposit which was left behind when the flood subsided. The superior worth of simplicity of life, the enervating and demoralising effect of the trammels and hypocrisies of artificial society, are ideas which have never been entirely absent from cultivated minds since Rousseau wrote; and they will in time produce their due effect, though at present needing to be asserted as much as ever, and to be asserted by deeds, for words, on this subject, have nearly exhausted their power.

from On Liberty, JOHN STUART MILL

NOTE received opinion = *generally accepted,* i.e. *orthodox opinion.*

A: 1 *Heresy* is often a word implying condemnation. Which is the phrase in the first sentence which conveys the same idea in objective terms?
2 Recapitulate the arguments previously used to justify liberty of expression.
3 What common view of both 'received opinion' and 'heresy' is expressed in lines 14–24?
4 Why ought 'every opinion to be considered precious' (line 36)?
5 Why are ordinary people (as opposed to 'sober judges' – line 38) often indignant about heretics?
6 What argument is put forward to suggest that even 'unpopular truth' should have 'one-sided assertors' (line 44)?
7 Show how the general thesis of the passage is illustrated by the case of Rousseau.
8 What would be the features of the 'stage of intellectual advancement' which seems to Mill to be 'at an incalculable distance' (lines 3–4)?

B: 1 In what style of language is this passage cast? What influences may have been working upon it? Would you describe it as pompous, or is it well devised for its purpose?
2 Show how the author carefully indicates the steps of his argument.
3 What is the importance of the qualification contained in the words 'not palpable to sense' (line 15)?
4 Comment on the metaphor in lines 28–29. To what extent does the passage as a whole make use of metaphor?
5 Comment on the sentence structure at line 31. 'improvement consisting chiefly in this, that. . . .'
6 'No sober judge of human affairs' (line 38). Is there any element of irony here? Or elsewhere, for example in lines 48–55?
7 What kind of 'deeds' might the author be hinting at (line 72)?

3.3
Civilisation

I have not yet defined civilisation; but perhaps I have made definition superfluous. Anyone, I fancy, who has done me the honour of reading so far will by now understand pretty well

what I mean. Civilisation is a characteristic of societies. In its crudest form it is the characteristic which differentiates what anthropologists call 'advanced' from what they call 'low' or 'backward' societies. So soon as savages begin to apply reason to instinct, so soon as they acquire a rudimentary sense of values – so soon, that is, as they begin to distinguish
10 between ends and means, or between direct means to good and remote – they have taken the first step upward. The first step towards civilisation is the correcting of instinct by reason: the second, the deliberate rejection of immediate satisfactions with a view to obtaining subtler. The hungry savage, when he catches a rabbit, eats it there and then, or instinctively takes it home, as a fox might, to be eaten raw by his cubs; the first who, all hungry though he was, took it home and cooked it was on the road to Athens. He was a pioneer, who with equal justice may be described as the first decadent. The
20 fact is significant. Civilisation is something artificial and un-natural. Progress and Decadence are interchangeable terms. All who have added to human knowledge and sensibility, and most of those even who have merely increased material comfort, have been hailed by contemporaries capable of profiting by their discoveries as benefactors, and denounced by all whom age, stupidity, or jealousy rendered incapable, as degenerates. It is silly to quarrel about words: let us agree that the habit of cooking one's victuals may with equal pro-priety be considered a step towards civilisation or a falling
30 away from the primitive perfection of the upstanding ape.

From these primary qualities, Reasonableness and a Sense of Values, may spring a host of secondaries: a taste for truth and beauty, tolerance, intellectual honesty, fastidiousness, a sense of humour, good manners, curiosity, a dislike of vulgarity, brutality, and over-emphasis, freedom from super-stition and prudery, a fearless acceptance of the good things of life, a desire for complete self-expression and for a liberal education, a contempt for utilitarianism and philistinism, in two words – sweetness and light. Not all societies that
40 struggle out of barbarism grasp all or even most of these, and fewer still grasp any of them firmly. That is why we find a considerable number of civilised societies and very few highly civilised, for only by grasping a good handful of civil-ised qualities and holding them tight does a society become that.

But can an entity so vague as a society be said to have or to hold qualities so subtle? Only in the vaguest sense. Societies

49

express themselves in certain more or less permanent and
more or less legible forms which become for anthropologists
50 and historians monuments of their civility. They express
themselves in manners, customs and conventions, in laws
and in social and economic organisation, above all, in the
literature, science and art they have appreciated and encouraged: less surely they tell us something about themselves
through the literature, science and art, which they may or
may not have appreciated, but which was created by artists
and thinkers whom they produced. All these taken together
may be reckoned – none too confidently – to compose a
legible symbol of a prevailing attitude to life. And it is this
60 attitude, made manifest in these more or less public and
permanent forms, which we call civilisation.

from *Civilisation*, CLIVE BELL

A: 1 How could definition of a topic such as this be 'superfluous'
(line 2)?
2 Discuss the principal criteria of 'civilisation' suggested.
3 What was the difference between the 'savage' who takes a rabbit
home to be eaten raw by his children and the one who took a rabbit
home to cook it?
4 Is the author as impartial in distinguishing between Progress
and Decadence as he claims? What motives does he attribute to
traditionalists?
5 Consider in turn each of the 'secondary qualities' of civilisation,
and show how it derives from the 'primary' ones.
6 Does 'civilisation' seem a characteristic of a community, or of
individual members?

B: 1 Observe and discuss the transitions between 1st person singular,
1st person plural, and 3rd person in this passage.
2 Point out phrases in this passage which give an effect of col-
loquiality in spite of the intellectual tone.
3 Why does the author draw support from 'anthropologists' (line
49) in his differentiation between 'advanced' and 'backward'
societies?
4 What is the significance of the tense differences between
catches, eats, takes
and   was, took, cooked (lines 15–18)?
5 Do you regard lines 21–27 as an unnecessary digression?
6 Can you explain more clearly the two kinds of 'literature, science
and art' referred to in lines 50–57?
7 What do you gather from the 'above all' (line 52)?

3·4

Language and Thought

It is evident that there is a close connection between the capacity to use language and the capacities covered by the verb 'to think'. Indeed, some writers have identified thinking with using words: Plato coined the aphorism, 'In thinking the soul is talking to itself'; J. B. Watson reduced thinking to inhibited speech located in the minute movements or tensions of the physiological mechanisms involved in speaking; and although Ryle is careful to point out that there are many senses in which a person is said to think in which words are not
10 in evidence, he has also said that saying something in a specific frame of mind is thinking a thought.

Is thinking reducible to, or dependent upon, language habits? It would seem that many thinking situations are hardly distinguishable from the skilful use of language, although there are some others in which language is not involved. Thought cannot be simply identified with using language. It may be the case, of course, that the non-linguistic skills involved in thought can only be acquired and developed if the learner is able to use and understand language. How-
20 ever, this question is one which we cannot hope to answer in this book. Obviously being able to use language makes for a considerable development in all one's capacities but how precisely this comes about we cannot say.

At the common-sense level it appears that there is often a distinction between thought and the words we employ to communicate with other people. We often have to struggle hard to find words to capture what our thinking has already grasped, and when we do find words we sometimes feel that they fail to do their job properly. Again when we report or
30 describe our thinking to other people we do not merely report unspoken words and sentences. Such sentences do not always occur in thinking, and when they do they are merged with vague imagery and the hint of unconscious or subliminal activities going on just out of range. Thinking, as it happens, is more like struggling, striving, or searching for something than it is like talking or reading. Words do play their part but they are rarely the only feature of thought. This observation is supported by the experiments of the Wurzburg psychologists reported in Chapter Eight who showed that
40 intelligent adaptive responses can occur in problem-solving

situations without the use of either words or images of any kind. 'Set' and 'determining tendencies' operate without the actual use of language in helping us to think purposefully and intelligently.

Again the study of speech disorders due to brain injury or disease suggest that patients can think without having adequate control over their language. Some patients, for example, fail to find the names of objects presented to them and are unable to describe simple events which they witness;
50 they even find it difficult to interpret long written notices. But they succeed in playing games of chess or draughts. They can use the concepts needed for chess playing or draughts playing but are unable to use many of the concepts in ordinary language. How they manage to do this we do not know. Yet animals such as Kohler's chimpanzees can solve problems by working out strategies such as the invention of implements or climbing aids when such animals have no language beyond a few warning cries. Intelligent or 'insightful' behaviour is not dependent in the case of monkeys on
60 language skills: presumably human beings have various capacities for thinking situations which are likewise independent of language.

from *The Psychology of Thinking*, ROBERT THOMSON

A: 1 Give your own survey of the 'capacities covered by the verb *to think*' (line 3).
2 Explain the theory of 'thought' devised by J. B. Watson. What does the author indicate by his use of the word 'reduced'?
3 Describe a typical 'thinking situation' which is hardly distinguishable from the 'skilful use of language' (line 14).
4 How could 'non-linguistic skills' (lines 17–18) involved in thought be dependent upon language?
5 Survey the evidence for believing that 'language' and 'thought' are not identical.
6 What features does the author seem to be attaching to 'talking and reading' (line 36)?
7 How do the concepts involved in playing draughts and chess differ from those used in language?

B: 1 Illustrate the orderliness of procedure in this passage, and note the devices by which 'cohesion' is maintained.
2 Consider the use of question in exposition, as in lines 12–13.
3 '... which we cannot hope to answer in this book' (lines 20–21) – What does this imply?
4 'At the common-sense level' (line 24) – What verbal signal indicates

that the author is passing to another level, and what is that level?

5 How satisfied are you with the statement that 'thinking is more like struggling, striving, or searching for something' (line 35)?

6 How much do you actually learn about the experiments of the Wurzburg psychologists?

7 Kohler's chimpanzees' (line 55). What is the relationship between Kohler and the chimpanzees?

3·5

Primitive

To some extent it is for these reasons that various attempts have been made to find some other appellation by which these most recently discovered peoples might be designated. Such terms as 'native' and 'aboriginal' are inappropriate, since all persons are native to particular areas, while aboriginal peoples are the prehistoric populations of the world. 'Nonliterate' and 'tribal' are other terms frequently used, but these, too, are unsatisfactory. 'Nonliterate' was coined especially to replace 'primitive' and can only mean peoples
10 who are not literate – that is, who have not learned to read; this designation is applicable to all of the illiterate peoples of many countries and hence has a restricted usage. The word 'tribal' is little more satisfactory as a replacement, since a good number of primitive peoples are not organised in a tribal pattern, and it is erroneous to consider them in this way; at the same time, numerous tribes, such as those of the Islamic peoples, have high cultures.

What word, then, is suitable to define these peoples, called by their discoverers 'primitive'? Since the last war, they have
20 been categorised as the peoples of 'underdeveloped' areas. This cannot mean, however, underdeveloped with respect to the history of their own cultures, but only by comparison with the technological standards of the high cultures of the world. It is apparent that the term 'primitive' was not used because of its derogatory implications, and to discredit them as being so is only out of a false respect for the sensitive feelings of these peoples who have so recently become 'our brothers'. Perhaps even a sense of guilt, a remembrance of past exploitations and intentional disruptions of their ways of life, is
30 somewhat responsible for the concept of these peoples as 'underdeveloped'. It would seem that by far the word most

applicable to these societies is the one given to them historically, namely 'primitive'. But this is not because they represent the fumbling, early beginnings of civilisation; rather, it is because these cultures show developments more closely allied to the fundamental, basic, and essential drives of life that have not been buried under a multitude of parasitical, non-essential desires. These are not, in so many of their aspects, simpler cultures; and certainly, within their own
40 tenets, they have had a long and evolved development. That the rate of change has been slow is a consequence of their conservatism, a concomitant of their close adherence to tradition, that is, to those ideas and practices which, through time, have been established as valid. It seems highly desirable to accept 'primitive' as a reasonable term, and to make clear that its use in designating these cultures must be thoroughly understood.

Used in this way, 'primitive' refers largely to the Negro peoples south of the Sahara in Africa; to the Eskimo and
50 the American Indian, excluding the high cultures of the Andean region, Central America, and Mexico; and to the peoples who inhabited the islands of the Pacific Ocean, Australia, and certain areas of the islands off the coast of South-east Asia at the time of their discovery. In relation to these cultures, 'primitive' is a meaningful word of historical status, which refers to the cultures existent largely in those parts of the world brought to light during the Age of Discovery and subsequent explorations. When used in this context, it has no derogatory connotations, and to give it
60 such shows a lack of knowledge or a personal bias.

from *Primitive Art*, PAUL S. WINGERT

A: 1 State the object of the 'various attempts' (line 1).
   2 Why has there been general dissatisfaction with the word 'primitive'?
   3 Why are the following terms in turn rejected:
      native, aboriginal, nonliterate, tribal, underdeveloped.
   4 What conclusion does the author come to in his search for a 'suitable appellation'?
   5 Explain the meaning he proposes to attach to the old term in order to make it more acceptable.
   6 What argument is used to explain the 'conservatism' of so-called primitive cultures.
   7 Show how the author indicates the geographical limits of the word he has rehabilitated.

B: 1 'What's in a word?' Do you consider the care shown by this author to be necessary, or pedantic?

2 Into what register does the style of this passage fall: of art appreciation, of ethnology, of racialism, of philosophical discussion, or what?

3 Consider the use of words such as
appellation (line 2) for name
designated (line 11) for called
erroneous (line 15) for wrong
categorised (line 20) for described.

4 Give a brief history of the word 'native'.

5 What does the author imply are the principal characteristics of the 'high cultures' (line 23)?

6 Consider the implications of the phrase 'recently discovered' (line 3).

7 Comment on the reasons for the word 'underdeveloped' being more recently replaced by 'developing'.

Section 3 PRACTICAL

C: 1 Choose one of the urgent social problems of your own community at the present time (e.g. unemployment, poverty, malnutrition, corruption, underdevelopment, disharmony, materialism, fanaticism, etc. etc.). Analyse clearly the factors which have contributed to its existence, and indicate the lines along which in your opinion it can be solved.

2 What are the reasons for valuing the famous 'freedoms' – of expression, of movement, of association, and of belief, in a modern community?

3 How can the tendency to revert to forms of military government in many parts of the world in the latter part of the twentieth century be explained? Can it also in any cases be justified?

4 Discuss the role of 'force' or 'compulsion' in human affairs, considering its application at various levels, e.g. in the family, in a school or college, nationally, internationally.

5 Give your account of the qualities and capacities you associate with the idea of being 'educated'.

6 Consider the ways in which 'developing' countries may expect to benefit from 'developed' countries. Is there a reciprocal process which is, or ought to be, in operation?

7 Describe and discuss any instances known to you in which scientific methods of investigation and experiment have been applied to the solution of any social problem or disaster, e.g. a crime, an air crash, an epidemic, etc.

8 Describe clearly the stages by which men have arrived at a correct understanding of any of the following:

[a] the tendency of things to 'fall downwards'.
[b] the shape of the Earth.
[c] the nature of the Universe
[d] the constitution of light
[e] the cause of 'Consumption' (i.e. 'T.B.')
  of 'Madness'
  of Malaria.
[f] the meaning that can be attached to the word 'God'.

9 Write an orderly account of 'the Novel', including the essential elements from the following quotations, and embodying any other knowledge you have available:

[a] A fictitious prose narrative of considerable length, in which characters and actions representative of real life are portrayed in a plot of more or less complexity.

Shorter Oxford Dictionary

[b] 'And what are you reading, Miss ——?' 'Oh! it is only a novel!' replies the young lady; while she lays down her book with affected indifference, or momentary shame. 'It is only *Cecilia*, or *Camilla*, or *Belinda*'; or, in short, only some work in which the greatest powers of the mind are displayed, in which the most thorough knowledge of human nature, the happiest delineation of its varieties, the liveliest effusions of wit and humour, are conveyed to the world in the best chosen language.

from Northanger Abbey, JANE AUSTEN

[c] Now I absolutely flatly deny that I am a soul, or a body, or a mind, or an intelligence, or a brain, or a nervous system, or a bunch of glands, or any of the rest of these bits of me. The whole is greater than the part. And therefore, I, who am man alive, am greater than my soul, or spirit, or body, or mind, or consciousness, or anything else that is merely a part of me. I am a man, and live. I am man alive, and as long as I can, I intend to go on being man alive.

For this reason I am a novelist. And being a novelist, I consider myself superior to the saint, the scientist, the philosopher, and the poet, who are all great masters of different bits of man alive, but never get the whole hog.

The novel is the one bright book of life. Books are not life. They are only tremulations on the ether. But the novel as a tremulation can make the whole man alive tremble. Which is more than poetry, philosophy, science, or any other book-tremulation can do.

from Why the Novel Matters, D. H. LAWRENCE

[d] Where have modern intellectuals learned, together with their anti-intellectualism, these diffident gestures of the spirit?

The answer is: in the novel. ... Unlike tragedy, voluminous and explicit, the novel depicts life with cruel educational intent, has been the text book of increasingly plain manners, a manual of resentful self-consciousness. ... The novel knows no magnanimity or logic and makes the most trivial traits indicative. ... No wonder modern man has grown suspicious of himself and others, devious, ironic.

from *The House of Intellect,* JACQUES BARZUN

10 Plan your approach, including the forms of expression you would use, for any of the following needs:

[*a*] To recover a long outstanding loan from a friend you would not sue.

[*b*] To apologise for an unintended insult.

[*c*] To recommend someone, when you feel there is a danger that your recommendation may be a disadvantage.

[*d*] To make suggestions to a superior, without seeming officious.

[*e*] To make enquiries about someone, without seeming inquisitive.

[*f*] To discourage someone who occupies too much of your time.

[*g*] To explain why you have not returned something borrowed from a friend for a short time only.

[*h*] To inform someone of an accident to a beloved person or prized possession.

[*i*] To bring about a reconciliation between two 'third parties'.

[*j*] To deter a friend from taking a disastrous decision.

[*k*] To express condolence for the death of someone generally disliked.

[*l*] To gain credence for an incredible story.

[*m*] To recommend a project of your own to someone who is likely to be unsympathetic.

[*n*] To admit a change of plan to someone who has already given much time and trouble to help you make a decision.

Section 4

LANGUAGE FOR PERSUASION

The urge to convey one's needs effectively to other people is one of the funda-mental origins of language, and this becomes successively more complex as the individual develops and as human affairs become more intricate. The ancient Greeks studied this aspect of language under the title of Rhetoric, one of the earliest intellectual and manipulative disciplines in the history of language study. Language of course may be used for the promotion of both worthy and unworthy causes, using either valid or invalid methods, and the use of language for persuasion should be attended by a rational critical consciousness. Nevertheless any mastery of a language must include the capacity to marshal facts and arguments in such a way as to gain maxi-mum attention to them.

4.1

Racial Equality

The truth is that our Christian civilisation is riddled through and through with dilemma. We believe in the brotherhood of man, but we do not want it in South Africa. We believe that God endows men with diverse gifts, and that human life depends for its fullness on their employment and enjoyment, but we are afraid to explore this belief too deeply. We believe in help for the underdog, but we want him to stay under. And we are therefore compelled, in order to preserve our belief that we are Christian, to ascribe in Almighty God, Creator
10 of Heaven and Earth, our own human intentions, and to say that, because He created white and black, He gives the Divine Approval to any human action that is designed to keep black men from advancement. We go so far as to credit Almighty God with having created black men to hew wood and draw water for white men. We go so far as to assume that He blesses

58

any action that is designed to prevent black men from the full employment of the gifts He gave them. Alongside of these very arguments we use others totally inconsistent, so that the accusation of repression may be refuted. We say we withhold
20 education because the black child has not the intelligence to profit by it; we withhold opportunity to develop gifts because black people have no gifts; we justify our action by saying that it took us thousands of years to achieve our own advancement, and it would be foolish to suppose that it will take the black man any lesser time, and that therefore there is no need for hurry. We shift our ground again when a black man does achieve something remarkable, and feel deep pity for a man who is condemned to the loneliness of being remarkable, and decide that it is a Christian kindness not
30 to let black men become remarkable. Thus even our God becomes a confused and inconsistent creature, giving gifts and denying them employment. Is it strange then that our civilisation is riddled through and through with dilemma? The truth is that our civilisation is not Christian; it is a tragic compound of great ideal and fearful practice, of high assurance and desperate anxiety, of loving charity and fearful clutching of possessions. . . .

from *Cry the Beloved Country*, ALAN PATON

NOTE *This is an excerpt from one of the papers left by the engineer, Arthur Jarvis, a noted opponent of apartheid in South Africa, who ironically was shot by a young African attempting to rob his house.*

A: 1 What is the specific topic that these remarks relate to?
2 To whom are the remarks addressed?
3 Who are the 'we' (line 2 and elsewhere)?
4 What are the arguments used by the opposite party to refute the accusation that they are repressive (line 19)?
5 Explain the 'deep pity' which is felt for 'black men who have done something remarkable' (line 27).
6 In view of other comments adjoining, how precise is the statement that 'our civilisation is not Christian' (line 34)?
7 What is the ultimate implication of these remarks?

B: 1 What degree of importance do you give to the expression 'The truth is . . .' (line 1)?
2 Examine the pattern of sentences in lines 2–7, and comment on their effect.
3 Can you express more lucidly the content of the sentence in lines 7–13?

4 What is the effect of 'we go so far as to . . .' (lines 13 and 15)?
5 Explain in detail the relevance of the metaphor 'We shift our ground' (line 26).
6 'our God becomes . . .' (lines 31–32). What light does this throw on the nature of meaning in words?
7 What is the nature of the question, (lines 32–33)?
8 Examine the antithesis of words in the final sentence.
9 What meaning can be inferred from the context for the word 'tragic' (line 34)?

4.2

Independence

When, in the course of human events, it becomes necessary from one people to dissolve the political bands which have connected them with another, and to assume, among the powers of the earth, the separate and equal station to which the laws of nature and of nature's God entitle them, a decent respect to the opinions of mankind requires that they should declare the causes which impel them to the separation.

We hold these truths to be self-evident, that all men are created equal; that they are endowed by their Creator with
10 certain unalienable rights; that among these are life, liberty, and the pursuit of happiness. That, to secure these rights, governments are instituted among men, deriving their just powers from the consent of the governed; that, whenever any form of government becomes destructive of these ends, it is the right of the people to alter or to abolish it, and to institute a new government, laying its foundation on such principles, and organising its powers in such form, as to them shall seem most likely to effect their safety and happiness. Prudence, indeed, will dictate that governments long established should
20 not be changed for light and transient causes; and, accordingly, all experience hath shown, that mankind are more disposed to suffer, while evils are sufferable, than to right themselves by abolishing the forms to which they are accustomed. But, when a long train of abuses and usurpations, pursuing invariably the same object, evinces a design to reduce them under absolute despotism, it is their right, it is their duty, to throw off such government, and to provide new guards for their future security. Such has been the patient sufferance of these colonies, and such is now the
30 necessity which constrains them to alter their former systems of government.

The history of the present King of Great Britain is a history of repeated injuries and usurpations, all having, in direct object, the establishment of an absolute tyranny over these states. To prove this, let facts be submitted to a candid world:

He has refused his assent to laws the most wholesome and necessary for the public good.

He has forbidden his governors to pass laws of immediate and pressing importance, unless suspended in their operation 40 till his assent should be obtained; and, when so suspended, he has utterly neglected to attend to them. . . .

He is, at this time, transporting large armies of foreign mercenaries to complete the works of death, desolation, and tyranny, already begun, with circumstances of cruelty and perfidy scarcely paralleled in the most barbarous ages, and totally unworthy the head of a civilised nation.

He has constrained our fellow-citizens, taken captive on the high seas, to bear arms against their country, to become the executioners of their friends and brethren, or to fall them- 50 selves by their hands.

He has excited domestic insurrections amongst us, and has endeavoured to bring on the inhabitants of our frontiers, the merciless Indian savages, whose known rule of warfare is an undistinguished destruction of all ages, sexes, and conditions.

In every stage of these oppressions, we have petitioned for redress, in the most humble terms; our repeated petitions have been answered only by repeated injury. A prince, whose character is thus marked by every act which may define a tyrant, is unfit to be the ruler of a free people.

60 Nor have we been wanting in attention to our British brethren. We have warned them, from time to time, of at-tempts made by their legislature to extend an unwarrantable jurisdiction over us. We have reminded them of the circum-stances of emigration and settlement here. We have appealed to their native justice and magnanimity, and we have conjured them, by the ties of our common kindred, to disavow these usurpations, which would inevitably interrupt our connections and correspondence. They, too, have been deaf to the voice of justice and consanguinity. We must, therefore, acquiesce in 70 the necessity which denounces our separation, and hold them, as we hold the rest of mankind, enemies in war, in peace, friends.

We, therefore, the representative of the United States of America, in general Congress assembled, appealing to the Supreme Judge of the world for the rectitude of our inten-

tions, do, in the name, and by the authority of the good people
of these colonies, solemnly publish and declare, that these
united colonies are, and of right ought to be free and independent states; that they are absolved from all allegiance to the
80 British Crown, and that all political connection between
them and the state of Great Britain is, and ought to be, totally
dissolved; and that, as free and independent states, they
have full power to levy war, conclude peace, contract alliances,
establish commerce, and to do all other acts and things which
independent states may of right do. And, for the support of
this declaration, with a firm reliance on the protection of
Divine Providence, we mutually pledge to each other our lives,
our fortunes, and our sacred honour.

selected from *Declaration of American Independence*,

THOMAS JEFFERSON

NOTE *This is a shortened form of the Declaration of Independence: the
sections omitted are merely some of the 'facts' in the middle part.*

A: 1 What reasons do the authors give for publishing the Declaration
to mankind?
   2 What kind of sanctions are claimed in the opening and closing
paragraphs in support of Independence?
   3 Explain the theory of 'government' which is being put forward
in this document.
   4 How do the authors indicate that they are not lightly changing
their form of government?
   5 'Let facts be submitted . . .' (line 35). What is the hope expressed
in the word 'candid' (lines 35)?
   6 List as unemotionally as possible the grievances which are
asserted as grounds for the assumption of independence.
   7 Explain the distinction between 'prince' (line 57) and 'brethren'
(line 61).
   8 Explain the special force of the expression 'acquiesce in the
necessity' (lines 69–70).

B: 1 Give your own impression of the effect produced by this document?
Has it achieved fame because of its occasion, or because of its
inherent qualities?
   2 Illustrate the combination of modesty with firmness with which
the declaration is put forward.
   3 Examine the rhythmic relationships of the sentences from lines
1–18.
   4 Why are the 'truths' (line 8) said to be self-evident?
   5 Illustrate the use made of [a] legal, and [b] religious registers to
add solemnity to the declaration.

6 What is the nature of the transition from 'right' to 'duty' (lines 26–27)?
7 What is inexact about the expression 'The history of the present King of Great Britain' (line 32)?
8 How objectively would you say the 'facts' in paragraphs 4–9 are presented?
9 What comment do you make on the reference to the American Indians (lines 53–54)?
10 Can you justify the use of the word 'denounces' as in line 70?
11 What is the emotional effect of the final sentence?

4·3

The Second World War

In these pages I attempt to recount some of the incidents and impressions which form in my mind the story of the coming upon mankind of the worst tragedy in its tumultuous history. This presented itself not only in the destruction of life and property inseparable from war. There had been fearful slaughters of soldiers in the First World War, and much of the accumulated treasure of the nations was consumed. Still, apart from the excesses of the Russian Revolution, the main fabric of European civilisation remained erect at the close
10 of the struggle. When the storm and dust of the cannonade passed suddenly away, the nations, despite their enmities, could still recognise each other as historic racial personalities. The laws of war had on the whole been respected. There was a common professional meeting-ground between military men who had fought one another. Vanquished and victors alike still preserved the semblance of civilised States. A solemn peace was made which, apart from unenforceable financial aspects, conformed to the principles which in the nineteenth century had increasingly regulated the relations of enlight-
20 ened peoples. The reign of law was proclaimed, and a World Instrument was formed to guard us all, and especially Europe, against a renewed convulsion.

In the Second World War every bond between man and man was to perish. Crimes were committed by the Germans under the Hitlerite domination to which they allowed themselves to be subjected which find no equal in scale and wickedness with any that have darkened the human record. The wholesale massacre by systematised processes of six or seven

millions of men, women, and children in the German execu-
30 tion camps exceeds in horror the rough-and-ready butcheries
of Genghis Khan, and in scale reduces them to pigmy proportions. Deliberate extermination of whole populations was
contemplated and pursued by both Germany and Russia in
the Eastern war. The hideous process of bombarding open
cities from the air, once started by the Germans, was repaid
twenty-fold by the ever-mounting power of the Allies, and
found its culmination in the use of the atomic bombs which
obliterated Hiroshima and Nagasaki.

We have at length emerged from a scene of material ruin
40 and moral havoc the like of which had never darkened the
imagination of former centuries. After all that we suffered
and achieved we find ourselves still confronted with problems
and perils not less but far more formidable than those through
which we have so narrowly made our way.

It is my purpose, as one who lived and acted in these days,
to show how easily the tragedy of the Second World War could
have been prevented; how the malice of the wicked was reinforced by the weakness of the virtuous; how the structure
and habits of democratic States, unless they are welded into
50 larger organisms, lack those elements of persistence and
conviction which can alone give security to humble masses;
how, even in matters of self-preservation, no policy is pursued
for even ten or fifteen years at a time. We shall see how the
counsels of prudence and restraint may become the prime
agents of mortal danger; how the middle course adopted
from desires for safety and a quiet life may be found to lead
direct to the bull's-eye of disaster. We shall see how absolute
is the need of a broad path of international action pursued
by many States in common across the years, irrespective of
60 the ebb and flow of national politics.

from *The Gathering Storm*, WINSTON CHURCHILL

A: 1 In what ways, according to the author, was the First World
War less 'tragic' (line 3) than the Second?

2 What predilections of the author are signified by the word 'tumultuous' (line 3), especially in its context here?

3 With what other factors are 'life and property' (lines 4–5) compared? What value-assumptions does the author seem to be making?

4 In what specific way did the horrors of the Second World War
'exceed' (line 30) those attributed to Genghis Khan?

5 What means are used to maintain an element of impartiality in
lines 24–28?

6 What ethical anomalies does the author intend to illustrate?

7 What general political wisdom does he intend to convey by means of his historical survey?

B: 1 Select some of the words or expressions which are slightly unexpected in their present context, thus giving a personal character to the narration.

2 Point out details which add a sensational 'dramatic' flavour to the historical writing.

3 Observe how the oratorical character of the writing is assisted in various places by the use of repeated consonants (alliteration).

4 What is the effect of the adjective formed from the name *Hitler* – Hitlerite?

5 Comment on the use of the work 'darkened' at line 27, and again at line 40.

6 How deeply felt is the word 'hideous' (line 34) in relation to other concepts in the same sentence?

7 Discuss the logic of lines 48–51. Is it true that 'larger organisms' necessarily have 'elements of persistence and conviction'?

8 Consider the general quality of metaphor in this passage?

9 Knowing the historic role of this particular author, comment on the use of First Person Singular in this extract.

4·4

The Renaissance

Michael Angelo's great painting of the newly created Adam on the ceiling of the Sistine Chapel might be taken as a symbol of the Renaissance, of the time when man was, as it were, re-created more glorious than before, with a body naked and unashamed, and a strong arm, unimpaired by fasting, out-stretched towards life and light.

Definitions are generally misleading, and it is easier to represent the Renaissance by a symbol than to define it. It was a movement, a revival of man's powers, a reawakening
10 of the consciousness of himself and of the universe – a move-ment which spread over Western Europe, and may be said to have lasted over two centuries. It was between 1400 and 1600 that it held full sway. Like other movements, it had fore-runners, but, unlike other movements, it was circumscribed by no particular aim, and the fertilising wave which passed over Italy, Germany, France, England and, in a much fainter degree, over Spain, to leave a fresh world behind it, seems

more like a phenomenon of nature than a current of history –
rather an atmosphere surrounding men than a distinct course
20 before them. The new birth was the result of a universal
impulse, and that impulse was preceded by something like a
revelation, a revelation of intellect and of the possibilities
in man. And like the Christian revelation in the spiritual
world, so the Renaissance in the natural, meant of a temper
of mind, a fresh vision, a source of thoughts and works,
rather than shaped results. When it crystallised into an aesthetic ritual, it fell into decadence and corruption.

But before that happened, its real task had been accomplished – a complex task, in which certain elements stand out.
30 Two main things there were which the Renaissance of Western
Europe signified; it signified Emancipation and Expression.
The Renaissance is a loose term which has served to cover
many issues – the Revival of Learning, the regeneration of
art, the revolt against the Schoolmen, the expansion of
men's thought with the expansion of the world beyond the
seas. And it has been ascribed to many external causes greater
and less. The death of feudalism had given free play to the
individual and had weakened authority. The famous taking of
Constantinople by the Turks in 1453, which put an end to the
40 Greek Empire, had sent Greek scholars wandering over the
world and shipped west into Italy a glorious cargo of looted
manuscripts and sculptures. The discovery of printing, with
the consequent circulation of books and of thought, produced
a change that was immeasurable; while the discovery of
America and the obvious effect that it produced upon trade
profoundly modified the laws of wealth and the possibilities
of transit. But all these outward events were only visible
signs of a great motive power that grew from within; of the
reassertion of Nature, and of her rights, against asceticism;
50 of the disinterested desire for knowledge for its own sake –
not the Schoolman's desire for logical results, or that of the
alchemist who regarded science as a means to find the philosopher's stone, but for something far wider. Rabelais' giant
baby, Prince Gargantua, born in the open air, in the midst
of a festival, wakening to life parched with thirst and calling
loudly for drink, must have been a conscious symbol of the
child of the Renaissance, who came forth into the World
unswaddled, and athirst, to drink deep and grow strong
enough for the overturning of false barriers, and the rein-
60 statement of those senses which religion had taught him to
condemn. Beauty was manifested to man afresh – beauty and

66

joy which he had learnt to regard as the deadly foes of
Christianity. And, inspired by new-found marbles and manuscripts, in a kind of intoxication, he once more embraced
Paganism and Nature, and acknowledged man's body to be
the exponent, not the adversary, of his soul.

Here there comes in the second great element of the
Renaissance – Expression. Expression implies a consciousness
of that which is expressed. In the Middle Ages expression
70 in words or stone or painting was naïf, a matter of narrative
and of symbols prescribed mostly by tradition. If personal
force pierced through, it was accidental – when men of exceptional gifts happened to be employed. But as people became
more conscious to themselves and the world, and began to
want to define their relations towards it, and when they finally
reawakened to a sense of beauty, emotion was kindled and
expression sought and found. There arose, first in Italy, then
in other lands, a perfect passion for language. The fuel was
ready, the re-discovery of the classics set it alight. The
80 unearthing of manuscripts in remote and forgotten monas-
teries, the publication of the works of Virgil and Seneca,
Plato and Aristotle, with a score of other ancient authors,
acted upon men's imaginations. Scholarship in those days was
no set science; it involved risk, it unfolded unknown vistas.
Like all else, like science itself, it was bathed in an atmosphere
of poetry. Men approached new-found manuscripts with
excitement and reverence.

from *The Renaissance*, EDITH SICHEL

A: 1 How could definitions be 'misleading' (line 7)?
   2 Give an outline of the historical factors which led to the Renaissance.
   3 What is implied by the statement that the Renaissance was 'more
     like a phenomenon of nature than a current of history' (line 18)?
   4 Explain the analogy between the Renaissance and the 'Christian
     revelation'. How did the Renaissance come to be in antagonism to
     later aspects of that revelation?
   5 How could the Renaissance become 'crystallised into an aesthetic
     ritual' (lines 26–27)?
   6 Discuss the effect of the symbols of Michael Angelo's Adam and
     Rabelais' Gargantua?
   7 How does the author represent the 'Middle Ages' in contrast
     to the Renaissance?
   8 What assumptions does the author seem to make about 'science'
     and 'scholarship' (lines 83–84)?

B: 1 Would you say that the language of this passage is in general appropriate to the subject, as expounded by the author? In what ways?

2 Note any of the recurrent sentence patterns here used for rhetorical effect.

3 List the principal 'extreme' expressions in paragraph 2.

4 '... a glorious cargo of looted manuscripts' – Do you find anything in this expression (line 41) open to possible objection?

5 How clear is the distinction between 'knowledge for its own sake' (line 50) and 'the Schoolman's desire for logical results' (line 51)?

6 Which seems to you the most beautiful or eloquent sentence in this passage?

7 What is your general opinion of the quality of the thinking in this passage?

8 'emotion was kindled ...' (line 77) – Observe points in this passage of which this statement is true.

4.5

World Government

If a World Government is to work smoothly, certain economic conditions will have to be fulfilled. One of these, which is beginning to receive widespread recognition, is the raising of the standard of life in what are now under-developed countries to the level which prevails among the most prosperous populations of the West. Until a certain economic equality among the different parts of the world has been achieved, the poorer nations will envy the richer ones, and the richer ones will dread violent action on the part of those who are less
10 prosperous.

But this is not the most difficult economic measure that may be necessary. Various raw materials are essential to industry. Of these, at present, oil is one of the most important. Probably uranium, though no longer needed for purposes of war, will be essential for the industrial use of nuclear energy. There is no justice in the private ownership of such essential raw materials – and I think we must include in undesirable private ownership, not only that by individuals or companies, but also that by separate States. The raw materials without which
20 industry is impossible should belong to the International Authority and be granted to separate nations in accordance with the two principles of justice and aptitude for their use. Nations which are lacking in this aptitude should be helped to acquire it.

In a stable world such as we are envisaging, there could be

in many ways a great deal more freedom than there is at present. There would, however, be some new limitations on freedom, since it would be necessary to inculcate loyalty to the International Government and to curb incitements to
30 war by single nations or groups of nations. Subject to this limitation, there should be freedom of the Press, freedom of speech, and freedom of travel. There should be a very radical change in education. The young should no longer be taught to over-emphasise the merits of their own countries, to feel pride in those of their compatriots who had shown most skill in killing foreigners, or to adopt Mr Podsnap's maxim: 'Foreign nations, I am sorry to say, do as they do do.' History should be taught from an international point of view with little emphasis on wars and much emphasis upon peaceful achieve-
40 ments, whether in knowledge or art, or in exploration or adventure. The education authorities of a single country should not be permitted by the International Government to stir up chauvinist feeling or to advocate armed rebellion against the International Government. Apart from these limitations, there should be a much greater freedom in education than there is at present. Unpopular opinions, unless they were such as to cause a danger of war, should be tolerated in teachers. The whole emphasis, in all teaching of history or social subjects, should be on Man and not on
50 separate nations or groups of nations.

from *Has Man a Future?*, BERTRAND RUSSELL

A: 1 Why does the author regard economic equality as a necessary preliminary to World Government?

2 What grounds are given, or implied, for the assertion that there is 'no justice in private ownership' (line 16) of some 'essential raw materials'?

3 What extension of the idea of 'private ownership' is advanced in paragraph 2?

4 What 'limitations on freedom' does the author regard as necessary under World Government?

5 What changes does the author consider to be necessary in 'education'?

6 Express more specifically the meaning conveyed in Mr Podsnap's maxim (lines 36–37).

B: 1 Examine this text as an illustration of the possible uses of *would, should, could, will have to*, etc.

2 Why has the author selected the particular form of the Conditional he has in paragraph 1?

3 Allowing for the fact that this is only a short extract from a longer book, what impressions do you form about the quality of the thinking it embodies?

4 Would it be useful to make a distinction between 'World Government' and 'International Government', both of which occur in this passage? Has the author himself any such distinction in mind?

5 What is the value of 'a certain' (line 6)?

6 Examine carefully the structure and thought sequence of the sentence at lines 15–19.

7 Taking evidence from the passage, how would you either attack or defend the assertion that this author seems to make complex problems seem light?

8 How far is the author's view of contemporary education true in your own experience?

9 Comment on the view that history should be taught 'with little emphasis on wars and much emphasis on peaceful achievements' (lines 38–39).

10 Is the author consistent in suggesting that educational authorities should not be allowed to advocate armed rebellion against International Government?

Section 4 PRACTICAL

C: 1 Write speeches which might be used in some circumstances to answer the point of view expressed in 4.1. One version could be 'emotive and rhetorical'; another as 'logical and rational' as possible.

2 Prepare a speech or essay which would state a case against the excessive valuation of 'political independence', e.g. in the 'developing countries'.

3 Write a speech in support of the policy of the government or national leader whom you most favour. Then write the most effective answer to it that you can devise.

3 Compose an appeal which is likely to be effective, addressed to the person (or persons) indicated in each of the following circumstances:

[a] To a bank manager, for an unusually large loan.

[b] To a political representative, for the remedy of a local abuse.

[c] To the editor of a newspaper, for a change of policy.

[d] To the general public (through a newspaper) advocating an unpopular view.

[e] To an international agency, to support a local project.

[f] To employees on strike, to return to work.

[g] To the management, to enable strikers to return to work.

[h] To the Head of State, for the award of a national distinction to a candidate whom you support.

[i] To a publisher, to publish a highly deserving work.
[j] To a national leader, for a social reform which is urgently needed.

5 Prepare speeches either For or Against any of the following motions for debate:

[a] That patriotism is not enough.
[b] That science requires us to dispense with religion.
[c] That we need a more technical education.
[d] That the O.A.U. is an unpractical dream.
[e] That crabbed age and youth cannot live together.
[f] That history is bunk.
[g] That we are too much hampered by tradition.
[h] That we should drive on the right.
[i] That travel broadens the mind.
[j] That Western civilisation is in decline.
[h] That there is urgent need for the redistribution of wealth.
[l] That State enterprise must replace private capitalism.

6 Prepare further suitable topics for formal debate, on more topical and local issues.

Section 5

LANGUAGE AS PERSONAL
EXPRESSION

Language is for most people the most important way of 'expressing' and exploring their individuality — art, costume, and behaviour are others. This roughly is what was meant by the celebrated little girl who remarked 'I never know what I think until I see what I say.' Personal uses of language usually occur on less public occasions, when the more formal elements (e.g. grammar, cohesion, specific register) may be in abeyance.

5.1
An Early Twentieth-Century Schooling

I left my public school in 1910, an intelligent young barbarian. I had an extensive knowledge of Latin and Greek literature, could write reasonably good Latin and Greek verses, had 'done' mathematics as far as conic sections and the differential calculus, and knew a certain amount of Greek and Roman history and French grammar. On the strength of my knowledge of Latin and Greek I gained a scholarship to Balliol. I went there a good classic but a complete ignoramus. Looking back I am astonished at the nature and
10 extent of my ignorance. I was, I must presume, one of the most successful products of our public-school system of education. For a year and a half I had been the head boy in the Classical Sixth. Whatever they had to teach me I had assimilated. Admittedly I had learned nothing for myself; but then I had never been encouraged to think that learning for oneself was either possible or desirable. As a result I went up to Oxford ignorant of the major events that have determined the history of the Western world and made our civilisation what it is. My acquaintance with the physical sciences
20 was confined to their smells. I had never been in a laboratory;

I did not know what an element was or a compound. Of biology I was no less ignorant. I knew vaguely that the first Chapter of Genesis was not quite true, but I did not know why. Evolution was only a name to me and I had never heard of Darwin. Of botany, geology and astronomy I knew absolutely nothing; I had never heard of psychology and the existence of the so-called social sciences was unknown to me. Among great men I knew a little of Plato and Socrates, in so far as they were figures in Greek history; but beyond
30 the information derived from the *Apology* that Socrates had been put to death for not believing in the country's gods and corrupting its youth, I did not know what their teaching was or why it was important. Aristotle was just a name, and of the great philosophers Descartes, Spinoza, Locke, Berkeley, Hume, Kant, Hegel and Goethe I had not heard at all. Of the discoverers and inventors whose original insight has changed the face of human life I knew nothing; I had never heard of Copernicus or Galileo or Harvey or Lister or Faraday or Pasteur. Newton was, however, known to me
40 through the incident of the apple.

History was an abyss of darkness in which there glowed three little points of intense light: Greece from 500 to 380 B.C., Rome from about 200 B.C. to 100 A.D., and the period of English history from the Norman Conquest to the end of the Middle Ages. Why I had knowledge of this last I cannot say; it must have been just chance that set us studying it in the sixth during my two years of membership. In the cycle of recurring periods this obscure tract of English history had come round again about the time when I entered the sixth.
50 But at no time did the cycle go beyond the battle of Waterloo. Had I stayed in the sixth until Doomsday, I should never have learned anything about the nineteenth century. Of the existence of pre-history I did not know.

My conception of the Industrial Revolution was limited to stories about James Watt, George Stephenson, Arkwright and spinning jennies, which I had inherited from my preparatory school. Of the history of the last fifty years, of the origin of the forces that lay behind the movements of my own times and of those movements themselves I knew nothing at all.
60 As to economics I was not aware that such a branch of study existed. But I had a cursory acquaintance with the Protection-Free Trade controversy, and had astonished and alarmed the school by becoming a Liberal on my own initiative and introducing that class-conscious, revolutionary paper the *Daily*

News into the school library, where it fermented dangerously, an irritant leaven in the otherwise untroubled dough of school Toryism. Besides myself there were only two Liberals in the school, and, consciously forlorn, I had written as the lone supporter of an unpopular cause to Mr Lloyd George
70 for material for a School Debating Society speech in defence of the famous 1909 Budget. It came abundantly accompanied by a courteous note from L. G. himself, and on the strength of it I made a successful speech against overwhelming odds, converting two boys in the process.

My knowledge of literature was confined to an acquaintance with some of the reasons which have led people erroneously to suppose that Bacon wrote Shakespeare, our head master being a Baconian enthusiast, who was unable to discourse on any literary subject for five minutes without making off in
80 the direction of the loved controversy from which he never returned. I had also some knowledge of Sheridan's *The Rivals* and *The School for Scandal*, through having acted the parts of Bob Acres and Charles Surface in school plays. But outside the literature of Greece and Rome, my reading was to all intents and purposes non-existent. I had never read for pleasure a single book worth reading. Of the writers of my own times I knew nothing, and, when I went up to Oxford in the autumn of 1910, I had not so much as heard the names of Hardy or Bernard Shaw.
90 Looking back upon my education I am not only astonished at its irrelevance but indignant at its inadequacy.

from *The Book of Joad*, C. E. M. JOAD

A: 1 Explain in general terms the features of his education that the author recalls at the time of writing.
2 What is implied by the inverted commas with 'done' (line 4)?
3 What can you infer about the curriculum of the Classical Sixth of the British Public School at that time?
4 List in general terms the topics of which the author was ignorant when he left school.
5 In what ways may the first Chapter of Genesis be considered 'not quite true' (line 23)?
6 Discuss the considerations implied in the use of 'so-called' (line 27).
7 What is intended to be conveyed by the remark that Newton was known to him 'through the incident of the apple' (line 40)?
8 What is the author's opinion of the truth of the 'Baconian' theory?

B: 1 If the predominant mood aimed at in this passage is one of

74

'indignation' (line 91), consider the means by which the author attempts to convey it.

2 What features of the language employed contribute to the impression of energy and economy it gives?

3 Consider the frequent use of the first person singular pronoun in this passage.

4 Observe the effect of sharp antithesis as in 'good classic ... absolute ignoramus' (lines 8–9) and point out other examples.

5 Can you suggest anything more specific than 'just chance' which determined the pattern of his historical studies?

6 Is the term 'pre-history' (line 53) self-contradictory? What meaning can you attach to it from its context here?

7 What is the particular concept presented in 'stories' (line 55)?

8 In what general ways has your own education so far differed from this author's? (Generalise; don't just quote 'subjects'.)

5.2

A Writer in War-time

Higher Tregerthen, Zennor,
St Ives, Cornwall.
Wednesday, April 26th, 1916

MY DEAR LADY CYNTHIA

It seems as if we were all going to be dragged into the *danse macabre*. One can only grin, and be fatalistic. My dear nation is bitten by the tarantula, and the venom has gone home at last. Now it is dance, *mes amis*, to the sound of the knuckle-bones.

It is very sad, but one isn't sad any more. It is done now, and no use crying over spilt milk. 'Addio' to everything. The poor dear old ship of Christian democracy is scuttled at last, the breach is made, the veil of the temple is torn, our epoch
10 is over. *Soit!* I don't care, it's not my doing, and I can't help it. It isn't a question of 'dancing while Rome burns,' as you said to me on the omnibus that Sunday evening – do you remember? It is a question of bobbing about gaily in chaos. 'Carpe diem' is the motto now: pure gay fatalism. It makes me laugh. My good old moral soul is *crevé*.

Will you tell me, if you can, what it would be wisest for me to do, at this juncture? Ought one to attest, and if so, what sort of job can I do? I don't *want* to do anything; but what will

be, will be, and I haven't any conscience in the matter. If I
20 have to serve, all right: only I should like a job that was at
least sufferable. Do think a little, and advise me: or ask
Herbert Asquith to tell me what I could do. I think it is all
rather ridiculous – even when it is a question of life and death;
such a scurry and a scuffle and a meaningless confusion that
it is only a farce.

It is very lovely down here, the slopes of desert dead grass
and heather sheering down to a sea that is so big and blue. I
don't want a bit to have to go away. But it will keep. And the
cottage is *very nice*, so small and neat and lovely. There is one
30 next door, the same as this, that you must have when the pot
bubbles too hard out there in the world. Will you be coming
this way, when you are making your round of visits?

I am still waiting for my book of *Italian Sketches* to appear.
Now there is a strike among the printers in Edinburgh. But it
won't be long. It is quite a nice book. I will send you a copy.

I am doing another novel – that really occupies me. The
world crackles and busts, but that is another matter, external,
in chaos. One has a certain order inviolable in one's soul.
There one sits, as in a crow's nest, out of it all. And even if
40 one is conscripted, still I can sit in my crow's nest of a soul
and grin. Life mustn't be taken seriously any more, at least,
the outer, social life. The social being I am has become a
spectator at a knockabout dangerous farce. The individual
particular me remains self-contained and grins. But I should
be mortally indignant if I lost my life or even too much of
my liberty, by being dragged into the knockabout farce of
this social life.

I hope we shall see you soon. We might have some good
times together – real good times, not a bit macabre, but jolly
50 and full. The macabre touch bores me excessively.

Frieda is boiling the washing in a saucepan. I am, for the
moment, making a portrait of Taimur-i-lang –Tamerlane,
the Tartar: copying it from a 15th-century Indian picture.
I like it very much.

Mila salute di cuore.

from *Selected Letters*, D. H. LAWRENCE

A: 1 Outline the historical events alluded to in this letter.
 2 What impact of the 'social world' upon himself does the writer
   envisage as possible?
 3 What attitude towards external events does the writer express?

4 Why is the writer unenthusiastic about the 'outer, social life' (line 42)?

5 Trace the connection between the verb *suffer* and 'sufferable' (line 21).

B: 1 Consider the mixture of 'I' and 'one' in this letter.

2 What possible reasons does this letter suggest for the casual epistolatory style?

3 What features of the language employed (apart from the references to books) indicate that the writer is a literary person?

4 What attitude is expressed in the phrase 'My dear nation' (line 2) in this context?

5 Interpret the reference to the 'knuckle-bones' (lines 4–5).

6 Examine the extent to which features of the language employed here are a transcription of speech.

7 With what metaphor earlier in the letter is the 'crow's nest' related? Discuss its aptness.

8 Comment on the grammar of the expression 'the individual particular me' (lines 43–44).

9 How far can you accept the attitude expressed in this letter?

5·3

The Insult

20 July 1921

We are in a funny whirl. I have been *Insulted*, but you are not going to be as angry as you expect, for it was an official insult. The Agent to the Governor General for Central India came in state to visit us, and according to custom H.H. calls on him first at the Guest House. Whole programme arranged beforehand – how many steps everyone is to advance and all the rest of it. Down we went and sat in a row in A.G.G.'s tent, we on one side and they opposite. Attar and pan were then distributed to our side by the other – the usual ceremonial. There
10 had already been talks between H.H. and Colonel Adams the P.A. as to whether I should receive these ingredients from A.G.G.'s Chief of Staff (who is English) or from his Indian attaché, H.H. wishing for former, but saying latter would not offend him. Moment comes. Chief of Staff works down line and stops above me. I resign myself without too much of a shock to receiving from Indian and get ready handkerchief for the scent. P.A. opposite begins genial but anxious motions towards me with his hands. A.G.G. holds H.H. in

close converse. When Indian attaché takes up his duties it is
20 *below* me so that I am excluded from the honours altogether.
What this means in an Indian Court you can't imagine and I
could scarcely. I merely felt a little flat. As soon as our
procession returned to the Palace I mentioned it to H.H., who
grew livid with passion – partly, and I know largely, for my
sake, but partly for his own, because the omission implied
that the A.G.G. would not recognise his right to have
Europeans under him. Since the Govt of India has recognised
my appointment, it does seem absurd. The upshot of the
Insult was that I had a very pleasant time with nothing to do.
30 I was at once forbidden to dance attendance on the Visitors,
and the printed programme was drastically altered. In due
course my absence was remarked. 'Where is Mr Forster?'
asks the P.A. at the Tennis Party, to which H.H. replies: 'I
am not sure whether he will come. He is rather out of spirits.'
Glances between P.A. and A.G.G. When Mr Forster does
come H.H. rises, leaves company, and greets him effusively.
I sit down far away from officials. P.A. and Chief of Staff seek
me out with remarks about weather. But the A.G.G. remains
aloof and glares – an elderly Colonel. Official banquet in
40 evening. Icy speeches on both sides. Subtle expressions of
annoyance and contempt from H.H. By this time I was
annoyed myself – the surrounding atmosphere engendered it,
and when half the company is violently upholding you against
the remainder you become self-conscious. So when A.G.G.
who had ignored me the whole day held out his hand after the
cinema, I bowed stiffly, and grasped it not until it was held
out a second time. A.G.G. went. P.A. remains (unofficially)
and is still here, profuse in unofficial regrets. But this is not to
suffice. Our Prime Minister is to draft a protest which will go
50 to A.G.G. and, if he ignores it, to the Govt of India.

from *The Hill of Devi*, E. M. FORSTER

NOTE *The above is a letter written to his mother by the English novelist,*
who as a young man had taken service as personal secretary to the
ruler of an Indian Native State.

A: 1 How does the fact that it was an 'official' insult lessen its serious-
ness to the writer?
2 What general picture is presented of the relationship between
British India of that period and the Native States?
3 Explain exactly how the 'insult' arose?
4 Was the insult accidental or deliberate?

5 Why did H.H. take offence, and what were the consequences?
6 Why presumably did A.G.G. 'remain aloof' (lines 38–39) even after the P.A. and the Chief of Staff had made polite overtures?
7 'This is not to suffice' 'Our Prime Minister is to draft' (line 49). This statement of the facts appears very impersonal. In what way is the writer understating the facts?

B: 1 'all the rest of it' (lines 6–7). What light does this small phrase throw on the writer's attitude to the whole incident?
   2 What pattern or significance can you find in the frequent change of Tense in this letter?
   3 What effect does the writer wish to convey by putting the word *below* (line 20) in italics?
   4 What attitude is revealed when the author uses the words 'I resign myself . . .' (line 15)?
   5 Which word suggests that the author was under strict obedience to his employer?
   6 What is the significance of the 'remarks about weather' (line 38)?
   7 What general impression of the author is given by the general nature of the language employed here?

5.4

Reminiscences

One day, putting my finger on a spot in the very middle of the then white heart of Africa, I declared that some day I would go there. My chums' chaffing was perfectly justifiable. I myself was ashamed of having been betrayed into mere vapouring. Nothing was further from my wildest hopes. Yet it is a fact that, about eighteen years afterwards, a wretched little stern-wheel steamboat I commanded lay moored to the bank of an African river.
    Everything was dark under the stars. Every other white man
10 on board was asleep. I was glad to be alone on deck, smoking the pipe of peace after an anxious day. The subdued thundering mutter of the Stanley Falls hung in the heavy night air of the last navigable reach of the Upper Congo, while no more than ten miles away, in Reshid's camp just above the Falls, the yet unbroken power of the Congo Arabs slumbered uneasily. Their day was over. Away in the middle of the stream, on a little island nestling all black in the foam of the broken water, a solitary little light glimmered feebly, and I

said to myself with awe, 'This is the very spot of my boyish
20 boast'.

A great melancholy descended on me. Yes, this was the
very spot. But there was no shadowy friend to stand by my
side in the night of the enormous wilderness, no great haunting memory, but only the unholy recollection of a prosaic
newspaper 'stunt' and the distasteful knowledge of the vilest
scramble for loot that ever disfigured the history of human
conscience and geographical exploration. What an end to
the idealised realities of a boy's daydreams! I wondered what
I was doing there, for indeed it was only an unforeseen
episode, hard to believe in now, in my seaman's life. Still,
30 the fact remains that I have smoked a pipe of peace at midnight in the very heart of the African continent, and felt very
lonely there.

But never so at sea. There I never felt lonely, because there
I never lacked company. The company of great navigators,
the first grown-up friends of my early boyhood. The un-
changeable sea preserves for one the sense of its past, the
memory of things accomplished by wisdom and daring
among its restless waves. It was those things that commanded
my profoundest loyalty, and perhaps it is by the professional
40 favour of the great navigators ever present to my memory
that, neither explorer nor scientific navigator, I have been
permitted to sail through the very heart of the old Pacific
mystery, a region which even in my time remained very
imperfectly charted and still remote from the knowledge of
men.

It was in 1888, when in command of a ship loading in
Sydney a mixed cargo for Mauritius, that, one day, all of a
sudden, all the deep-lying historic sense of the exploring
adventures in the Pacific surged up to the surface of my being.
50 Almost without reflection I sat down and wrote a letter to my
owners suggesting that, instead of the usual southern route,
I should take the ship to Mauritius by way of Torres Strait. I
ought to have received a severe rap on the knuckles, if only
for wasting their time in submitting such an unheard-of
proposition.

I must say I awaited the reply with some trepidation. It
came in due course, but instead of beginning with the chiding
words, 'We fail to understand,' etc., etc., it simply called my
attention in the first paragraph to the fact that 'there would
60 be an additional insurance premium to pay for that route,'
and so on, and so on. And it ended like this: 'Upon the whole,

however, we have no objection to your taking the ship through the Torres Strait if you are certain that the season is not too far advanced to endanger the success of your passage by the calms which, as you know, prevail at times in the Arafura Sea.'

I read, and in my heart I felt compunctious. The season was somewhat advanced. I had not been scrupulously honest in my argumentation. Perhaps it was because I never expected 70 it to be effective. And here it was all left to my responsibility. My letter must have struck a lucky day in Messrs H. Simpson and Sons' offices – a romantic day. I won't pretend that I regret my lapse from strict honesty, for what would the memory of my sea life have been for me if it had not included a passage through Torres Strait, in its fullest extent, from the mouth of the great Fly River right on along the track of the early navigators.

from Last Essays, JOSEPH CONRAD

A: 1 Why did the author's chums 'chaff' him (line 3)?
 2 In what ways was the heart of Africa 'then white' (line 2)?
 3 How would you account for the 'awe' (line 19) felt by the author?
 4 Why did the great 'melancholy' descend on him (line 21)?
 5 In what sense was he 'never lonely' (line 33) at sea?
 6 What prompted him to request permission to take a route through the Torres Strait?
 7 Why was that an unexpected thing to propose?
 8 Explain his feelings on learning that his request had been granted.
 9 Why must his letter have reached the office on a 'romantic' day (line 72)?

B: 1 While this is a passage of personal reminiscence, show how it differs from the three previous ones.
 2 Explain the difference between 'vapouring' and 'fact' in paragraph 1.
 3 What mood is created in paragraph 2?
 4 Comment on the etymology and associations of the word 'stunt' (line 25).
 5 In what way does the sentence structure change at lines 34–37?
 6 Discuss the effect of the generalisations 'wisdom and daring' in line 37.
 7 'Neither explorer nor scientific navigator' (line 41). Make clear both the grammatical and the logical relation between this expression and the rest of the sentence?
 8 What account can you give of the 'official' language used by Messrs H. Simpson and Sons.
 9 In what ways had he not been 'scrupulously honest' (line 68)?

The True Purpose of Life

Both my brother and I were away, during the last war, when our father was seriously ill at home. Amos (The Rev. A. S. Solarin) was away in Burma and I was in Britain. Father swore, so our eldest sister reported, that he would not die until one or the other of his two boys had returned home. He turned the critical corner of his illness and he lived.

Amos returned home first and father, with everybody else, ate, drank and made merry. Three weeks later he had company and neighbours remarked how well the rich
10 laughter had returned. He went to bed that night in the gayest of spirits – but he never woke up the following morning!

What a wonderful way to die! I am one of the millions of Nigerians whose childhood days were spent away from 'home', away from father. I could reproduce on no more than four pages of an ordinary exercise book all the conversations I ever had with my father. We were very good friends but we were always separated by long distances and when we did meet, we were usually very correct and very discreet. I therefore never had the opportunity of discussing ethics and
20 principles with the man to whom I owe so much.

I could have asked him, for example, what he thought of life. Most of my ideas on life I have therefore picked up from my favourite authors. To these ideas I have naturally blended what I have imbibed from being alive myself.

The Christians and the Moslems believe in doing everything for God's sake. To them life would be meaningless without a perpetually solid anchorage in their beliefs.

During my school days and early adolescence, I thought with the crowd and accepted all the norms without a doubt,
30 let alone a challenge. I never developed a taproot. I never had the courage to stand on my own. I used my lamp post as did Professor Lester Smith's drunk, for physical support only.

But I outgrew this. Today, I believe that life must be spent, and spent buoyantly and in entirety, in the service of one's fellow men.

'I shall pass through this world but once; any good thing, therefore, that I can do, or any kindness that I can show any human being, let me do it now. Let me not defer nor neglect it, for I shall not pass this way again.' I just cannot improve
40 on Mr Stephen Grellet in those very well-chosen words.

But to be a Nigerian is to be a real gambler. Of every 100 children born in Lagos today only 75 reach the age of four years. In Ibadan more than fifty per cent die before the age of four! And I am not counting motor accidents on our roads as one of the items of this slaughter. It is, therefore, essential that anybody living in this country wastes no time in working out what his purpose in life is.

I want to live and serve man. I would like to offer a job, if I am in the position to do so, to the next man or woman
50 qualified, not because he is, like myself, an Ibo, or Hausa, but because, like myself, this job seeker deserves to live.

'Confound my enemies, O Lord.' I don't want my enemies confounded. I don't want my enemies shamed. I would like to offer a renewed arm of friendship to my enemy, and say, 'Come, let us anew, our journey pursue.'

I want to get up in the morning and start to work on a programme that is directly beneficial to my fellow men. I want to finish up at the end of the day fully convinced that I have not for one minute veered or backed from the goal set before
60 me when the day began.

When a life time has been spent, and I find myself folding up, I should like to think I have devoted my entire span to the service of my fellow men.

Looking round and seeing the infinite possibilities there are for man, I might, like the old empire builder, Cecil Rhodes, be tempted to cry, 'so much to do, so little done,' but I want to make sure that that 'little done' was for the betterment of my fellow men.

They say Methuselah lived for almost a thousand years. If
70 true, what for? We read nowadays of many men and women who linger on into the uninterrupted idleness of prolonged longevity. I don't want to be one of them. I don't want any overtime on top of the 'normal' seventy years.

When, therefore, the end comes, be it on the open field, or in my bed, I want those who heard me last to be able to say – 'we heard his tremendous laughter only a short while ago.'

from *Thinking With You*, TAI SOLARIN

A: 1 What was 'wonderful' (line 12) about the circumstances of his father's death?
2 What was the relationship between the writer and his father?
3 Enumerate and evaluate the sources of his 'ideas on life' (line 22).

4 Explain the distinction he draws between his ideas and those of 'the Christians and the Moslems' (line 25).
5 With what result did he outgrow his adolescent ideals?
6 In what sense, according to this author, is the Nigerian a gambler (line 41)?
7 What benefit may be derived from that kind of 'gamble'?
8 What appears to be, by implication, strange about the policy advocated in lines 48–51?
9 What is his opinion about 'longevity' (line 72)?

B: 1 Remembering that the author of the passage uses English as a second language, observe any ways in which it diverges from standard English?
2 What may he have in mind when he refers to the 'so much' he owed his father?
3 Can you comment on the accuracy of his representation of the Christian and the Moslem religions (lines 25–27)?
4 Explain the metaphor of a 'taproot', with reference to the context.
5 Examine the accuracy of the metaphor 'offer a renewed arm of friendship' (line 54).
6 What implications are conveyed in the 'but' (line 67)?
7 What rational comments would you make on the idea of 'service', as expressed in this article?
8 What sense of the character of the writer do you obtain from his selection of language?

Section 5 PRACTICAL

C: 1 Write some excerpts from your own candid autobiography.
2 As a variant on 1, write an account of your own life as you would expect to see it written in an 'official publication' (e.g. an obituary notice in the London 'Times'). Then follow this by a frank account such as you might have left in your own personal records. You may imagine if you like that you have attained a position of national or international celebrity!
3 Write an account of the origins and career of the person you would *like to have been.*
4 Select one of the key 'experiences' in your own life, whether in the realm of physical exploration, intellectual illumination, human relationships, or possibly combining elements of all these, and give as vivid an account of it as possible.
5 Based on the information available in 5.1, write an imaginary conversation between the author of that passage and a university acquaintance about one year after he had left school.
6 Avoiding customary formulae and trite sentiments, write a letter to a close friend surveying the events of the present term, casting it as far as possible in the style and manner of 5.2.

84

7 Study the episode in 5.3; then write two letters, referring to it,

[a] as it might have been reported officially either by H.H. (His Highness) or by A.G.G. (Agent to the Governor General).

[b] as it might have been written in a personal letter by the P.A. (Personal Assistant), taking note of the sentence 'P.A. remains (unofficially) and is still here, profuse in unofficial regrets' (lines 47–48).

8 On the lines of 5.4, describe one of your own childhood ambitions or fantasies, and contrast it with the situation you find yourself in at present!

9 Write a personal letter in the style of 5.2 upon the episode referred to in 5.4.

10 Write a letter to the family as it might have been written by the author of 5.5 (or, if you wish, his brother) when he was away from home.

11 On the lines of 5.5, attempt a statement of your own personal aims and ideals.

Section 6

LANGUAGE AS ART

Here we think of an approach which arises out of all those so far described, but which goes beyond them in that the 'artist' deliberately contrives new arrangements and inventions of language, sometimes to the extent of offending against linguistic 'propriety', in order to deliver his message with greater truth. This of course is one of the ways in which languages grow, as successful experiments become absorbed into the main stream.

6.1

Stream of Consciousness

'Yes, of course, if it's fine tomorrow,' said Mrs Ramsay. 'But you'll have to be up with the lark,' she added.

To her son these words conveyed an extraordinary joy, as if it were settled the expedition were bound to take place, and the wonder to which he had looked forward, for years and years it seemed, was, after a night's darkness and a day's sail, within touch. Since he belonged, even at the age of six, to that great clan which cannot keep this feeling separate from that, but must let future prospects, with their joys and
10   sorrows, cloud what is actually at hand, since to such people even in earliest childhood any turn in the wheel of sensation has the power to crystallise and transfix the moment upon which its gloom or radiance rests, James Ramsay, sitting on the floor cutting out pictures from the illustrated catalogue of the Army and Navy Stores, endowed the picture of a refrigerator as his mother spoke with heavenly bliss. It was fringed with joy. The wheelbarrow, the lawn-mower, the sound of poplar trees, leaves whitening before rain, rooks cawing, brooms knocking, dresses rustling—all these were so
20   coloured and distinguished in his mind that he had already

86

his private code, his secret language, though he appeared the image of stark and uncompromising severity, with his high forehead and his fierce blue eyes, impeccably candid and pure, frowning slightly at the sight of human frailty, so that his mother, watching him guide his scissors neatly round the refrigerator, imagined him all red and ermine on the Bench or directing a stern and momentous enterprise in some crisis of public affairs.

'But,' said his father, stopping in front of the drawing-room window, 'it won't be fine.'

Had there been an axe handy, a poker, or any weapon that would have gashed a hole in his father's breast and killed him, there and then, James would have seized it. Such were the extremes of emotion that Mr Ramsay excited in his children's breasts by his mere presence; standing, as now, lean as a knife, narrow as the blade of one, grinning sarcastically, not only with the pleasure of disillusioning his son and casting ridicule upon his wife, who was ten thousand times better in every way than he was (James thought), but also with some secret conceit at his own accuracy of judgement. What he said was true. It was always true. He was incapable of untruth; never tampered with a fact; never altered a disagreeable word to suit the pleasure or convenience of any mortal being, least of all of his own children, who, sprung from his loins, should be aware from childhood that life is difficult; facts uncompromising; and the passage to that fabled land where our brightest hopes are extinguished, our frail barks founder in darkness (here Mr Ramsay would straighten his back and narrow his little blue eyes upon the horizon), one that needs, above all, courage, truth, and the power to endure.

'But it may be fine—I expect it will be fine,' said Mrs Ramsay, making some little twist of the reddish-brown stocking she was knitting, impatiently. If she finished it tonight, if they did go to the Lighthouse after all, it was to be given to the Lighthouse keeper for his little boy, who was threatened with a tuberculous hip; together with a pile of old magazines, and some tobacco, indeed whatever she could find lying about, not really wanted, but only littering the room, to give those poor fellows who must be bored to death sitting all day with nothing to do but polish the lamp and trim the wick and rake about on their scrap of garden, something to amuse them. For how would you like to be shut up for a whole month at a time, and possibly more in stormy weather, upon a rock

the size of a tennis lawn? she would ask; and to have no
letters or newspapers, and to see nobody; if you were
married, not to see your wife, not to know how your children
were—if they were ill, if they had fallen down and broken
their legs or arms; to see the same dreary waves breaking week
70 after week, and then a dreadful storm coming, and the
windows covered with spray, and birds dashed against the
lamp, and the whole place rocking, and not be able to put
your nose out of doors for fear of being swept into the sea?
How would you like that? she asked, addressing herself
particularly to her daughters. So she added, rather differently,
one must take them whatever comforts one can.

from *To the Lighthouse*, VIRGINIA WOOLF

A: 1 What question might have been put just before this passage opens?
  2 Show how three different temperaments are revealed by the author
    in between the few remarks exchanged between husband and wife.
  3 By what process was James able to 'endow the picture of the
    refrigerator with heavenly bliss' (lines 15–16)?
  4 In what way did James's external appearance belie his inner state
    of mind?
  5 What pictures did Mrs Ramsay form of her son in the future?
  6 Why did James regard his mother as 'ten thousand times better'
    than his father?
  7 What was to be the object of the visit to the lighthouse?

B: 1 Explain the effect of the combination of Direct Speech with narra-
    tive in this excerpt.
  2 Examine some of the effects of sentence variety as employed here.
  3 Illustrate how a long sentence can be organised to bring maximum
    effect upon the final word.
  4 Illustrate and comment upon this author's tendency to use double
    expression, e.g. 'crystallise and transfix' (line 12).
  5 Examine the means by which the author registers a sudden change
    of feeling (lines 31–33).
  6 What exactly was James's 'secret language' (line 21)?
  7 What is the exact force of 'should be aware' in its context (line 45)?
  8 What is the full grammatical context of 'facts uncompromising'
    (line 46)?
  9 Comment on the effect of including more than the normal amount
    of information within the usual sentence limits, e.g. lines 54–62.

Under the Arch

Standing alone under a railway arch out of the wind, I was
looking at the miles of sands, long and dirty in the early dark,
with only a few boys on the edge of the sea and one or two
hurrying couples with their mackintoshes blown around them
like balloons, when two young men joined me, it seemed out
of nowhere, and struck matches for their cigarettes and illu-
minated their faces under bright-checked caps.

One had a pleasant face; his eyebrows slanted comically
towards his temples, his eyes were warm, brown, deep, and
10 guileless, and his mouth was full and weak. The other man
had a boxer's nose and a weighted chin ginger with bristles.

We watched the boys returning from the oily sea; they
shouted under the echoing arch, then their voices faded. Soon
there was not a single couple in sight; the lovers had disappeared among the sandhills and were lying down there
with broken tins and bottles of the summer passed, old paper
blowing by them, and nobody with any sense was about. The
strangers, huddled against the wall, their hands deep in their
pockets, their cigarettes sparkling, stared, I thought, at the
20 thickening of the dark over the empty sands, but their eyes
may have been closed. A train raced over us, and the arch
shook. Over the shore, behind the vanishing train, smoke
clouds flew together, rags of wings and hollow bodies of great
birds black as tunnels, and broke up lazily; cinders fell
through a sieve in the air, and the sparks were put out by the
wet dark before they reached the sand. The night before,
little quick scarecrows had bent and picked at the track-line
and a solitary dignified scavenger wandered three miles by
the edge with a crumpled coal sack and a park-keeper's steel-
30 tipped stick. Now they were tucked up in sacks, asleep in a
siding, their heads in bins, their beards in straw, in coal-
trucks thinking of fires, or lying beyond pickings on Jack
Stiff's slab near the pub in the Fishguard Alley, where the
methylated-spirit drinkers danced into the policemen's arms
and women like lumps of clothes in pool waited, in doorways and holes in the soaking wall, for vampires or firemen.
Night was properly down on us now. The wind changed.
Thin rain began. The sands themselves went out. We stood in
the scooped, windy room of the arch, listening to the noises
40 from the muffled town, a goods train shunting, a siren in the

docks, the hoarse trams in the streets far behind, one bark of a dog, unplaceable sounds, iron being beaten, the distant creaking of wood, doors slamming where there were no houses, an engine coughing like a sheep on a hill.

The two young men were statues smoking, tough-capped and collarless watchers and witnesses carved out of the stone of the blowing room where they stood at my side with nowhere to go, nothing to do, and all the raining, almost winter, night before them. I cupped a match to let them see my face in
50 a dramatic shadow, my eyes mysteriously sunk, perhaps, in a startling white face, my young looks savage in the sudden flicker of light, to make them wonder who I was as I puffed my last butt and puzzled about them. Why was the soft-faced young man, with his tame devil's eyebrows, standing like a stone figure with a glow-worm in it? He should have a nice girl to bully him gently and take him to cry in the pictures, or kids to bounce in a kitchen in Rodney Street. There was no sense in standing silent for hours under a railway arch on a hell of a night at the end of a bad summer when girls were
60 waiting, ready to be hot and friendly, in chip shops and shop doorways and Rabbiotti's all-night café, when the public bar of the 'Bay View' at the corner had a fire and skittles and a swarthy, sensuous girl with different coloured eyes, when the billiard saloons were open, except the one in High Street you couldn't go into without a collar and tie, when the closed parks had empty, covered bandstands and the railings were easy to climb.

A church clock somewhere struck a lot, faintly from the night on the right, but I didn't count.
70 The other young man, less than two feet from me, should be shouting with the boys, boasting in lanes, propping counters, prancing and clouting in the Mannesmann Hall, or whispering around a bucket in a ring corner. Why was he humped here with a moody man and myself, listening to our breathing, to the sea, the wind scattering sand through the archway, a chained dog and a foghorn and the rumble of trams a dozen streets away, watching a match strike, a boy's fresh face spying in a shadow, the lighthouse beams, the movement of a hand to a fag, when the sprawling town in a
80 drizzle, the pubs and the clubs and the coffee-shops, the prowlers' streets, the arches near the promenade, were full of friends and enemies? He could be playing nap by a candle in a shed in a wood-yard.

from *Portrait of the Artist as a young Dog*, DYLAN THOMAS

90

A: 1 Bring together concisely as many facts as you can about the scene presented in this extract.
2 What is the general sociological-historical background to the passage?
3 With what feeling does the writer present this scene and the humans who feature in it? What, for example, is the implication of 'he should have . . .' (line 55)?
4 Why are the scavengers who were there the previous night not there now?
5 How were some of them 'beyond pickings' on Jack Stiff's slab (lines 32–33)?
6 What change in the sense impression occurs in the course of paragraph 3?
7 What might be the use of 'empty covered bandstands' (line 66)?
8 Show how the writer suggests different types of 'fulfilment' for two of his characters. What seems to be preventing that kind of fulfilment?
9 What picture is called up by 'whispering round a bucket in a ring corner' (line 73)?

B: 1 Show how the rhythm of the opening sentence reflects the time sequence referred to.
2 What meaning do you attach to 'sense' (line 17)?
3 Comment on the unfamiliar 'collocation' in: 'the thickening of the dark' (line 20), 'the sands went out' (line 38), 'hoarse trams' (line 41), 'an engine coughing' (line 44), and 'I cupped a match' (line 49).
4 'All the raining, almost winter, night . . .' (line 48). Comment on the unexpectedness of this phrase.
5 What is the special meaning of 'the boys' (line 71) here?
6 Comment on the assortment of information in the sentence at lines 73–82.

6.3
Molly's Reverie

NOTE *Molly Bloom lies awake in bed, waiting for her husband to come home.*

Ill go out Ill have him eyeing up at the ceiling where is she gone now make him want me thats the only way a quarter after what an unearthly hour I suppose theyre just getting up in China now combing out their pigtails for the day well soon have the nuns ringing the angelus theyve nobody coming in to spoil their sleep except an odd priest or two for his night office the alarmclock next door at cockshout clattering the brains out of itself let me see if I can doze off 1 2 3 4 5 what

kind of flowers are those they invented like the stars the wall-
10 paper in Lombard street was much nicer the apron he gave me
was like that something only I only wore it twice better lower
this lamp and try again so as I can get up early Ill go to
Lambes there beside Findlaters and get them to send us some
flowers to put about the place in case he brings him home
tomorrow today I mean no no Fridays an unlucky day first
I want to do the place up someway the dust grows in it I think
while Im sleep then we can have music and cigarettes I can
accompany him first I must clean the keys of the piano with
milk whatll I wear shall I wear a white rose or those fairy cakes
20 in Liptons I love the smell of a rich big shop at 7½d a lb or
the other ones with the cherries in them and the pinky sugar
11d a couple of lbs of course a nice plant for the middle of
the table Id get that cheaper in wait wheres this I saw them
not long ago I love flowers Id love to have the whole place
swimming in roses God of heaven theres nothing like nature
the wild mountains then the sea and the waves rushing then
the beautiful country with fields of oats and wheat and all
kinds of things and all the fine cattle going about that would
do your heart good to see rivers and lakes and flowers all
30 sorts of shapes and smells and colours springing up even out
of the ditches primroses and violets nature it is as for them
saying theres no God I wouldnt give a snap of my two fingers
for all their learning why dont they go and create something
I often asked him atheists or whatever they call themselves go
and wash the cobbles off themselves first then they go howling
for the priest and they dying and why why because theyre
afraid of hell on account of their bad conscience ah yes I know
them well who was the first person in the universe before
there was anybody that made it all who ah that they dont know
40 neither do I so there you are they might as well try to stop
the sun from rising tomorrow the sun shines for you he said
the day we were lying among the rhododendrons on Howth
head in the grey tweed suit and his straw hat the day I got
him to propose to me yes first I gave him the bit of seedcake
out of my mouth and it was leapyear like now yes 16 years ago
my God after that long kiss I near lost my breath yes he said I
was a flower of the mountain yes so we are flowers all a
womans body yes that was one true thing he said in his life and
the sun shines for you today yes that was why I liked him
50 because I saw he understood or felt what a woman is and I
knew I could always get round him and I gave him all the
pleasure I could leading him on till he asked me to say yes and

I wouldnt answer first only looked out over the sea and the sky
I was thinking of so many things he didnt know of Mulvey and
Mr Stanhope and Hester and father and old captain Groves
and the sailors playing all birds fly and I say stoop and washing up dishes they called it on the pier and the sentry in front
of the governors house with the thing round his white helmet
poor devil half roasted and the Spanish girls laughing in their
60 shawls and their tall combs and the auctions in the morning
the Greeks and the Jews and the Arabs and the devil knows
who else from all the ends of Europe and Duke street and the
fowl market all clucking outside Larby Sharons and the poor
donkeys slipping half asleep and the vague fellows in the
cloaks asleep in the shade on the steps and the big wheels of
the carts of the bulls and the old castle thousands of years old
yes and those handsome Moors all in white and turbans like
kings asking you to sit down in their little bit of a shop and
Ronda with the old windows of the posadas glancing eyes a
70 lattice hid for her lover to kiss the iron and the wine-shops
half open at night and the castanets and the night we missed
the boat at Algeciras the watchman going about serene with
his lamp and O that awful deepdown torrent O and the sea
the sea crimson sometimes like fire and the glorious sunsets
and the figtrees in the Alameda gardens yes and all the
queer little streets and pink and blue and yellow houses
and the rose-gardens and the jessamine and geraniums
and cactuses and Gibraltar as a girl where I was a Flower of
the mountain yet when I put the rose in my hair like the
80 Andalusian girls used or shall I wear a red yes and how he
kissed me under the Moorish wall and I thought well as well
him as another and then I asked him with my eyes to ask
again yes and then he asked me would I yes to say yes my
mountain flower and first I put my arms around him yes and
drew him down to me so he could feel my breasts all per-
fume yes and his heart was going like mad and yes I said yes
I will Yes.

from *Ulysses*, JAMES JOYCE

A: 1 What is the most conspicuous departure of this piece of writing
   from conventional forms?
   2 What particular problems has Molly on her mind?
   3 How do you interpret in the context '1 2 3 4 5' (line 8)?
   4 Show in detail how trivial and more significant details are woven
   together.
   5 What is Molly's attitude towards atheists? Of what inconsistencies

does she accuse them? With what other argument does she reckon
to confute them?

6 Where have her 'thoughts' gone in lines 56–74?

7 What meaning do you attach to 'well as well him as another'
(line 81)?

8 What impression does this stream of language give of Molly's
history and temperament?

9 In what ways is Molly made to seem a part of 'nature' here? In what
sense does she herself employ the term, e.g. line 25 and line 31?

B: 1 In the absence of customary signs of sentence boundaries, how do
you make 'sense' of this? Why has the author chosen to employ this
unusual form of written representation?

2 Make your specific interpretation of 'well' (line 4).

3 Indicate the sense groups in 'the apron he gave me was like that
something only I only wore it twice' (lines 10–11), and in 'in case
he brings him home tomorrow today I mean no no Fridays on
unlucky day' (lines 14–15).

4 Comment on 'the dust grows in it' (line 16).

5 How do you fit 'all birds fly and I say stoop' (line 56) into the
context?

6 What special function is attached to the word 'yes' in this passage?

6.4

The Perfect Gentleman

As they were travelling along in this endless forest when the
complete gentleman in the market that the lady was following,
began to return the hired parts of his body to the owners and
he was paying them the rentage money. When he reached
where he hired the left foot, he pulled it out, he gave it to the
owner and paid him, and they kept going; when they reached
the place where he hired the right foot, he pulled it out and
gave it to the owner and paid for the rentage. Now both feet
had returned to the owners, so he began to crawl along on
10 the ground, by that time, that lady wanted to go back to her
town or her father, but the terrible and curious creature or the
complete gentleman did not allow her to return or go back to
her town or her father again and the complete gentleman said
thus: 'I had told you not to follow me before we branched
into this endless forest which belongs to only terrible and
curious creatures, but when I became a half-bodied incomplete gentleman you wanted to go back, now that cannot be

done, you have failed. Even you have never seen anything yet, just follow me.'

20 When they went furthermore, then they reached where he hired the belly, ribs, chest, etc., then he pulled them out and gave them to the owner and paid for the rentage.

Now to this gentleman or terrible creature remained only the head and both arms with neck, by that time he could not crawl as before but only went jumping on as a bull-frog and now this lady was soon faint for this fearful creature whom she was following. But when the lady saw every part of this complete gentleman in the market was spared or hired and he was returning them to the owners, then she began to try 30 all her efforts to return to her father's town, but she was not allowed by this fearful creature at all.

When they reached where he hired both arms, he pulled them out and gave them to the owner, he paid for them; and they were still going on in this endless forest, they reached the place where he hired the neck, he pulled it out and gave it to the owner and paid for it as well.

Now this complete gentleman was reduced to head and when they reached where he hired the skin and flesh which covered the head, he returned them, and paid to the owner, 40 now the complete gentleman in the market reduced to a 'SKULL' and this lady remained with only 'Skull'. When the lady saw that she remained with only skull, she began to say that her father had been telling her to marry a man, but she did not listen to or believe him.

from *The Palm-wine Drinkard*, AMOS TUTUOLA

NOTE *The author of this 'folk novel' from western Nigeria was not in the normal sense an 'educated' man.*

A: 1 To what literary mode does this writing belong, e.g. the realistic novel, science fiction, fantasy, allegory, etc.?
   2 Why do we presume the lady was following the 'complete gentle-man'?
   3 What does the author convey in the symbolic return of the various parts of the body?
   4 Explain the effect of the gentleman's reduction to a SKULL.

B: 1 How has the term 'drinkard' in the title been formed?
   2 What variety of the English language is being employed here?
   3 Enumerate features which distinguish this from a piece of con-ventional standard English, in [a] sentence structure, [b] vocabu-lary, and [c] cohesion.

4 Comment on the formations – 'branched' (line 14), 'rentage' (line 4), and 'furthermore' (line 20).

5 How can it be argued that the language of this narrative has special appropriateness to the subject?

6 Comment on any effects of special vividness you find in this unsophisticated style.

6.5
Breaking Off

And today I was in Quauhnahuac as usual when I received from my lawyers news of our divorce. This was as I invited it. I received other news too: England is breaking off diplomatic relations with Mexico and all her Consuls – those, that is, who are English – are being called home. These are kindly and good men, for the most part, whose name I suppose I demean. I shall not go home with them. I shall perhaps go home but not to England, not to that home. So, at midnight, I drove in the Plymouth to Tomalin to see my Tlaxcaltecan friend
10 Cervantes the cockfighter at the Salon Ofelia. And thence I came to the Farolito in Parian where I sit now in a little room off the bar at four-thirty in the morning drinking *ochas* and then *mescal* and writing this on some Bella Vista notepaper I filched the other night, perhaps because the writing paper at the Consulate, which is a tomb, hurts me to look at. I think I know a good deal about physical suffering. But this is worst of all, to feel your soul dying. I wonder if it is because tonight my soul has really died that I feel at the moment something like peace.
20   Or is it because right through hell there is a path, as Blake well knew, and though I may not take it, sometimes lately in dreams I have been able to see it? And here is one strange effect my lawyer's news has had upon me. I seem to see now, between mescals, this path, and beyond it strange vistas, like visions of a new life together we might somewhere lead. I seem to see us living is some northern country, of mountains and hills and blue water; our house is built on an inlet and one evening we are standing, happy in one another, on the balcony of this house, looking over the water. There are saw
30 mills half hidden by trees beyond and under the hills on the other side of the inlet, what looks like an oil refinery, only softened and rendered beautiful by distance.
    It is a light blue moonless summer evening, but late, per-

haps ten o'clock, with Venus burning hard in daylight, so we
are certainly somewhere far north, and standing on this
balcony, when from beyond along the coast comes the
gathering thunder of a long many-engined freight train,
thunder because though we are separated by this wide strip
of water from it, the train is rolling eastward and the changing
40 wind veers for the moment from an easterly quarter, and we
face east, like Swedenborg's angels, under a sky clear save
where far to the north-east over distant mountains whose
purple has faded, lies a mass of almost pure white clouds,
suddenly, as by light in an alabaster lamp, illumined from
within by gold lightning, yet you can hear no thunder, only
the roar of the great train with its engines and its wide shunting echoes as it advances from the hills into the mountains;
and then all at once a fishingboat with tall gear comes running
round the point like a white giraffe, very swift and stately,
50 leaving directly behind it a long silver scalloped rim of wake,
not visibly moving inshore, but now stealing ponderously
beachward towards us, this scrolled silver rim of wash striking
the shore first in the distance, then spreading all along the
curve of beach, its growing thunder and commotion now
joined to the diminishing thunder of the train, and now
breaking reboant on our beach, while the floats, for there
are timber diving floats, are swayed together, everything
jostled and beautifully ruffled and stirred and tormented in
this rolling sleeked silver, then little by little calm again, and
60 you see the reflection of the remote white thunderclouds in
the water, and now the lightning within the white clouds in
deep water, as the fishing-boat itself with a golden scroll of
travelling light in its silver wake beside it reflected from the
cabin vanishes round the headland, silence, and then again,
within the white white distant alabaster thunderclouds beyond
the mountains, the thunderless gold lightning in the blue
evening, unearthly . . .

from *Under the Volcano*, MALCOLM LOWRY

A: 1 What can be inferred about the status and affairs of the narrator?
    To whom does he appear to be writing?
  2 What combination of disasters have recently afflicted him?
  3 What state of mind is the narrator expressing? and what kind of
    'peace' is he experiencing? (line 19).
  4 What is the full meaning of the saying by Blake referred to, and how
    might it apply to the narrator?
  5 'our house is built' (line 27); 'There are sawmills' (line 29); 'we are

certainly somewhere far north' (line 35). What is the status in the present context of these statements in the present tense?

6 Comment on the details in which the 'vision' is presented.

7 What is particularly tragic about 'though I may not take it' (line 21). What force do you give to 'may' in this clause?

B: 1 What is the partly expressed antithesis to 'I think I know a good deal about physical suffering' (line 15)?

2 Comment on the linguistic form of 'mescals' (line 24).

3 What is the effect of the contrast between the Mexican setting (and place-names), and the vision of 'some northern country' (line 26)?

4 Discuss the possible symbolism of the contrast between the freight train and the fishingboat in the vision.

5 Investigate the significance of the reference to Swedenborg's angels (line 41).

6 Explain the image of 'shunting echoes' (lines 46–47).

7 What is the effect of the sentence structure in lines 35–47?

8 How would you explain the suggestion that the waves produced by the fishingboat produce their own 'thunder' (line 54), like the train?

9 How does the writer quietly emphasise by grammatical means that this is no more than a rather desperate vision?

Section 6 PRACTICAL

C: 1 Write a parallel passage to 6.1, but imagine the thoughts and remarks which might occur to a child and its parents in your own family circle.

2 Select a particular period (say one hour) from the last few days and, using the technique of 6.1, write out a transcript of all the thought, sensations which passed through your consciousness, interweaving them with any external events which occurred during the same period.

3 Choose a particular moment at a specific time of the day and write a survey under the title 'Now', describing in as much detail as you can all the different things, no matter how incongruous, which will be happening simultaneously.

4 List twelve people known to you, either personally or through the media of public information, and think of a series of epithets (adjectives) defining the peculiar qualities of each in as candid a way as possible.

5 List twelve of the characteristic phenomena of life in your area, and devise a series of similes to give an original impression of their qualities, e.g.

a woman pounding yams . . . . . like the throbbing of a strong and steady heart a countryman visiting a large modern city . . . . . like Lazarus wandering around the Celestial City.

6 Select suitable topics for which to compose sentences on the following lines:
    i As long a sentence as possible, while still being grammatical and artistically appropriate.
    ii A series of short separate sentences.
    iii A sequence in which narrative and speech are rapidly alternated.
    iv A series of sentences marked by strong antithesis.

7 Using the principal consonants in turn (e.g. b, d, k, p, s, t, etc.) construct sentences making intensive use of each ('Hunting the letter'!)

8 Imagine yourself, like the narrator in 6.3, lying awake and compose a similar sequence as it might occur to you.

9 Using all the resources of language, describe one of the following:
    [a] The take-off of a great jet-plane.
    [b] A riotous mob rushing through a town
    [c] A 'beat' (jazz, or high-life) session.

10 Write a short story, a fable, or a poem suggested by the following cartoon:

11 Write an account of an unexpected meeting and conversation between yourself and one of the following: (sketch in as much of the circumstances of the meeting as possible)
    God
    Noah
    Muhammad
    A visitor from the moon
    Karl Marx
    Your great-grandfather

12 Describe a real dream. Perhaps prepare for this by keeping writing materials near your bed and record a dream as soon as you wake up.

13 Retell a well-known legend, folk-tale, or animal fable from the traditional literature of your country, but adding some strikingly contemporary detail.

14 Listen to a piece of music of any kind, and try to imagine the kind of 'pictures' it can call up in your mind's eye. Transpose these into words.

15 Think of six phenomena within your experience for which there is
   no word in the English language. Invent new words to refer to these
   concepts, and illustrate them in use in some suitable contexts.

16 Invent six new words which could occur in the English language
   (e.g. perhaps *ungletip, spream, kwiroo, spiritizer*) and describe phenomena for which they could possibly be found useful.

Section 7

DIALECT

Most languages which are spread over a wide area produce 'dialects' —
forms which are recognisable as belonging to the parent language but
possess regular distinctive variations in pronunciation, vocabulary, gram-
matical structure, and cultural features such as idioms, allusions and
set-phrases. Dialect has traditionally been thought of as geographical in
origin, but it is also common to find 'dialects' which characterise particular
social groups or strata.

Dialect often gives rise to social prejudice, to ridicule — and also to
humour: many writers and entertainers have exploited this feature of
language, though it may be suspected that their dialects have not always
been accurate representations of actual forms of speech.

The enlightened approach to language includes a genuine respect for
all kinds of dialect, but suggests the need in a modern community for all
users of a language to be familiar with the standard form.

7.1
Stephen Blackpool

'Now, what do you complain of?' asked Mr Bounderby.

'I ha' not coom here, Sir,' Stephen reminded him, 'to complain. I coom for that I were sent for.'

'What,' repeated Mr Bounderby, folding his arms, 'do you
people, in a general way, complain of?'

Stephen looked at him with some little irresolution for a
moment, and then seemed to make up his mind.

'Sir, I were never good at showin' o 't, though I ha' had'n
my share in feeling o 't. 'Deed we are in a muddle, Sir. Look

10 round town – so rich as 'tis – and see the numbers o' people as
has been broughten into bein heer, fur to weave, an' to card,
an' to piece out a livin', aw the same one way, somehows,
'twixt their cradles and their graves. Look how we live, an'
wheer we live, an' in what numbers, 'an by what chances, and
wi' what sameness; and look how the mills is awlus a goin,
and how they never works us no nigher to onny dis' ant
object – ceptin awlus, Death. Look how you considers of us,
and writes of us, and talks of us, and goes up wi' yor deputa-
tions to Secretaries o' State 'bout us, and how you are awlus
20 right, and how we are awlus wrong, and never had'n no
reason in us sin ever we were born. Look how this ha' growen
an' growen, Sir, bigger an' bigger, broader an' broader,
harder an' harder, fro year to year, fro generation unto
generation. Who can look on 't, Sir, and fairly tell a man 'tis
not a muddle?'

'Of course,' said Mr Bounderby. 'Now perhaps you'll let
the gentleman know, how you would set this muddle (as
you're so fond of calling it) to rights.'

'I donno, Sir. I canna be expecten to 't. 'Tis not me as
30 should be looken to for that, Sir. 'Tis them as is put ower me,
and ower aw the rest of us. What do they tak upon themseln,
Sir, if not to do 't?'

'I'll tell you something towards it, at any rate,' returned
Mr Bounderby. 'We will make an example of half-a-dozen
Slackbridges. We'll indict the blackguards for felony, and get
'em shipped off to penal settlements.'

Stephen gravely shook his head.

'Don't tell me we won't, man,' said Mr Bounderby, by this
time blowing a hurricane, 'because we will, I tell you!

40 'Sir,' returned Stephen, with the quiet confidence of absolute
certainty, 'if yo was t' tak a hundred Slackbridges – aw as there
is, and aw the number ten times towd – an' was t' sew 'em up in
separate sacks, an' sink 'em in the deepest ocean as were made
ere ever dry land coom to be, yo'd leave the muddle just
wheer 'tis. Mischeevous strangers!' said Stephen, with an
anxious smile; 'when ha' we not heern, I am sure, sin ever
we can call to mind, o' th' mischeevous strangers! 'Tis not by
them the trouble's made, Sir. 'Tis not wi' *them* 't commences.
I ha' no favour for 'em – I ha' no reason to favour 'em – but 'tis
50 hopeless and useless to dream o' takin them from their trade,
'stead o' takin their trade from them! Aw that's now about me
in this room were heer afore I coom, an' will be heer when I
am gone. Put that clock aboard a ship an' pack it off to

102

Norfolk Island, an' the time will go on just the same. So 'tis wi' Slackbridge every bit.'

from *Hard Times*, CHARLES DICKENS

NOTE *Josiah Bounderby, a self-made capitalist in the northern industrial city of Coketown, is interviewing one of his workers, Stephen Blackpool, in the presence of a parliamentary investigator. Slackbridge, the interfering stranger referred to, is a professional agitator.*

A: 1 What does the gesture of Bounderby's folding his arms indicate?
   2 State concisely the grounds of Stephen's dissatisfaction.
   3 In what tone of voice does Bounderby say "Of course" (line 26)?
   4 'them as is put ower me' (line 30). What kind of social philosophy does the speaker seem to possess?
   5 What is Stephen's attitude towards political agitators?
   6 What would 'takin their trade from them' (line 51) involve?
   7 Explain the comparison drawn between Slackbridge and the clock (line 54).

B: 1 Read off, or write out, a transcription of the dialect speech in standard English.
   2 Explain the force of the juxtaposition of the 'we' and the 'you' in paragraph 5.
   3 Point out the linguistic forms in Stephen's speech which differ from those in standard English.
   4 Although Stephen is represented as an uneducated, inarticulate man, point out those passages in his remarks which have rhetorical power.
   5 What is the effect of the series of repetitions in lines 21–24?
   6 Consider the adequacy of the word 'muddle' (lines 9 and 25) for what it is intended to refer to.
   7 Do you find any earlier indications that Mr Bounderby was preparing to 'blow a hurricane' (line 39)?
   8 What part in the argument at that point is played by the word 'separate' (line 43)?
   9 How suitable to the context is the word 'trade' (line 50). Why does Stephen have to use it?

7.2
Congo Sermon

The voice of the Superior reached them from across the road. He was preaching in a mixture of French and Creole; even a Flemish phrase crept in here and there, and a word or two that

Querry assumed to be Mongo or some other tongue of the river tribes.

'And I tell you truth I was ashamed when this man he said to me, "You Klistians are all big thieves – you steal this, you steal that, you steal all the time. Oh, I know you don't steal money. You don't creep into Thomas Oslo's hut and take his new radio set, but you are thieves all the same. Worse thieves than that. You see a man who lives with one wife and doesn't beat her and looks after her when she gets a bad pain from medicines at the hospital, and you say that's Klistian love. You go to the courthouse and you hear a good judge, who say to the piccin that stole sugar from the white man's cupboard, 'You're a very sorry piccin. I not punish you, and you, you will not come here again. No more sugar palaver,' and you say that's Klistian mercy. But you are a mighty big thief when you say that – for you steal this man's love and that man's mercy. Why do you not say when you see man with knife in his back bleeding and dying, 'There's Klistian anger'?"'

'I really believe he's answering something I said to him,' Querry said with a twitch of the mouth that Colin was beginning to recognise as a rudimentary smile, 'but I didn't put it quite like that.'

'Why not say when Henry Okapa got a new bicycle and someone came and tore his brake, "There's Klistian envy." You are like a man who steals only the good fruit and leaves the bad fruit rotting on the tree.

'All right. You tell me I'm number one thief, but I say you make big mistake. Any man may defend himself before his judge. All of you in this church, you are my judges now, and this is my defence.'

'It's a long time since I listened to a sermon,' Dr Colin said. 'It brings back the long tedious hours of childhood, doesn't it?'

'You pray to Yezu,' the Superior was saying. He twisted his mouth from habit as though he were despatching a cheroot from one side to the other. 'But Yezu is not just a holy man. Yezu is God and Yezu made the world. When you make a song you are in the song, when you bake bread you are in the bread, when you make a baby you are in the baby, and because Yezu made you, he is in you. When you love it is Yezu who loves, when you are merciful it is Yezu who is merciful. But when you hate or envy it is not Yezu, for everything that Yezu made is good. Bad things are not here – they are nothing. Hate means no love. Envy means no justice. They are just empty spaces, where Yezu ought to be.'

50 'He begs a lot of questions,' Dr Colin said.

'Now I tell you that when a man loves, he must be Klistian. When a man is merciful he must be Klistian. In this village do you think you are the only Klistians – you who come to church? There is a doctor who lives near the well beyond Marie Akimbu's house and he prays to Nzambe and he makes bad medicine. He worships a false God, but once when a pic-cin was ill and his father and mother were in the hospital he took no money; he gave bad medicine but he took no money: he made a big God palaver with Nzambe for the piccin but

60 took no money. I tell you then he was a Klistian, a better Klistian than the man who broke Henry Okapa's bicycle. He did not believe in Yezu, but he a Klistian. I am not a thief, who steal away his charity to give to Yezu. I give back to Yezu only what Yezu made. Yezu made love, he made mercy. Everybody in the world has something that Yezu made. Everybody in the world is that much a Klistian. So how can I be a thief? There is no man so wicked he never once in his life show in his heart something that God made.'

from *A Burnt-Out Case*, GRAHAM GREENE

NOTE *Querry, a famous architect, has taken refuge from the world in a leper colony far up the Congo River. Here he comments on a sermon being preached to the African Christians in the settlement by the Catholic Superior. Dr Colin is the dedicated medical officer, whose inspiration is humanist rather than religious. The previous night, the following words occurred in a conversation between Querry and the Superior:*

You try to draw everything into the net of your faith, father, but you can't steal all the virtues. Gentleness isn't Christian, self-sacrifice isn't Christian, charity isn't, remorse isn't. I expect the caveman wept to see another's tears. Haven't you even seen a dog weep? . . .

A: 1 Why does the Superior, an educated man, preach in this kind of language?

2 What exactly was the 'Christian kind of theft' which the Superior is talking about?

3 Who was this man' (line 6)?

4 How is the idea of 'Christian love' represented to these members of the river tribes?

5 What point is the Superior trying to emphasise in saying that Yezu is not just a 'holy man' (line 40)?

6 If 'begging the question' means 'assuming the truth of what needs to be proved', what questions does the Superior beg in this sermon?

7 How, according to the Superior, was Nzambe a Christian without knowing it?

B: 1 How closely does the author transcribe the 'dialect' he describes (line 2)?

2 How does the language of his sermon differ principally from standard English?

3 Which consonant (or *phoneme*) appears to be difficult for the speakers of *Mongo* to produce?

4 Show how the Superior develops his theme with the help of examples within the experience of his listeners.

5 Examine the means used to convey to the listeners the idea of God/Yezu as the source of life.

7·3

The Balloon

It was a noble big balloon, and had wings and fans and all sorts of things, and wasn't like any balloon you see in pictures. It was away out toward the edge of town, in a vacant lot, corner of Twelfth street; and there was a big crowd around it, making fun of it, and making fun of the man – a lean pale feller with that soft kind of moonlight in his eyes, you know – and they kept saying it wouldn't go. It made him hot to hear them, and he would turn on them and shake his fist and say they was animals and blind, but some day they would find they
10 had stood face to face with one of the men that lifts up nations and makes civilisations, and was too dull to know it; and right here on this spot their own children and grand-children would build a monument to him that would outlast a thousand years, but his name would outlast the monument. And then the crowd would burst out in a laugh again, and yell at him, and ask him what was his name before he was married, and what he would take to not do it, and what was his sister's cat's grandmother's name, and all the things that a crowd says when they've got hold of a feller that they
20 see they can plague. Well, some things they said *was* funny – yes, and mighty witty too, I ain't denying that – but all the same it warn't fair nor brave, all them people pitching

on one, and they so glib and sharp, and him without any
gift of talk to answer back with. But, good land! what did he
want to sass back for? You see, it couldn't do him no good,
and it was just nuts for them. They *had* him, you know. But
that was his way. I reckon he couldn't help it; he was made
so, I judge. He was a good enough sort of cretur, and hadn't
no harm in him, and was just a genius, as the papers said,
30 which wasn't his fault. We can't all be sound: we've got
to be the way we're made. As near as I can make out, geniuses
think they know it all, and so they won't take people's advice,
but always go their own way, which makes everybody forsake
them and despise them, and that is perfectly natural. If they
was humbler, and listened and tried to learn, it would be
better for them.

The part the professor was in was like a boat, and was big
and roomy, and had water-tight lockers around the inside to
keep all sorts of things in, and a body could sit on them, and
40 make beds on them, too. We went aboard, and there was twenty
people there, snooping around and examining, and old
Nat Parsons was there, too. The professor kept fussing around
getting ready, and the people went ashore, drifting out one
at a time, and old Nat he was the last. Of course it wouldn't
do to let him go out behind us. We mustn't budge till he was
gone, so we could be last ourselves.

But he was gone now, so it was time for us to follow. I
heard a big shout, and turned around – the city was dropping from under us like a shot! It made me sick all through,
50 I was so scared. Jim turned gray and couldn't say a word,
and Tom didn't say nothing, but looked excited. The city
went on dropping down, and down, and down; but we didn't
seem to be doing nothing but just hang in the air and stand
still. The houses got smaller and smaller, and the city pulled
itself together, close and close, and the men and wagons
got to looking like ants and bugs crawling around, and the
streets like threads and cracks; and then it all kind of melted
together, and there wasn't any city any more: it was only
a big scar on the earth, and it seemed to me a body could
60 see up the river and down the river about a thousand miles,
though of course it wasn't so much. By and by the earth
was a ball – just a round ball of a dull colour, with shiny
stripes wriggling and winding around over it, which was rivers.
The Widder Douglas alway told me the earth was round like a
ball, but I never took any stock in a lot of them superstitions
o' hers, and of course I paid no attention to that one, because

I could see myself that the world was the shape of a plate,
and flat. I used to go up on the hill, and take a look around
and prove it for myself, because I reckon the best way to get
70 a sure thing on a fact is to go and examine for yourself, and
not take anybody's say-so. But I had to give in now that the
widder was right. That is, she was right as to the rest of
the world, but she warn't right about the part our village is
in; that part is the shape of a plate, and flat, I take my oath!

from *Tom Sawyer Abroad*, MARK TWAIN

A: 1 What kind of symbolism is indicated in the opposition between
the balloonist professor and the crowd?
2 Why is the balloon a particularly appropriate symbol?
3 Why do 'geniuses', according to the author, so often meet with
opposition?
4 What difference did it make when Nat Parsons stepped out of
the 'boat'-like thing?
5 What indicates that the balloon ascended to a very considerable
height?
6 Why had the narrator been in the habit of going up on the hill?
7 How did the narrator appear to find it difficult to reconcile the
general and the particular?

B: 1 Point out features of the language here which relate to the
American vernacular.
2 In what terms was the crowd expressing its contempt of the professor?
3 'The part ... was like a boat' (line 37). Why had the author no
more precise name for this part of the balloon?
4 How does the author convey the speed with which the balloon
ascended?
5 Discuss the narrator's way of indicating the continued upward
movement of the balloon.
6 What is the grammatical origin of 'say-so' (line 71)?
7 Can you distinguish in this narrative between the comments of
the author himself and those of his narrator?

7.4
The Playboy's Story

CHRISTY It's a long story; you'd be destroyed listening.
WIDOW QUINN Don't be letting on to be shy, a fine, gamey,
treacherous lad the like of you. Was it in your house
beyond you cracked his skull?
CHRISTY It was not. We were digging spuds in his cold,
sloping, stony, divil's patch of a field.

WIDOW QUINN And you went asking money of him, or making talk of getting a wife would drive him from his farm?

CHRISTY I did not, then; but there I was, digging and digging, and 'You squinting idiot,' says he, 'let you walk down now and tell the priest you'll wed the Widow Casey in a score of days.'

WIDOW QUINN And what kind was she?

CHRISTY A walking terror from beyond the hills, and she two score and five years, and two hundred-weights and five pounds in the weighing scales, with a limping leg on her, and a blinded eye, and she a woman of noted misbehaviour with the old and young.

WIDOW QUINN And what did he want driving you to wed with her?

CHRISTY He was letting on I was wanting a protector from the harshness of the world, and he without a thought the whole while but how he'd have her hut to live in and her gold to drink.

WIDOW QUINN There's maybe worse than a dry hearth and a widow woman and your glass at night. So you hit him then?

CHRISTY I did not. 'I won't wed her,' says I, 'When all knows she did suckle me for six weeks when I came into the world, and she a hag this day with a tongue on her has the crows and seabirds scattered, the way they wouldn't cast a shadow on her garden with the dread of her curse.'

WIDOW QUINN That one should be right company.

SARA Don't mind her. Did you kill him then?

CHRISTY 'She's too good for the like of you,' says he, 'and go on now or I'll flatten you out like a crawling beast has passed under a dray.' 'You will not if I can help it,' says I. 'Go on,' says he, 'or I'll have the devil making garters of your limbs tonight.' 'You will not if I can help it,' says I.

SARA You were right surely.

CHRISTY With that the sun came out between the cloud and the hill, and it shining green in my face. 'God have mercy on your soul,' says he, lifting a scythe: 'Or on your own,' says I, raising the loy.

HONOR He tells it lovely.

CHRISTY He gave a drive with a scythe, and I gave a lep to the east. Then I turned around with my back to the north, and I hit a blow on the ridge of his skull, laid him stretched out, and he split to the knob of his gullet.

from *The Playboy of the Western World*, J. M. SYNGE

NOTE *Christy Mahon arrives at a remote Irish inn and gains rapid popularity by claiming to have killed his father.*

A: 1 Outline the circumstances of Christy's alleged deed.
  2 What were his father's reasons for wishing him to marry the Widow Casey?
  3 What were his reasons for being unwilling to marry her?
  4 In what way were Christy's remarks not entirely tactful as far as the Widow Quinn was concerned?
  5 What is Christy's aesthetic aim in telling his story?
  6 What attitude is expressed in the comments of the Widow Quinn, Sara, and Honor?

B: 1 Why does he apologise in advance for the length of his story?
  2 What is the equivalent in standard English of these expressions: destroyed (line 1)   the like of (line 3)   beyond (line 4)   let you walk (line 10)   a score of days (line 12)   letting on (lines 2 and 21)   right company (line 33)   don't mind her (line 34)
  3 What other examples can you find of the structure 'and she two score and five years' (line 15)?
  4 What attitude towards his son do the words attributed to the father indicate?
  5 'A walking terror from *beyond the hills*' (line 14). What does this expression indicate about these Irish peasants?
  6 What picturesque detail is given to illustrate the Widow Casey's harsh tongue?
  7 What was the 'it' (line 42)?
  8 What on reflection does the detail about the father being split to the 'knob of his gullet' suggest?

7.5
Caveat Emptor

'Reuben, don't make such a mess o' tapping that barrel as is mostly made in this house,' Mrs Dewy cried from the fireplace. 'I'd tap a hundred without wasting more than you do in one. Such a squizzling and squirting job as 'tis in your hands! There, he always was such a clumsy man indoors.'

'Ay, ay; I know you'd tap a hundred beautiful, Ann – I know you would; two hundred, perhaps. But I can't promise. This is a' old cask, and the wood's rotted away about the tap-hole. The husbird of a feller Sam Lawson – that ever I should
10 call'n such, now he's dead and gone, poor heart! – took me in completely upon the feat of buying this cask. "Reub," says he – 'a always used to call me plain Reub, poor old heart!

– "Reub," he said, says he, "that there cask, Reub, is as good as new; yes, good as new. 'Tis a wine-hogshead; the best port-wine in the commonwealth have been in that there cask; and you shall have en for ten shillens, Reub," – 'a said, says he – "he's worth twenty, ay, five-and-twenty, if he's worth one; and an iron hoop or two put round en among the wood ones will make en worth thirty shillens of any man's money, if –"'

20 'I think I should have used the eyes that Providence gave me to use afore I paid any ten shillens for a jimcrack wine-barrel; a saint is sinner enough not to be cheated. But 'tis like all your family was, so easy to be deceived.'

'That's as true as gospel of this member,' said Reuben.

Mrs Dewy began a smile at the answer, then altering her lips and refolding them so that it was not a smile, commenced smoothing little Bessy's hair; the tranter having meanwhile suddenly become oblivious to conversation, occupying him-self in a deliberate cutting and arrangement of some more

30 brown paper for the broaching operation.

'Ah, who can believe sellers?' said old Michael Mail in a carefully-cautious voice, by way of tiding-over this critical point of affairs.

'No one at all,' said Joseph Bowman, in the tone of a man fully agreeing with everybody.

'Ay,' said Mail, in the tone of a man who did not agree with everybody as a rule, though he did now; 'I knowed a' auction-eering feller once – a very friendly feller 'a was too. And so one hot day as I was walking down the front street o' Caster-

40 bridge, jist below the King's Arms, I passed a' open winder and see him inide, stuck upon his perch, a-selling off. I jist nodded to en in a friendly way as I passed, and went my way, and thought no more about it. Well, next day, as I was oilen my boots by fuel-house door, if a letter didn't come wi' a bill charging me with a feather-bed, bolster, and pillers, that I had bid for at Mr Taylor's sale. The slim-faced martel had knocked 'em down to me because I nodded to en in my friend-ly way; and I had to pay for 'em too. Now, I hold that that was coming it very close, Reuben?'

50 ''Twas close, there's no denying,' said the general voice.

from *Under the Greenwood Tree*, THOMAS HARDY

A: 1 What relationship seems to exist between Reuben and Mrs Dewy?
  2 What exactly is the 'tapping' operation referred to?
  3 Why was it likely to be difficult?
  4 Illustrate Reuben's tendency to digression.

5 What is the principal motive of Michael Mail's entry into the conversation?

6 Explain the anecdote of the episode involving Michael Mail and the auctioneer.

7 How closely does the anecdote fit the earlier question 'who can believe sellers' (line 31)?

8 'coming it very close' (line 49). What does this seem to indicate? Can you suggest a metaphorical origin to the expression?

B: 1 Discuss the effect of the words 'squizzling and squirting' (line 14) in this context.

2 'indoors' (line 5). What does this imply otherwise about Reuben?

3 What kind of meaning seems to attach to the word 'husbird' (line 9)?

4 Indicate some of the subtle variations of attitude represented in those participating in this conversation.

5 Explain 'That's as true as gospel of this member' (line 24).

6 List any deviations in this passage from standard English. In what way would the passage entirely fail if written in the standard form?

Section 7 PRACTICAL

C: 1 Write an adapted version of 7.1, changing the characters to another period and environment with which you are familiar, and representing a vernacular dialect in contrast with an élite dialect.

2 On the lines suggested in 7.2, write part of a public address (or sermon) to an audience for whom a particularly simplified form of English is necessary.

3 Imagining yourself the correspondent of a modern newspaper, write a report of the events described in 7.3 but in standard educated English.

4 Without at first referring to the original play, write a continuation of the dialogue in 7.4 between Christy and the girls in a manner which fits the style of Synge's play.

5 Using a tape-recorder if available, collect some samples of the different dialects of spoken English in your own area. Transcribe these into written form using the standard characters of written English. (Phonetic transcription may be introduced if available.)

6 On the basis of the evidence collected in the previous question (5), write some imaginary conversation or stories, introducing the dialects you have 'collected', featuring particularly the effect of contrast between different dialects (whether on a regional or 'class' basis).

7 Consider how you would set up an investigation to test the authenticity of the 'dialects' represented in the passages collected in Section 7.

Section 8

LANGUAGE FOR GOVERNMENT

No matter what techniques, technologies and 'powers' are available, there is no doubt that language is an essential element in the control and regulation of communities, especially in furthering the aims of government. There is need for dispensing information (some of it unwelcome!), for encouraging co-operation, reconciling differences, as well as for the rational investigation and solution of particular problems. Governments are rightly becoming increasingly aware how much can be achieved by the selection of language appropriate to each kind of occasion, though presumably throughout the centuries they have been past-masters at the art of conveying confidence without giving any kind of specific undertaking!

8.1

The Breathalyser

WHY A NEW LAW?

To drive under the influence of drink has been an offence in this country since 1925. Why do we need this new law and the new tests for detecting drivers who have drunk more than they should?

The simple answer is that we need to be much more precise and accurate about measuring the effects of drinking on driving. It's a fact, well established by medical authorities, that alcohol in the bloodstream affects the reflexes and impairs judgement. It's another fact, well established from accident
10 statistics gathered over the years, that drinking by drivers plays a part in nearly 10,000 fatal and serious accidents every year.

A driver may actually feel more confident after a few drinks. He may not feel, look or act drunk. But his judgement may be so impaired by drink that he is a danger at the wheel.

113

The old law often misses drivers in this condition. It really only works in the case of drivers who are pretty obviously *drunk* – the really bad cases. We need a much more scientific and precise test to pinpoint drivers who have had more than
20 they should. The new law makes it an offence to be in charge of a vehicle if you have more than 80 milligrammes of alcohol in every 100 millilitres of blood.

The aim of the new law is not to stop people drinking. The aim is to stop the minority who drink too much for safety, and then drive.

HOW DOES THE NEW TEST WORK?

Anybody can be asked to take the first stage of the test. Any driver stopped by the police for a normal caution arising out of some quite minor traffic infringement (such as crossing a white line), any driver involved in an accident (whether it's
30 his fault or not) or any driver whom the police suspect has been drinking can be asked to take the test.

Stage 1. At the roadside the driver will be asked to blow through a small glass tube into a plastic bag. Inside the tube are chemically treated crystals which change colour if the driver has alcohol on his breath. If the colour change goes beyond a certain line marked on the tube this indicates that the driver is probably over the specified limit. If the colour change does not reach the line the driver is in the clear under the new law. But if the colour change *does* reach the line then
40 the test has proved positive and the driver will be asked to go to the police station for . . .

Stage 2. At the police station the driver can repeat the first test – the one he has already taken at the roadside – if he wants to. This check is for his protection. But if he does not take a second breath test, or if the second test also proves positive, he goes on to . . .

Stage 3. Still at the police station, the driver is required to give a sample of blood. This is provided quite painlessly by pricking a finger or the lobe of an ear. If the driver refuses a
50 blood sample he is required to give two samples of urine within one hour. After this, the driver can leave immediately provided he is not going to drive. If he *is* going to drive he will be detained in the station until the police are satisfied he is below the limit.

Stage 4. The driver's blood or urine samples are sent to the forensic laboratories where they are analysed by the latest scientific equipment. If the analysis shows that the driver has more than 80 milligrammes of alcohol in every 100 millilitres of his blood then the driver has broken the law and will be prosecuted.

60   It is the evidence of this analysis which the police will use in court and once the blood alcohol level has been established there is no room for argument.

But the driver does have this reassurance: At Stage 3 (see above) he can ask for an extra sample of his blood or urine, taken at the same time. He can send this sample to a doctor of his own choice for independent analysis. In this, as in the opportunity to take a second breath test, the driver's rights are protected twice over and every care is taken to
70 eliminate the chance of error.

WHAT ARE THE PENALTIES?
A driver convicted as a result of the test will be disqualified from driving for one year. The fact that he needs his licence to make his living – as a lorry-driver, salesman or doctor for example – will make no difference. But a doctor who is called out to an emergency on a night when he is not 'on call', could plead that there was a special and inescapable reason why he had to drive when over the limit. Under the new law the courts can take a very few such 'special reasons' into account.

As well as disqualification a convicted driver may also be
80 fined up to £100 or he may be sent to prison for up to four months – or both.

WHAT IF A DRIVER REFUSES TO TAKE THE TEST?
If a driver refuses to take the roadside breath test and the court decides that he had no good reason for doing so then he will be fined up to £50.

If he refuses to take the roadside test – and has been drinking – he will still be asked to come to the police station. There, if he refuses to provide blood or urine samples, he will be treated as if he had taken the tests and these had proved positive. This means that he will face exactly the same penal-
90 ties – including disqualification – as if he had been proved scientifically to have more than the alcohol limit in his blood.

from *The New Law on Drink and Diving*, H.M.S.O

NOTE *This is extracted from a leaflet explaining a new law passed in Britain in 1968.*

A: 1 What is the relation between the consumption of alcoholic drinks and road accidents?
 2 What is the difference between the old law and the new law on this matter?
 3 How does the new law define the amount of alcohol a person may consume if he intends to drive a motor vehicle?
 4 How is [a] the initial test, [b] the final test of a suspected person carried out?
 5 Why may a suspected person need 'protection' (line 44), and what protection does the new law provide?
 6 Is punishment of guilty persons automatic, or may there be any extenuating circumstances?
 7 What penalties may a guilty person incur?
 8 An important principle of many codes of justice is that a person is 'presumed innocent until proved guilty'. In what way does the new law, as described here, appear to violate that principle?

B: 1 What is the attitude of the government towards the public evident in this leaflet?
 2 What linguistic devices are used to gain the confidence of those who read the leaflet?
 3 How does the leaflet attempt to gain authority from medical and scientific sources?
 4 'drunk' (line 18); 'drinking' (line 23). What meanings have become attached to these words, over and above their literal meanings?
 5 What argument is advanced against any who try to suggest that the new law is intended to stop 'drinking'?
 6 Comment on the grammar, and the origin, of the expression 'in the clear' (line 38).
 7 What features of language are employed in this leaflet to ensure maximum comprehension of the matters explained?
 8 If you were a counsel defending someone who was being accused under this law, what would be your line of defence?

8.2

Commonwealth Aid

13. *Teachers for the Commonwealth Conference* The recommendations of the Working Party were placed before the Teachers for the Commonwealth Conference, held in London on the 23rd February 1960. This Conference was convened by the then Minister of Education for England and Wales, and attended by United Kingdom Ministers, representatives of Commonwealth countries and the remaining Colonial territories, as well as by some 250 representatives of local

education authorities, associations of teachers, and other in-
10 terested bodies. Speakers representing teachers' and local
education authorities' organisations agreed in principle to the
Working Party's recommendations, which were also wel-
comed by the overseas representatives attending the Conference. The Commonwealth Teachers' Act was at that time
under discussion in Parliament and the Minister of Education
was able to announce that Her Majesty's Government had
agreed to make available an annual sum, rising to £700,000
by 1964, to provide, *inter alia*:

    [a]   special allowances for augmenting the emoluments
20   paid by overseas governments to cover the addi-
            tional personal expense involved in teaching over-
            seas, where necessary:

    [b]   resettlement grants providing a lump sum to
            teachers on returning to the United Kingdom;
            and

    [c]   an interview fund which could help teachers serving
            overseas to meet the expense of returning to the
            United Kingdom for interview if short-listed for the
            headship of a large school, or for a comparable
30   post, due to fall vacant about the time of their
            return from overseas.

14. *The Next Stage* With the Conference's seal of approval
on the Working Party's recommendations the way was now
open for their implementation. In September 1960 the three
Education Departments issued parallel circulars to all local
education authorities, formally notifying them of the
measures which Her Majesty's Government now proposed to
take to give effect to the undertakings which they had assumed
as a result of the Commonwealth Education Conference.

40 15. In these Circulars the findings of the first Commonwealth Education Conference were reviewed, and the
addressees' attention drawn to the severe shortage of teachers
in developing Commonwealth countries and the Colonies.
The long term objective of these countries was so to develop
their own educational resources as to be able largely to dispense with outside assistance, but until this was achieved
short term assistance would be required with both the training
and the supply of teachers. To ensure that the available
resources were used to best advantage, efforts would be
50 directed primarily to filling 'key' posts in developing countries with staff from other countries more favourably placed,
and to training in the latter students from the former, who

would themselves fill 'key' posts on their return home. The
British contribution would be to offer an average of 400
additional teacher training places annually over the next five
years, with bursaries for the students filling them, and to
provide the financial assistance required to encourage the
recruitment by 1964 of 400 British teachers to fill 'key' educational posts in the developing countries of the Common-
60 wealth. The bulk of these would be expected to serve in
secondary schools, teacher training colleges, and technical
colleges on short term contracts of from two to five years.
The target for 1960 was set at 75.
16. The Circulars recognised the difficulties facing the
implementation of this undertaking. British education was
itself facing severe manpower difficulties, but it was pointed
out that the 400 British teachers required to fill 'key' posts
overseas would represent an accretion to the teaching strength
of the developing countries out of all proportion to the
70 numbers involved, which, in turn, were only marginal in relation to the total numbers of teachers in the United Kingdom.

from *The First Seven Years*, National Council for
Supply of Teachers Overseas, H.M.S.O. 1967

A: 1 Explain the stages by which government policy is formed and
carried out in a project of the kind treated here?
  2 What measures were taken to ensure the widest knowledge of, and
support for, the recommendations of the Working Party?
  3 Can you tell exactly how much money the government had agreed
to provide?
  4 How was the money allocated by the government to be used to
encourage British teachers to teach in other Commonwealth
countries?
  5 What exactly was the function of the Conference in relation to
the powers of the government?
  6 What happened on this matter between 23rd February 1960 and
September in the same year?
  7 What was the exact purpose of the 'circulars' (line 35)? Who were
the 'addressees' (line 42)?
  8 What was the aim of the government in relation to educational
needs in developing countries?
  9 How did the circulars deal with anticipated objections to the
government proposals?

B: 1 What kind of readers does the pamphlet from which this extract
is taken seem to address?
  2 What features give the passage a certain degree of formality?
  3 How appropriate is the formality to the issues being discussed?

118

4 How else could the following be expressed:
  [a] augmenting the emoluments (line 19)
  [b] dispense with outside assistance (lines 45–46)
  [c] countries more favourably placed (line 51)
  [d] severe manpower difficulties (line 66)?
5 'first (line 40). What implications does this word carry?
6 It has been said that the words 'former' and 'latter' can always be avoided. Does this seem possible here (line 52)?
7 Explain the metaphor of the 'key' post (line 67)?
8 Rewrite the information contained in this extract in the manner of 8.1.

8.3
English at the University

English continues in most areas to be used even more intensively as a medium of instruction when the pupil goes on to further education beyond school, notably at training colleges, and the university.

At the university level the main emphasis switches to the written form of English, and a student's written English often needs attention throughout his whole university period, *see* para. 54. The oral approach is best for the earlier stages of education, *see* paras. 15 and 16; yet the very success of this
10 approach is likely to have had effects on the student's written style, and the university student needs supplementary practice in what is, after all, a separate and equally necessary idiom, that of written English. The attainment of the Oversea School Certificate or its equivalent does not guarantee that the candidate will write perfect idiomatic English at the university. Accordingly, continuous attention to students' English composition is necessary if they are to derive the full profit from their course.

The final aim should be to produce a student whose English
20 will give him full control of the type of writing and reading required to master his subject successfully at degree level, and to use his attainments afterwards both in his professional life and in society in general. Since, therefore, adequate English for an engineer, for example, may be different from the English adequate for a student of English literature (cf. para. 65, sub-para. 2), any supplementary English course required at higher specialisation stage or university should be based on

a survey of these varying needs. Several courses of this type
will probably be required to cover the range of subjects being
30 studied.

The need for training students in efficient methods of study
is a universal educational problem, but when it is related to
study through the medium of English as a second language
the two aspects interact with particularly important consequences. If a student is taught to use his skill in language
methodically, he will avoid dissipating energy on problems
that may not be language problems at all.

A special problem arises with a student who proceeds by
scholarship or other means to a university or other institution
40 in the United Kingdom or in any other English-speaking
country. He now faces the ultimate test of his use of English,
namely, direct competition with students who speak and write
English as native speakers. The student from overseas who has
learned his English as a second language can seldom compete
on absolutely equal terms. For this reason attention is drawn
to our proposals for supplementary courses in English, *see*
paras. 52, 53 and 54.

from *The Makerere Report on the Teaching of English as a Second
Language, 1962*, Government of Uganda

A: 1 What distinction seems to be drawn between English at the level of
'further education' and at 'lower' levels?

2 What special assistance is it suggested that the university student
needs with English?

3 What is the connection of the Oversea School Certificate with the
problems being considered here?

4 Distinguish between the kinds of skill required by the graduate at
the three stages, (i) 'mastering his subject . . . at degree level'
(line 21), (ii) 'his professional life' (line 22), and (iii) 'in society in
general' (line 23).

5 What different kinds of supplementary course in English might
be required at universities?

6 What might be the 'other means' (line 39)?

7 What is described as the 'ultimate test' for the overseas student
studying in native-English-speaking countries?

B: 1 From which part of the whole Report do you suppose this extract
is taken?

2 What features distinguish this as typical of a government report?

3 What indication do you find of a mingling of formal and less
formal elements in the language?

4 Comment on the logic of the sentence 'If a student . . . problems
at all' (lines 35–37).

5 What would be the nature and purpose of the supplementary courses referred to in 'paras. 52, 53, 54' (line 46)?

6 How do you assess this as a piece of official writing? How quickly and efficiently does it achieve its purpose?

8.4
Trade Centres

We have visited two of these for boys and one for girls, and are aware of plans for the development of others. We were very pleased with what we saw, and consider that the general planning of these centres is on sound lines and that the quality of the teaching is, on the whole, of a high order, and that the instructors are doing their work faithfully and with success. The fact that they are boarding schools naturally puts extra responsibilities upon the staff and in all the centres we visited these responsibilities were being accepted
10 with good grace and worthy spirit.

We have, however, had some evidence regarding the planning of training centres which we feel bound to accept and to report. Firstly, it would seem that in the provision of trade centres, the decision regarding what trades shall be taught, and even regarding what staff should be recruited, are matters which ought to be decided by a Western Region Committee at high level which has representatives of all groups concerned in the industrial and economic development of the Region and of the country. This would be Advisory Committee B to
20 which we have referred in Chapter II and Appendix No. 1.

This committee should have all relevant papers concerning plans for the development of the country and of the Western Region and in the light of this information would be able to form an overall view regarding the nature and location of trade centres to be established in the years ahead.

It is particularly important that there should be long-term planning of this kind, for in the existing trade centres boys are being prepared for work which is becoming less common and even very difficult to find, because of changes in industrial
30 methods.

It has been suggested to us, for instance, that it is much more important to train young men who will be expert in repairing air-conditioners and television sets than in cabinet making, and that courses in auto engineering are too few. It

has also been pointed out to us that although the number of applicants for vacancies at these centres is so great that high selection is possible, and is on the whole very well done, it is not of a kind which enables the specific suitability of the young man or woman for the type of trade for which he or
40 she is ultimately centered to be ascertained. There is, at present, no system of even elementary vocational guidance in the Western Region, so it is inevitable that some young men and women, who are anxious to get a trade training at almost any cost, get trained for work for which they are not naturally endowed.

from *The Banjo Report*, Government of Western Nigeria, 1962

A: 1 What grounds for satisfaction with trade centres did the members of the commission making the report have?
2 To what objections were the trade centres liable?
3 What would be the function of Advisory Committee B?
4 Why is 'long-term planning' regarded as 'particularly important' (lines 26–27)?
5 Illustrate the disproportion between current efforts at training and the needs which existed.
6 What was gratifying about the selection of applicants for training?
7 What would have been the great advantage if 'vocational guidance' (line 41) had been available? (Ref: 1.1, page 15–17)

B: 1 What linguistic features give this passage an official character?
2 Illustrate the easy but effective flow of ideas in the language in which this is written.
3 'which we felt bound to accept' (line 12). What alternative decision do these words imply might have been taken, and for what reasons?
4 What is likely to be the effect if some young men and women 'get trained' (line 44) for work for which they are not 'naturally endowed'?

8.5

Loans to Students

Loans to the few individual students who find themselves in financial difficulties are a normal feature of academic life and raise no special problems. Institutions have their own techniques for ascertaining needs and arranging terms of repayment; we have heard no complaints on this score. But the suggestion that students in higher education should in general

be financed either wholly or partly by loans rather than grants is a different matter. It is not completely novel: for there is a good deal of this abroad, and it has been tried in this country
10 in the past for intending teachers; but its introduction on a large scale would be a break with recent tradition. The case must therefore be examined with some care.

Apart from relief to the budget, there are two arguments in favour of this form of loan finance. The first is an argument on the distribution of burdens. Higher education, it is argued, is an investment that, in many cases at least, carries with it the prospect of earnings substantially higher than the earnings of those who have not had it. Admittedly it is highly desirable that this privilege should not be confined to those whose
20 family position enables the necessary finance to be forth- coming – *la carrière ouverte aux talents* is an important social objective. But if finance is provided by outright subsidy from public funds, it is said, a new position of privilege is created: the recipient of the subsidy is being put in a position to command a higher income in virtue of taxes paid, in part at least, by those whose incomes are smaller. It is therefore urged that what is needed is not outright subsidy but a system where- by young men and women who have the prospect of being able to improve their talents by further study are provided
30 with the necessary finance by loans repayable in the future on reasonable terms out of their taxable income; or, as a variant upon this, a provision in the tax law whereby those who have been thus helped are taxed at a suitably higher rate until the assistance can be judged to have been repaid.

The second argument is an argument of morals and incen- tive. It is said that the student financed by grants is sometimes apt to take his privilege for granted; and that this may have as a by-product the lack of any particular sense of obligation and need to work. By contrast, the student financed by loan is
40 likely to have a greater sense of individual responsibility. He knows that he has to pay the price later on and is therefore all the keener to get the most out of what he is buying. The advo- cates of this plan point out that already in this country more is spent from public funds on the individual student in higher education than elsewhere in the world; and they ask whether, if the system is to be extended as we hope, it is not right that the students themselves should bear part of the burden as soon as they are in a position to do so.

from *The Robbins Report*, H.M.S.O., 1963

A: 1 What is the difference between those loans which are 'a normal feature of academic life' (line 2) and those referred to in line 7?
 2 What is the difference between 'wholly' and 'partly' in the context here (line 7)?
 3 What initial grounds are there for giving consideration to the proposed system of loans?
 4 Why must the case be 'examined with some care' (line 12)?
 5 Examine the *three* principal arguments which favour the policy of loans.
 6 How would the loans be repaid?
 7 What social philosophy underlies the thought in this extract?
 8 Explain the new 'position of privilege' (line 23) which might be created. How would a policy of 'loans' counteract this?
 9 What bearing has the possible 'extension' (line 46) of higher education upon the proposed 'loans'?

B: 1 Consider the means by which the discussion in this passage is maintained at a high level of impersonality and abstraction.
 2 Investigate the incidence of verb forms in the Passive in this passage.
 3 Discuss the means used to indicate the 'realities' in the following expressions:
   [a] 'students who find themselves in financial difficulties' (lines 1–2)
   [b] 'Institutions have their own techniques' (lines 3–4)
 4 Do you detect any attitude towards the proposals under consideration in the expressions:
   [a] 'there is a good deal of this abroad' (line 9)
   [b] 'it has been tried in this country in the past for intending teachers' (lines 9–10)
 5 What is gained (if anything) by introducing a French expression 'la carrière ouverte aux talents' (line 21) – 'careers open to ability'?
 6 What valid arguments could be adduced against the policy of financing higher education by loans rather than grants to students?

Section 8   PRACTICAL

C: 1 Imagine a new law or government regulation which seems to you to be necessary. Assume that it has just been passed, and write a simple explanation of its justification, and the way it will operate, as if for a public information leaflet, or a radio or television broadcast.
 2 Imagine yourself a member of the commission which produced the report from which 8.3 is selected. Suppose that you have felt it necessary to produce a minority report in which you urge the need for the teaching of a language other than English (e.g. Welsh, Arabic, Yoruba) in a particular area. Write out your minority report in a style which is compatible with that of the main report.

3 Imagine yourself the President or Public Relations Officer of a Students' Union just after the Report 8.5 has been published. Prepare a public address opposing the idea of 'loans', for each of the following occasions:

[a] an Annual Conference of the Union

[b] an official statement of policy to be put before representatives of the government or other authorities.

4 Imagine yourself a government official who is being fiercely attacked by critics (in parliament, and in the press) on an issue about which you are still waiting for vital information before making a decision. Draft a public statement intended to pacify and conciliate your critics, and promote an atmosphere in which rational decisions can be taken.

5 Imagine yourself the secretary of an official commission which has been set up to enquire into a serious problem which has recently arisen in your community (local or national). Write a part of the final report, surveying the origins of the problem, the possible lines of solution and the commission's recommendations in the best official manner (i.e. lucid, precise, objective, etc.).

6 Collect examples of the 'language of government' from contemporary sources, discussing whether they are as effective (or otherwise) as they might be, and rewriting where you feel that improvement is possible.

Section 9

IRONY IN LANGUAGE

Here we come to one of the most difficult, though quite widespread, uses of language — 'the expression of one's meaning by language of opposite or contradictory tendency,' as the Oxford Dictionary defines it. Irony is never a simple phenomenon, and its recognition perhaps depends on a certain degree of intelligence in the reader or listener. It is not a single phenomenon either, for its presence is discernible sometimes under smaller, sometimes under larger stretches of language. When it is not recognised, misunderstanding may be complete; for example, it is on record that Swift's pamphlet from which 9.1 is taken was understood as a serious statement of policy by some foreign readers.

While irony may sometimes settle into an intellectual vice, which refuses ever to make a plain statement, in other ways it may be regarded as one of the distinctive features of civilised intercourse, enabling opinions and attitudes to be expressed without the coarser methods of abuse and invective.

9.1
The Irish Poor

It is a melancholy object to those who walk through this great town, or travel in the country, when they see the streets, the roads, and cabin doors, crowded with beggars of the female sex, followed by three, four, or six children, all in rags, and importuning every passenger for an alms. These mothers, instead of being able to work for their honest livelihood, are forced to employ all their time in strolling to beg sustenance for their helpless infants; who, as they grow up, either turn thieves for want of work, or leave their dear native

10 country to fight for the Pretender in Spain, or sell themselves
to the Barbadoes.

I think it is agreed by all parties that this prodigious
number of children in the arms, or on the backs, or at the
heels, of their mothers and frequently of their fathers, is in
the present deplorable state of the kingdom a very great additional grievance; and therefore whoever could find out a fair,
cheap, and easy method of making these children sound useful members of the commonwealth, would deserve so well of
the public, as to have his statue set up for a preserver of the
20 nation. . . .

I shall now therefore humbly propose my own thoughts,
which I hope will not be liable to the least objection.

I have been assured by a very knowing American of my
acquaintance in London, that a young healthy child, well
nursed, is at a year old a most delicious, nourishing, and
wholesome food, whether stewed, roasted, baked, or boiled;
and I make no doubt that it will equally serve in a fricassee
or a ragout.

I do therefore humbly offer it to public consideration that
30 of the 120,000 children already computed, 20,000 may be
reserved for breed, whereof only one-fourth part to be males;
which is more than we allow to sheep, black cattle, or swine;
and my reason is, that these children are seldom the fruits of
marriage, a circumstance not much regarded by our savages,
therefore one male will be sufficient to serve four females.
That the remaining 100,000 may, at a year old, be offered in
sale to the persons of quality and fortune through the kingdom; always advising the mother to let them suck plentifully
in the last month, so as to render them plump and fat for a
40 good table. A child will make two dishes at an entertainment
for friends; and when the family dines alone, the fore or hind
quarter will make a reasonable dish, and, seasoned with a little
pepper or salt, will be very good boiled on the fourth day,
especially in winter.

I have reckoned upon a medium that a child just born will
weigh 12 pounds, and in a solar year, if tolerably nursed,
will increase to 28 pounds.

I grant this food will be somewhat dear, and therefore very
proper for landlords, who, as they have already devoured
50 most of the parents, seem to have the best title to the children.

I can think of no one objection that will possibly be raised
against this proposal, unless it should be urged that the
number of people will be thereby much lessened in the king-

dom. This I freely own, and it was indeed one principal design in offering it to the world. I desire the reader will observe, that I calculate my remedy for this one individual kingdom of Ireland, and for no other that ever was, is, or I think ever can be, upon earth. Therefore let no man talk to me of other expedients: of taxing our absentees at 5s. a pound; of
60 using neither clothes nor household furniture except what is of our own growth and manufacture; of utterly rejecting the materials and instruments that promote foreign luxury; of curing the expensiveness of pride, vanity, idleness, and gaming, in our women; of introducing a vein of parsimony, prudence, and temperance; of learning to love our country, in the want of which we differ even from LAPLANDERS and the inhabitants of TOPINAMBOO; of quitting our animosities and factions, nor acting any longer like the Jews, who were murdering one another at the very moment their city was taken; of
70 being a little cautious not to sell our country and conscience for nothing; of teaching landlords to have at least one degree of mercy toward their tenants; lastly, of putting a spirit of honesty, industry, and skill into our shopkeepers; who, if a resolution could now be taken to buy only our native goods, would immediately unite to cheat and exact upon us in the price, the measure, and the goodness, nor could ever yet be brought to make one fair proposal of just dealing, though often and earnestly invited to it.

Therefore I repeat, let no man talk to me of these and the
80 like expedients, till he has at least some glimpse of hope that there will be ever some hearty and sincere attempt to put them in practice.

from *A Modest Proposal*, JONATHAN SWIFT

NOTE *The date of the pamphlet from which this extract is taken was 1729, the 'great town' Dublin.*

A: 1 What circumstances presumably 'forced' (line 7) the women to beg?
  2 Why is the prevalence of begging an '*additional* grievance' (lines 15–16)?
  3 What is the ground proposed for one fourth part of the children 'for breed' (line 31) being males?
  4 What were some of the real causes of national distress in Ireland at that time, in the author's analysis?
  5 How does Swift, himself an Irishman, distribute blame for the

condition of his country between other nations and his own people?

6 What attitudes are expressed towards Laplanders, Jews, the inhabitants of Topinamboo?

7 For which section of his community does Swift seem to express the greatest scorn?

B: 1 At the superficial level, what kind of document does Swift seem to be offering to the public?

2 At which points does the reader begin to detect the ironical nature of the proposal?

3 Examine the way in which Swift's anger is revealed at its most intense by the discrepancy between the language used and the realities it refers to.

4 Is there any point made in attributing the proposal to 'a very knowing American of my acquaintance in London' (lines 23–24)?

5 At which points does the ironical method change to more direct denunciation?

6 Contrast the uses of language represented in paragraph 1 and paragraph 8 (lines 58–78).

7 Note any words or structures which seem to you to differ from their modern equivalents.

9.2
The Early Christians

The sober discretion of the present age will more readily censure than admire, but can more easily admire than imitate, the fervour of the first Christians, who, according to the lively expression of Sulpicius Severus, desired martyrdom with more eagerness than his own contemporaries solicited a bishopric. The epistles which Ignatius composed as he was carried in chains through the cities of Asia breathe sentiments the most repugnant to the ordinary feelings of human nature. He earnestly beseeches the Romans that, when he should be
10 exposed in the amphitheatre, they would not, by their kind but unseasonable intercession, deprive him of the crown of glory; and he declares his resolution to provoke and irritate the wild beasts which might be employed as the instruments of his death. Some stories are related of the courage of martyrs who actually performed what Ignatius had intended, who exasperated the fury of the lions, pressed the executioner to hasten his office, cheerfully leaped into the fires which were kindled to consume them, and discovered a

sensation of joy and pleasure in the midst of the most ex-
20 quisite tortures. Several examples have been preserved of
a zeal impatient of those restraints which the emperors had
provided for the security of the church. The Christians sometimes supplied by their voluntary declaration the want of an
accuser, rudely disturbed the public service of paganism,
and, rushing in crowds round the tribunal of the magistrates,
called upon them to pronounce and to inflict the sentence of
the law. The behaviour of the Christians was too remarkable
to escape the notice of the ancient philosophers, but they
seem to have considered it with much less admiration than
30 astonishment. Incapable of conceiving the motives which
sometimes transported the fortitude of believers beyond the
bounds of prudence or reason, they treated such an eagerness
to die as the strange result of obstinate despair, of stupid
insensibility, or of superstitious frenzy. 'Unhappy men!'
exclaimed the proconsul Antoninus to the Christians of Asia,
'unhappy men! if you are thus weary of your lives, is it so
difficult for you to find ropes and precipices?' He was extremely cautious (as it is observed by a learned and pious
historian) of punishing men who had found no accusers but
40 themselves, the imperial laws not having made any provision
for so unexpected a case; condemning therefore a few as a
warning to their brethren, he dismissed the multitude with
indignation and contempt. Notwithstanding this real or
affected disdain, the intrepid constancy of the faithful was
productive of more salutary effects on those minds which
nature or grace had disposed for the easy reception of religious truth. On these melancholy occasions there were
many among the Gentiles who pitied, who admired, and who
were converted. The generous enthusiasm was communicated
50 from the sufferer to the spectators, and the blood of martyrs,
according to a well-known observation, became the seed of
the church.

from *Decline and Fall of the Roman Empire*, EDWARD GIBBON

A: 1 What are the general attributes of the early Christians presented
in this passage?
2 What were the relative prospects of the early Christians being
[a] imitated, [b] admired, [c] censured by the readers of Gibbon's
time?
3 In what way were the sentiments expressed by Ignatius 'repugnant
to the ordinary feelings of human nature' (line 8)?

4 How far do we gather Ignatius was able to carry out the 'sentiments' expressed in his epistles?

5 What appears to have been the attitude of the Romans towards the early Christians?

6 What were some of the ways in which the early Christians 'asked for trouble'?

7 How did the 'ancient philosophers' regard the early Christians?

8 How did the proconsul Antoninus deal with those Christians he had encountered?

9 What was the general result of the behaviour of the early Christians?

B: 1 Considering the topic from all points of view, how justified do you consider the ironical approach adopted by Gibbon in this section?

2 What appears to be the attitude of Gibbon himself to the early Christians?

3 How were his personal feelings possibly related to the prevailing opinions of his own time? What appear to have been the principal virtues recognized at that time?

4 What do you learn of the religious attitudes of the contemporaries of Sulpicius Severus? (line 4)?

5 Do you consider that Gibbon fails to do justice to the early Christians?

6 Consider the effect of the metaphor 'breathe' (line 7).

7 Consider the element of abstraction introduced by Gibbon into the presentation of this subject.

9.3
Prayer and Providence

Then Miss Watson she took me in the closet and prayed, but nothing come of it. She told me to pray every day, and whatever I asked for I would get it. But it warn't so. I tried it. Once I got a fish-line, but no hooks. It warn't any good to me without hooks. I tried for the hooks three or four times, but somehow I couldn't make it work. By and by, one day, I asked Miss Watson to try for me, but she said I was a fool. She never told me why, and I couldn't make it out no way.

I set down, one time, back in the woods, and had a long
10 think about it. I says to myself, if a body can get anything they pray for, why don't Deacon Winn get back the money he lost on pork? Why can't the widow get back her silver snuff-box that was stole? Why can't Miss Watson fat up? No, says I to myself, there ain't nothing in it. I went and told the widow about it, and she said the thing a body could get by praying for

it was 'spiritual gifts'. This was too many for me, but she
told me what she meant – I must help other people, and do
everything I could for other people, and look out for them
all the time, and never think about myself. This was including
20 Miss Watson, as I took it. I went out in the woods and turned
it over in my mind a long time, but I couldn't see no advantage about it – except for the other people – so at last I reckoned I wouldn't worry about it any more, but just let it
go. Sometimes the widow would take me on one side and talk
about Providence in a way to make a body's mouth water;
but maybe next day Miss Watson would take hold and knock
it all down again. I judged I could see that there was two
Providences, and a poor chap would stand considerable show
with the widow's Providence, but if Miss Watson's got him
30 there warn't no help for him any more. I thought it all out,
and reckoned I would belong to the widow's, if he wanted me,
though I couldn't make out how he was a-going to be any
better off then than what he was before, seeing I was so
ignorant and so kind of low-down and ornery.

from *Huckleberry Finn*, MARK TWAIN

NOTE *Huckleberry Finn is a young American, whose father is a vagrant,
and who is to some extent brought up by the widow Douglas, with
some help from Miss Watson.*

A: 1 What picture do you form of Miss Watson?
   2 How had Huck failed to understand Miss Watson's teaching?
   3 'Once I got a fish-line (line 4). How does Huck appear to have
     misinterpreted this fact?
   4 What ulterior motive does Huck discern in Miss Watson's teaching?
     Was he right in this?
   5 What conception does Huck form of 'Providence' as a result of
     the teaching of the two ladies? What for example is signified by 'he'
     (line 31)?
   6 What is Huck's attitude towards himself?
   7 What important concept of Christianity does Huck fail to grasp in
     lines 32–33?

B: 1 What variety of language is in use in this passage? Examine and
     describe its regular characteristics.
   2 What serious purpose underlies the writing of the passage, and
     what is the author's 'message'?
   3 'she said I was a fool' (line 7). Do you think Miss Watson actually
     said this? What might she actually have said, and what light is
     thrown on the nature of language by Huck's misreporting?

4 What is the author's general attitude towards his character Huck? Of scorn, contempt, or ...?
5 How did the widow apparently attempt to explain the concept of 'spiritual gifts', and why did she not succeed?
6 Where do you see the process of concept-formation taking place in Huck's mind?
7 How exactly does the irony in this passage arise?

9.4
Population Explosion

But I prefer to quote now, on this topic, the words of an ingenious young Scotch writer, Mr Robert Buchanan, because he invests with so much imagination and poetry this current idea of the blessed and even divine character which the multiplying of population is supposed in itself to have. 'We move to multiplicity,' says Mr Robert Buchanan. 'If there is one quality which seems God's, and his exclusively, it seems that divine philoprogenitiveness, that passionate love of distribution and expansion into living forms. Every animal
10 added seems a new ecstasy to the Maker; every life added, a new embodiment of his love. He would *swarm* the earth with beings. There are never enough: Life, life, life, – faces gleaming, hearts beating, must fill every cranny. Not a corner is suffered to remain empty. The whole earth breeds, and God glories.'
It is a little unjust, perhaps, to attribute to the Divinity exclusively this philoprogenitiveness, which the British Philistine, and the poorer class of Irish, may certainly claim to share with him; yet how inspiriting is here the whole strain
20 of thought! and these beautiful words, too, I carry about with me in the East of London, and often read them there. They are quite in agreement with the popular language one is accustomed to hear about children and large families, which describes children as *sent*. And a line of poetry, which Mr Robert Buchanan throws in presently after the poetical prose I have quoted, –
'Tis the old story of the fig-leaf time –
this fine line, too, naturally connects itself, when one is in the East of London, with the idea of God's desire to *swarm* the
30 earth with beings; because the swarming of the earth with beings does indeed, in the East of London, so seem to revive

the old story of *the fig-leaf time*, such a number of the people
one meets there having hardly a rag to cover them; and the
more the swarming goes on, the more it promises to revive
this old story. And when the story is perfectly revived, the
swarming quite completed, and every cranny choke-full, then,
too, no doubt, the faces in the East of London will be gleaming faces, which Mr Robert Buchanan says it is God's desire
they should be, and which every one must perceive they are
40 not at present, but, on the contrary, very miserable.

from Culture and Anarchy, MATTHEW ARNOLD

NOTE *Surveying the social problems of his time, Arnold names the
      complacent and materialistic middle classes the Philistines. The
      'East' – the East End – of London illustrated most of the social
      evils of the 1860s at their most pronounced.*

A: 1 What is the principal social problem under consideration in
      this passage?
  2 What were the principal social evils evident in the 'East of
      London'?
  3 What does the trade or profession of Mr Buchanan seem to have
      been?
  4 What view is being expressed by Mr Buchanan in the extract quoted
      from his writings, and how do they agree with the actual facts pre-
      sented by Arnold?
  5 What matter-of-fact considerations relating to increase of popula-
      tion is Arnold ironically referring to in the word *sent* (line 24)?
  6 What are the historical/mythological references in the line of
      poetry (line 27)?
  7 Show how the meaning attached by Arnold to the words 'swarm'
      (line 29) and 'the fig-leaf time' (line 32) differ from Buchanan's.
  8 At what points does irony give place to direct expression in this
      passage?
  9 What practical conclusions are implied by Arnold's treatment
      of this subject?

B: 1 Illustrate from this passage the difference between what might be
      called 'local' irony (e.g. in such phrases as 'an ingenious young
      Scotch writer' (lines 1–2), 'how inspiriting is here the whole train
      of thought' (line 19), 'no doubt' (line 37), and 'general' irony as
      conveyed in the quotation of Buchanan placed in a different context
      from the original.
  2 Deduce from the context the meaning of the word 'philopro-
      genitiveness' (line 8).
  3 From the present context, in what sense is Arnold using the word
      'poetry'? (line 3)

134

4 Why does Buchanan's phrase 'We move to multiplicity' (lines 5–6) seem particularly insensitive?

5 In what ways do the habits of the British Philistine now differ from those in Arnold's time (vide lines 17–18)?

6 'every cranny choke-full' (line 36). Comment on the aptness of this phrase in its context.

9.5

F**d

'Well, ladies and gentlemen of the jury, we have all heard a great deal this afternoon about "purity" and "compassion". We have been told that certain of the – er – words in this book have appeared before in technical works or that they can be found in early English literature. We have patiently listened to a number of learned quotations which are said to be "of historical interest". Some of us may feel that they contain not the slightest jot or tittle of interest whatsoever. We have been lectured at length about "our Anglo-Saxon heritage". In this
10 case, ladies and gentlemen, it is nothing more or less than a heritage of filth.

'For what we have to consider – and consider very carefully before we give our verdict – is not this passage or that, not some abstract idea, not some passing reference to contemporary furniture or clothes, but the effect and the tendency of the book taken as a whole. Not a book for specialists, or sophisticated people, or scholars in some museum: but a paperback edition, multiplied by the million, within the reach of any man – or any boy – or any young girl – with idle curios-
20 ity and half-a-crown to spend.

'And we have to consider this book not as remote academic professors, not as pedants, but as people, as men and women of the world. And let me remind you, ladies and gentlemen, that the world is not an ivory tower where there are no problems, no dangers, no human weaknesses. The world is full of temptations – temptations of the flesh. And what could be more calculated – more coldly, more callously, more unscrupulously calculated – to arouse temptation and inflame the appetites than passages such as this?
30 ' "... Her hungry eyes met his as, ever so slowly, she turned to reveal the warm, full curves of breast and leg. He watched, fascinated, as the covering fell away from the soft white skin. Eagerly, he bent forward. An instant later, lips

parted, her head thrown back, Estella surrendered to the moment's sudden succulence, the firm warm flesh that brought the secret juices welling from within her. All too soon they were replete, exhausted. On Sundays, they always bought too big a chicken" ...'

from *Encounter No. 137*, RICHARD MAYNE

NOTE *The article from which this is the concluding section was written soon after the public prosecution of a number of novels alleged to be 'corrupting', as they included various 'Anglo-Saxon' four-letter words normally subject to strong tabu.*

A: 1 What kind of person is presumed to be speaking and on what precise occasion?
   2 What kind of evidence and arguments have been produced by the Defence?
   3 What principal arguments are being used in the Prosecution?
   4 What is considered to be the most effective form of evidence being used by the Prosecution?
   5 How has the mass production of cheap books made the problem seem more urgent?
   6 At what point in this speech does the reader realise that he has been tricked? What has he been led to expect, and what has he actually been given?
   7 Why is there no point at the end in continuing the speech, or describing the conclusion of the trial?
   8 What do you take to be the underlying purpose of this ironical invention?

B: 1 Show how the irony in this extract depends principally on two different meanings of the word 'flesh' (line 26).
   2 Describe at least three different 'registers' or varieties of language which are represented in this extract.
   3 What is the rhetorical effect of the sequence 'within the reach of any man – or any boy – or any young girl ...' (lines 18–19)?
   4 What are the main lines of thought along which the issue of the moral censorship of books has to be considered?

Section 9 PRACTICAL

C: 1 Write out a concise and systematic statement of the data and the 'case' that Swift is presenting in 9.1.
   2 On the lines of 9.2, write an account of any historical event in the history of your own nation or community which might involve an

ironical method of reporting (especially where the attitudes, creeds, or behaviour of one or more parties seems to invite criticism).

3 Present a situation in which two codes of belief or conduct are in juxtaposition or conflict (cf. 9.3). Observe whether the use of irony has formed any part of your technique.

4 To what extent is irony a universal feature of language (i.e. not only of the English Language)? Collect examples of the ironical use of language from languages other than English.

5 Why is irony often associated with a critical frame of mind in the person who employs it?

6 Invent a denunciation of any of the following topics:
[a] Poverty in the midst of plenty
[b] The gullible public
[c] Democratic politics
[d] Pedantic educationalists
[e] Slaves of fashion
[f] Hypochondriacs
[g] Political hypocrisy
[h] 'How to make friends and influence people'
[i] Foreign travel
[j] Self-righteousness
[k] 'Experts'.

Observe whether irony enters into your treatment of the subject.

7 As though for an article in an average newspaper, write a short, descriptive article illustrating any of the following tendencies:
[a] of 'important' people to ignore humble people
[b] of educated people to despise the uneducated
[c] of uneducated people to despise the educated
[d] of 'virtuous' people to be unsympathetic
[e] of 'godly' people to be shrewd in business (sometimes)
[f] of the young to misunderstand the old
[g] of the old to misunderstand the young

Section 10

JOURNALISM

Few expressions used in the discussion of language are more ambivalent than this. At the less creditable end of the range are the kinds of writing in which truth and significance are sacrificed to crude sensationalism and compulsive appeal. The better types (not necessarily the prerogative of any one type of newspaper) bring considerable powers of insight, imagination and linguistic skill to bear upon the explanation and interpretation of contemporary issues.

10.1

Siamese Twins in 'clear all roads' Drama

Siamese twins, joined at the chest and born prematurely to a young wife on holiday, were raced 130 miles from Lincoln to London last night.

The twins – girls, with a combined weight of 8lb – were taken to Great Ormond Street Children's Hospital. They were said to be in 'fair' condition.

Police in five counties had joined in an emergency link-up to speed the ambulance. The order went out: *All road junctions must be kept clear.*

10 Inside the ambulance the twins were tucked up in an incubator. A doctor and two nurses watched over them.

Outside, police cars and motor-cycle outriders buzzed around in relays until, after three hours 25 minutes, the ambulance reached Great Ormond Street.

A CHANCE

A doctor at the Lincoln maternity home where they were born yesterday said: 'Apart from being a bit premature, they are reasonably satisfactory.'

They were transferred, he said, because specialised treatment
20 offered them the best chance of survival.

He added 'I think it will be very difficult to separate them.'

The mother, who is in her 20's, was an emergency admission at the hospital. Last night she was 'pretty well'.

She and her husband – they have no other children – were on holiday and are believed to be from Essex. The hospital said the parents did not want their names disclosed.

The doctor said: 'We had no idea the babies were joined until they were delivered.'

And that, for ambulance-men Ernest Skelton, aged 40, and
30 Eric Toyne, 25, meant a hectic dash to London.

AT 5.25 P.M. a call came through to their station.

The ambulance loaded an incubator – always kept heated at the ambulance station – and was soon heading south.

Drivers Skelton and Toyne, both married with two children, took turns at the wheel.

HIGH-SPEED

They reached the A1 at Newark, 14 miles from Lincoln and raced down the dual-carriageway, eating up the 120 miles to Hatfield.

40 AT 8.20 they stopped for petrol at Hatfield.

AT 8.35 – 15 minutes and 15 miles later – Hertforshire police handed them over to the Metropolitan Police for the final lap. Most of that was covered at speeds reaching 70 miles an hour.

James Wilkinson, Express medical reporter, writes: Siamese twins occur in only one in 50,000 births. But as the majority are still-born, the chances of live Siamese twins being born is much rarer.

Doctors will perform many tests and study X-rays before
50 deciding exactly how they should be separated.

The last separation operation in Britain was in June 1964 at St Bartholomew's Hospital, London, on the year-old Siamese twin daughters of Mr and Mrs James Fenwick, of Nottingham, who were joined at the head.

One of the girls died half an hour after the operation. The other survived.

from the *Daily Express*, London 17. 8. 68

A: 1 Where and when were the twins referred to in this article born?
  2 How frequently do such births occur?
  3 Why is the birth of Siamese twins attended with some anxiety?

4 What action was taken in this case?

5 What are the prospects of survival for Siamese twins?

B: 1 Examine the extent to which the actual sequence of events has been dislocated in this report. For what purpose?

2 What degree of repetition of information do you observe in the article, and can it be justified?

3 Show how the writer attempts to exploit the possibilities of drama in the situation presented.

4 Examine the incidence of dramatic words such as 'raced', 'buzzed', 'hectic', etc.

5 Show how the writer attempts to introduce 'human interest' into his account, whether relevant or not to the main purpose.

6 Consider the relationship between the general part of the report and the contribution of the 'medical reporter'.

7 Indicate the features of the writing which denote that it is 'reported'.

8 What degree of [a] knowledge, [b] human insight does this article convey?

10.2

Editorial

'TAIN'T WHAT YOU DO...

'It's not what you do but the way that you do it . . .' So go the lyrics of a song that was popular a few years ago.

It's advice to which many a Government department should pay greater attention. So many edicts and decrees of the last 16 months have been handled in such a hamfisted way as to create public resentment where it could easily have been avoided.

10 The more sophisticated critic tends to regard such short-comings as bad public relations, but to the more down-to-earth observer it is a case of doing the right thing in the wrong way.

The latest case in point is the announcement about restrictions on money going out of the country. What a sad state of affairs when a bank, for example, has to act upon a newspaper report! No reasonable person questions the motives behind these restrictions, but because little publicity was given all kinds of interpretations have been placed on them. Human nature being what it is, what more can you expect?

20 Our point is that it should not be left to the public to place its own construction on such legislation. Explanations should be given at the time it is introduced. It would cut the ground

from beneath the rumour-mongers; those, for instance, who saw it as a tit-for-tat move on the part of the Government because foreign investment had slowed down to a mere trickle.

The restoration of overseas confidence in Nigeria is one of the more vital tasks that face our diplomats and information services, but their work is not made easier when announce-
30 ments like this are made with no thought to the response they are likely to have on foreigners inside and outside the country.

We believe the Government had excellent reasons for introducing these restrictions and that they are in the wider interests of everyone – including those expatriates who threw up their arms in despair when they heard the news.

What is wrong, then with the Government taking the public into its confidence and thereby creating rather than destroying goodwill?

from *The New Nigerian*, Kaduna, 2.5.67

A: 1 To whom is the Editorial really being addressed?
  2 For what is the government in question being criticised?
  3 What is the underlying attitude of the editor towards the government?
  4 Outline the particular events which have given rise to the comments in this editorial. What seemed regrettable about them?
  5 What benefits would a government receive from better 'public relations'?

B: 1 Discuss the strategy of the opening paragraph. Why does the heading differ from the opening quotation? How relevant is the popular song to the topic of the editorial?
  2 Explain the origin and effect of the expression 'hamfisted' (line 6).
  3 How effective is the contrast offered in paragraph 3?
  4 'Human nature being what it is' (lines 19–20). What characteristics of human nature are implied here?
  5 Discuss the happiness of the expression 'rumour-monger'.
  6 Indicate the devices used to emphasise the essential points in this editorial.
  7 Do you consider this piece of writing a credit to the profession of journalism, or otherwise? Give your reasons.

10.3
Editorial

Put yourself in the boots of a railway guard. Why are you on strike and what will get you back to work? The immediate reason for stopping is that one of your colleagues, when detailed for 'second man' duties two days ago, refused to undertake them and was sent home without pay. Therefore, as instructed by your union, you stopped work. You are not at heart subversive or militant; you like a quiet life and a regular pay packet as much as anyone. But you're a bit browned off because the engine drivers won quite a lot extra under the
10 agreement, because you thought that you would get about the same, because the Railways Board seem to be such clods (doing their sums wrong over the 1965 agreement, for example), because you are uneasy about your future anyway with the rundown of railway employment, and because the basis of calculating your wage is so complicated.

Does it cut much ice when Ray Gunter talks about 'the conspiracy of communism'? No, none at all. He's a decent chap and as sound a Minister of Labour as any for twenty years, and he may be right about some of the trouble-makers
20 in the docks and on the building sites. But he was a railway-man and he ought to know that it doesn't apply to railways. Does it, then, cut much ice when he implies that a state of emergency may be declared next week? Yes, a little, but not too much. It has happened before and it doesn't affect the strikers greatly. But it reminds you that if the railways as a whole come to a stop the consequences for the country will be serious. Well, does that worry you? Yes, in a general way it does; but the union has told you to stop work – and you would probably have stopped even if it had not.

30 What about Mr Neal, of the British Railways Board, telling you that you ought to 'question the value of the sort of leadership' you've been getting from the union? You might admit that the union has made a mess of things – not explaining the 1965 agreement to you, not trying to get its implications for guards sorted out until 1967, not backing the Manchester protest at first, demanding a court of inquiry, and then rejecting the court's findings. All the same, 'To hell with Neal' is your feeling: he hasn't done any better and this is the last moment at which to accept that sort of advice from
40 him.

Well, then, what about George Woodcock saying that 'any move towards conciliation must be circumscribed by the incomes policy'? To hell with the incomes policy too may be your first reaction – it's not done me any good. But just possibly you might have second thoughts about that. If George Woodcock really says that 24s a week is right outside what the TUC could accept – and he has not said it yet – then you might take some notice of that. Maybe you would then retreat towards the court of inquiry's 12s (which is what British 50 Rail offered for those actually doing second man duties). At least you would think about it, even if you were also suspicious about the incomes policy, your union's involvement in it, and the way the Government has put it over on you.

That is probably how it looks at Euston, Longsight, or Motherwell. From Downing Street or St James's Square – or from the Conservative conference in Brighton – it has a different perspective. Mr Wilson and his Cabinet must be uncomfortably conscious of the direct link between the 1966 seamen's strike and the 1966 July measures, the severest 60 squeeze our economy has suffered. (Perhaps the Prime Minister should explain the point in simple terms when he next broadcasts.) The rail strike and the docks strike together, if not resolved soon, could plunge Britain into new difficulties. Yet if they are resolved by a settlement out of line with the prices and incomes policy they could wreck that policy – and the hope of halting inflation. A new formula will have to be worked out for the railway guards, probably with the help of the TUC. Something like a fraction over 12s for guards performing second man duties, plus a smaller sweetener for 70 other guards, may be the answer. The question is how long it will take to reach and how much damage must be done before it is seen by the railwaymen to be acceptable.

from the *Guardian*, London 21.10.67.

NOTE *This appeared as an Editorial during a strike of British railway guards in October 1967, during the office of Mr Harold Wilson, the Labour Prime Minister.*

A: 1 How had the strike originated?
 2 Distinguish between the principal parties involved in the strike?
 3 What are the more general causes said to be underlying the strike?
 4 To whom does this editorial seem to be addressed – nominally and actually?

5 How had the Minister of Labour apparently tried to deal with the strike?

6 What degree of patriotism, or public spirit, is attributed to the strikers?

7 What specific proposals and what kind of attitudes is the editorial seeking to encourage?

B: 1 Examine the development of this editorial by means of a method of question and answer.

2 Consider the replacement of the word 'shoes' by 'boots' (line 1).

3 Indicate the phrases which seem to belong to the speech customs of the railway employees. How accurately are they introduced?

4 What is the effect of the sentence in lines 8–15, with four 'because' clauses?

5 What category of language and tradition of discourse is implied in the quotation 'the conspiracy of communism' (lines 16–17)?

6 Can you trace any use of a method of persuasion by suggestion in this editorial?

7 Consider the symbolism intended in the two groups of place names, Euston, Longsight, Motherwell and Downing Street, St James's Square, Brighton.

8 In view of the content of the whole article, what is hinted at in the title 'The price of rail peace'? (i.e. price to whom?)

10.4

Tongue Twisting

OR HOW TO MAKE AN OMELETTE WITHOUT BREAKING EGGS

Every time I open a magazine devoted to food technology I get a sinking feeling in the pit of the stomach. Each new revolutionary breakthrough seems more ominous than the last. They've just discovered that you can get a finer, more uniform crumb in a bun by adding 0.5 per cent sodium stearoyl-2-lactate. They've worked out, too, that acetylated monoglycerides make dry base toppings taste and look more like whipped cream than ever before. And they've developed a
10 'flavour modifier' so that standard artificial sweeteners based on saccharins and cyclamates can be made to contain a ribonucleotide, or ribonucleoside, or their deoxy analogues.

I hope these preservatives, surfactants, anti-oxidants, emulsifiers, stabilisers, sequestrants, moisteners, colouring agents, non-nutritive sweeteners, anti-caking agents, thickeners, thinners, and bleaching agents are doing us a power of good because we're going to digest more of them in the future, not less. Increasingly the major food corporations are placing

pressure on caterers and the housewife to give up old-
20 fashioned raw materials and accept the factory prepared substitute. Whereas the television commercials still emphasise
taste and flavour ('Umm! It's scrumptious mum!') the copy in
the catering press appeals to more basic instincts: 'Needs no
preparation at all' (an instant plasticed GMS emulsifier);
'Quick delivery at economic prices' (sorbic acid for cakes,
propionic acid for bread); 'Instant success just add water'
(pastry mix); 'Bland flavour, consistent performance' (shor-
tening); 'Improved plasticity' (margarine); 'Above all gives
added shelf-life' (soya flour).
30   The appeal of all these products is their low cost, and
labour-saving economy. As F. H. James, a catering exec-
utive, observed the other day: 'We in the catering trade are
becoming grocers, in business to buy, sell, and make a profit.'
Perhaps the most formidable development is the careful
conditioning of the customer to accept what he is given. By
controlling supply the food technologist can control demand.
By the subtle use of television he can gradually persuade the
viewer that the factory substitute is in every way superior to
the natural product. Children begin to pine for *instant* mashed
40 potato and to reject 'boring old homemade' mashed potato.
    The extent to which a demand can be deliberately created
was revealed at a catering seminar last month by Mr P. D.
Galvani, the chairman of Express Dairy (Caterers) Ltd.
Talking of his supermarket experiences he admitted: 'We
put in prepacked meat for the first time in this country – and
the customers didn't want it. But I thought this is what they
should want, and we put it in and eventually it went.' Increasingly the consumer is getting what the food technologist
thinks he *should* want.
50   With a significant part of British industry in the hands of the
Americans it is obvious that any 'progress' on the food front
in the States will soon be introduced in Britain – our fate
tomorrow is theirs today.
    An increasing number of American 'food outlets' are rely-
ing entirely on preportioned frozen foods reheated in specialised ovens. Even a simple dish like an omelette no longer
has to be trusted to kitchen staff – it comes direct from the
factory as a homogenised frozen disc, and when needed it is
placed in the oven where it sets as it melts.
60   Already edible protein has been produced from sawdust,
straw, animal hides, cotton wool, grass, coal, and petrol.
The most accepted American source of non-animal protein

is the soya bean. Disguised as sausage, cutlet, luncheon roll, frankfurter, it is digested with no apparent resentment by millions of contented customers and is the first successful stage in the transition to the all-purpose artificial food.

from the *Guardian*, 4.7.68 (DEREK COOPER)

A: 1 What are the 'current developments' which the writer is referring to?
2 How are the food corporations 'placing pressure' on caterers and housewives (lines 19)?
3 What is the 'catering press' (line 23)?
4 What are the more 'basic instincts' appealed to in the catering press?
5 What 'developments' does the writer present as 'formidable' (line 34)?
6 Explain other developments which seem likely in this field.
7 What (if anything) is likely to be lost by the transition to 'the all-purpose artificial food' (line 66)?

B: 1 What seems strange about the phrase 'food technology' (line 2)?
2 Explain the play on words in the title and subtitle of this article.
3 In what spirit does the writer make use of the 'technical registers' of the chemistry of food technology?
4 What is insufficiently explained in lines 11–12?
5 Show how the list of expression in lines 13–16 introduces an element of special selection.
6 What is signified by members of the catering trade coming to think of themselves as 'grocers' (line 33)?
7 Examine the associations, or the 'collocations' of the words 'old' (line 40, and *'instant'* (line 39).
8 Why is 'progress' put in inverted commas in line 51?
9 What are 'food outlets' (line 54) and what is meant by 'pre-portioned'? Comment on the coinage of these new expressions.

10.5
And That Leaves the Fox

WHO ELSE PLAYS JUST FOR FUN?
As I pulled on my pink coat for the 93rd Secret Convention of the A A A A A, I felt a sharp twinge. Gout in the *navel*? I asked myself incredulously. Then I recognised the recurring spasm for what it was. Nervous melancholy. May was a-flying, June was soon, and Wimbledon had fallen – betrayed from within like Troy or did I mean Madrid, and with never a musket fired.

Sick at heart I mounted my tricycle and rode to the meet. Old Bellman lolloped after, chased by Toby the terrier.

We all wear full rig of one sort or another at the meetings of the Five A's (yes yes yes the All-rounders' And Absolute Amateurs' Association). It gives the occasion a kind of pageantry, in keeping with the splendour of the house and grounds where. . . But I must be discreet. Not only is the Press never admitted but no guests are invited, for our proceedings are arcane and we are bound by a Dread Oath. I can disclose merely that the morning session, chaired sternly by me, went well.

The day being fine, after luncheon we relaxed for an hour in the sunshine of the Great Terrace, overlooking the Old Adam folly and the famous vista by Culpability Brown. My heart was still heavy, though the umbilical pain had subsided. Standing wrapped in thought and oblivious to my surroundings, a bare yard or two from our august Patron by the by, I suddenly became aware that seated before me on the balustrade was a fox! And I smiled, or almost. For your fox is your true amateur. He runs, not for gold, but for love of the chase.

Reynard the wily. Charles James as they call him, in memory of the younger Pitt. He knew full well it was the close season. Cool as dammit he sat there, looking at Bellman and Toby and H*s R*y*l H*ghn*ss, at the self-styled croquet king of Salt Lake City, at the junior-amateur triple-yoyo champions of the Home Counties, at two youngsters behind me called Alekhin and Nimzowitsch who play draughts for Scotland, at Miss Simpson our leading lady tennis ornithologist, at little Marilyn Spellbound who is once again Miss Leapfrog (amateur) of Europe, at old Mother Thing who climbed Ben Hur on her motorbike, and many another celebrity. Bold Reynard surveyed them.

Well old friend, said I, so you and I meet here, while in Claridges, the Ritz and elsewhere the Handsome Eight and the Halfhandsome Half-hundred are lazing under sunray lamps as valets iron their iridescent shorts. And I fell to musing on the anatomy of the amateur, as it is variously anatomised.

For my Lord A declares a true amateur to be somebody *who has never benefited from his sport*, nay not even during a by-election. And Mr President B, meditating on Olympian heights, pronounces an amateur to be one *whose intentions are pure* – which shall be known to all on the Day of Judgment. And Mr C states with delight that an amateur is either stink-

50 ing rich, or fondly obsessed, or *not very good at his game*, a
most vile slander.

Is it for such reasons Reynard (I asked) that our potential
grandmasters and ambidextrous archers steadfastly reject
offers of Government aid, the wages of shamateurism. Is this
why I hunt *you* through every opening but a turnstile? What –
apart from the petty convenience of a tax-deductable loss –
can professionalism offer to me, proud Me, whose boots,
habit, hat, crop, breeches and daily breakfast cereal are
bona-fide tournament trophies, voucher-purchased and
60 hand-engraved with name and date?

It isn't their dirty money we envy, Reynard (I said). It's
their rigid dope-legislation we fear. As one man and as one
woman we amateur athletes suffer from headaches, consti-
pation, sexual fatigue, night terrors. Where would we stand
if our homely aperients were declared suspect? Where if our
time-hallowed tonics and proprietary remedies were snatched
from us? How do the arbiters of professional yachting or
bridge look on Hall's Wine, Friar's Balsam, Wincarnis,
Phospherine . . . How?

70 I am myself (I told him) like many a soldier and quondam
explorer, a martyr to spasms and to diarrhoea. The men of
Kitchener's Fighting Scouts are among those who vouch for
the only specific which gives me relief. So is Dr W Vesalius
Pettigrew of England. It contains – and I whispered the
words, as it were in small type – liquid extract of Opium . . .
Morphine . . . Chloroform . . . Proof Spirit . . . The fox
shuddered.

Its blessed name, I said defiantly, is Dr J Collis Browne's
Chlorodyne. The fox looked aghast. I realised with a spasm
80 that I had indeed been indiscreet, to the point of madness,
and my hand moved instinctively towards my side pocket. No
more than thirty drops. With water. *He* carried it, I said,
Edw Whymper Esq the celebrated Mountaineer. He used it
'effectively' on himself, on others, even on Mont Blanc. The
fox whimpered.

Roll on the bright cold months, I said, I'll have your guts
for garters.

from *Nova*, London, June 1968 (LINDLEY ABBAT)

NOTE *The hunting of foxes is regarded by some as a sport, but by others as
cruel and wasteful. In 1968 the Wimbledon tennis championships
were for the first time open to professional players.*

148

A: 1 What is the situation created in this passage?
  2 Why does the writer pretend to feel 'melancholy' (line 4)?
  3 Upon what topic does the passage revolve?
  4 Why does the author appear to fear 'dope-legislation' (line 62)?
  5 What does his attitude towards fox-hunting appear to be?
  6 Suggest any other objects of satire which you can discern in the passage.

B: 1 How do you describe the general management of language in this passage?
  2 Examine the passage for jokes, puns, jingles, humorous allusions, and decide whether they have a serious object or not.
  3 'he runs... for love of the chase' (line 25). What argument of the champions of fox-hunting does this relate to?
  4 Discuss the etymology of 'shamateurism' (line 54).
  5 In what sense is 'anatomy' (line 42) being used?
  6 What does the 'turnstile' (line 55) symbolise?
  7 Why does the writer long for the 'bright cold months' (line 86)?
  8 What is your final opinion of this piece of writing?

Section 10 PRACTICAL

C: 1 Choose a specific local event (e.g. a sports day, an arts festival, a public meeting, the visit of a celebrity, etc.) and report it in a number of different journalistic styles, e.g. the 'sensational' (cf. 10.1), the 'responsible/informal' (cf. 10.3), the 'playful/intellectual' (cf. 10.4), the stiff/formal (cf. 8.2).
  2 Imagine yourself a newspaper editor or leader-writer, and write a serious-minded editorial for your paper on a particular topical issue, whether local, national, or international. (This may be done also, as in Question 1, as for different types of newspaper.)
  3 In the manner of 10.1 write your report for a 'popular' newspaper of the hundredth birthday of a centenarian.
  4 Write an editorial for your favourite newspaper, which, while it makes clear a general support for the government in power, adversely criticises some aspect of its present policy.
  5 Write a newspaper article intended to sway public opinion very drastically in a certain direction. Consider afterwards how far your approach has been rational and how far rhetorical.
  6 Write an article for a particular newspaper on a public issue, which permits a 'light' or humorous approach while being fundamentally serious (e.g. perhaps, Dress, Attitude to Parents, Public Behaviour, Xenophobia, Conspicious Consumption).

Sections 11 and 12

SCIENTIFIC AND TECHNICAL REGISTERS

As an extension of the idea of 'dialect', we now recognise that many technical and professional occupations give rise to special 'registers' usually with vocabularies outside the range of the ordinary educated man and with distinctive sentence patterns, often of a restricted kind. The tendency of 'literary' people was formerly to scorn these 'languages' under such terms as Jargon. Now we are more willing to accept their existence, particularly because modern methods of investigation and operation produce numerous new concepts, materials and processes. This is still a matter for careful judgment however. There are problems concerned with the re-use of existing terms; also perhaps with the cult of novelty for novelty's sake: and not every piece of 'technical writing' need be regarded as automatically justified. Technical writers, too, are not spared the need to use more general forms of the language especially when they have to communicate with the general public. At their best, however, it must be recognised that technical registers provide a swift, economical, efficient, impersonal, sometimes international, means of exposition and discussion of specialised issues. In no way of course do they replace the need for cultivation of the more general, standard forms of the language.

11.1

Molecular Structure

SOLIDS AND SOLUBILITY

Let us cool the liquid still further and watch it solidify, still at the same magnification as before. As we abstract more heat the molecules, moving ever more slowly, are pulled closer together, and the liquid contracts. At length the molecules are so close that they can no longer pass between one another. The intermolecular force pulls them together so that they form a regular pattern (Fig. 1.8). Something similar can be

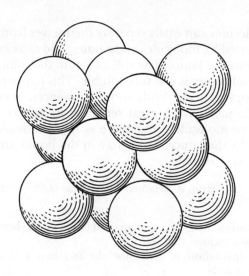

Fig. 1.8. Cubic crystal formed from spherical particles. Argon and other inert gases form crystals of this type, also many common metals.

seen if some marbles in the corner of a box are gently shaken. In this way the irregular arrangement of molecules in gas or
10 liquid is replaced by regular arrangement in a crystal. Such a regular arrangement is known as a *space lattice*, i.e. a lattice in three dimensions, as contrasted with the flat lattice or trellis common in gardens. In it each molecule occupies a kind of box made up of its neighbours, and in this space it vibrates, while its neighbours do the same in their spaces. As the temperature falls the vibration becomes less violent. This confinement of the molecules within a small space and close to one another permits chemical bonds to be formed more readily than before. Most molecules are not round, so the
20 way in which they fit together to form a crystal may be quite complicated.

The above description of the formation of crystalline solids deals with the solidification of pure liquids, i.e. of single substances. But frequently crystals separate from liquids which are mixtures, e.g. sugar from syrup. In this case the sugar molecules sort themselves out from the water molecules which they leave in the liquid. As with the separation of liquid from vapour, so there is really an equilibrium between molecules attaching themselves to the crystal and
30 those leaving the crystal and passing into the liquid. If

151

the molecules can easily separate themselves from the attraction exerted by molecules of the water, and can easily fit themselves into the lattice, few will be left in the solution, and we say the substance is not very soluble. This happens with boric acid (boracic acid). With some substances, such as sugar, the molecules have a great tendency to adhere to some of the water molecules, and there is more difficulty in fitting them into the lattice. More stay in the liquid and so we say sugar is very soluble.

from *A Structural Introduction to Chemistry*, E. T. HARRIS

A: 1 What kind of 'magnification' do you presume has been under consideration 'before' (line 2)?
2 What explanation is given for the fact that a liquid contracts as it is cooled?
3 What is the difference between the arrangement of molecules in a gas or liquid, and in a solid?
4 What is the perceptible effect of the 'vibration' (line 16) in the 'boxed up' molecules in a solid?
5 One kind of liquid under consideration here is called 'pure' (line 23). What is the other kind?
6 What explanation is given of the fact that some substances are more soluble than others?

B: 1 Examine the features which give impersonality to this exposition. Does the use of 'us' and 'we' (lines 1–2) violate this to any extent?
2 Do you classify the 'intermolecular force' (line 6) as a fact, a theory, a hypothesis, or a law?
3 Examine the use of metaphor and analogy in building up this explanation.
4 To what extent is the scientific information in this passage carried mainly by the nouns and nominal groups (see 12.2, page 166)?
5 Which of the concepts in the texts does the diagram most exactly illustrate?
6 Consider the status of the expression 'we say' (line 39). What does it suggest about the general purpose of this exposition?
7 What combination between scientific exactness and clarity of explanation do you find in this passage?

The 'Clutch'

FRICTION CLUTCH

This is invariably installed between the engine and gearbox and is almost always mounted directly on the output end of the engine, though occasionally both it and the gearbox are incorporated in the final drive unit. The clutch is always foot operated, the pedal being linked either by a direct mechanical linkage or, very often nowadays, by a hydraulic system, similar to that of hydraulic brakes. The latter method facilitates the accommodation of the considerably transverse movement of rubber mounted engines.

10   The most common form of clutch is the dry single plate type, as manufactured by Messrs Borg & Beck Ltd. Fig. 59 is a diagrammatic illustration to show the operating principle and it can be seen that there are three main elements. In the centre is the *clutch plate*, which is a steel disc to both sides of which are attached rings of special friction material, similar to that used for brake linings. This is mounted so that it can slide on the front end of the input shaft to the gearbox. The clutch plate is normally pushed firmly against the machined rear face of the flywheel by a spring-loaded *pressure* (or *presser*)

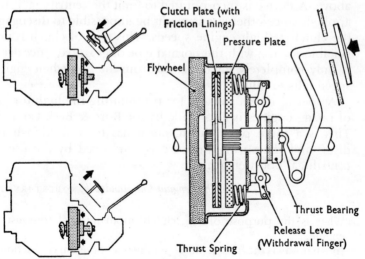

Fig. 59.   Principle of dry plate friction clutch.
a. Clutch pedal depressed – interrupts drive between engine and gearbox.
b. Pedal released – spring pressure restores drive.

20 *plate*. The depression of the clutch pedal moves the pressure plate back slightly and relieves pressure on the clutch plate, allowing slip to occur. Since all three main parts are normally revolving together, the movement of the clutch linkage is transferred to the pressure plate by a thrust bearing, which is either a heavy ball-race or a thick carbon ring, the latter type requiring no lubrication. The forward movement of the thrust bearing or collar is 'reversed' by three levers known as *release levers*. To aid the smooth take-up of the drive, the clutch plate is usually made with a flexible centre, 30 i.e. the outer portion is mounted upon a separate hub, with springs or rubber interposed to allow a limited amount of angular movement which absorbs torsional vibration.

A further refinement in some friction clutches is the use of centrifugal force to exert pressure on the clutch plate. Pivoted weights are used in conjunction with weaker springs than usual. By this means only a light pressure is required to disengage the clutch at low engine speed, but as the engine speed rises the weights are thrown outwards and, by suitable leverage system, provide additional force on the pressure plate. 40 This principle is extended further in the fully automatic centrifugal clutch in which the speeding up of the engine automatically engages the clutch in the manner described above. A device is incorporated to limit the centrifugal force applied, since otherwise it might be impossible to disengage the clutch at high engine speeds. This type of clutch is not suitable for use with the normal type of gearbox, since drive is only completely disconnected from the box when engine speed falls to idling.

A special clutch suitable for transmitting the high torque 50 of racing engines is also made by the Borg & Beck Co. Ltd. This is a three plate clutch, i.e. it has three friction-lined discs, and the spring pressure is reinforced by the use of centrifugal bob weights.

from *The Penguin Car Handbook*, ROBERT IRESON

A: 1 What is the purpose of the 'clutch' in an internal combustion engine?
  2 In what way is the 'clutch' based on the phenomenon of 'friction'?
  3 Why is the hydraulic system of operation apparently better than the directly mechanical method?
  4 Explain the effect of providing a 'flexible centre' (lines 29–30) to the clutch plate.
  5 What refinement can be applied to a clutch with the help of the

principle of centrifugal force (line 34)? How exactly is it a refinement'?

6 What is the possible danger of the use of centrifugal force to maintain pressure on the clutch plate?

B: 1 List all the verb forms in this passage and draw appropriate
conclusions.

  2 Has any particular character been given to this passage by a considerable avoidance of 'which' clauses?

  3 What tendency of technical English can be inferred from the
following expressions:
    [a] the output end of the engine (line 2)
    [b] the final drive unit (line 4)
    [c] foot operated (line 5)
    [d] rubber mounted engines (line 9)
    [e] dry single plate type (line 10)
    [f] special friction material (line 15)

  4 'considerably transverse movement' (lines 8–9). Could 'considerably' be changed without loss to 'considerable'?

  5 How necessary is the 'latter' (line 8) in this situation?

  6 At what points in this sample of writing do you see a tendency to
omit 'the'? What effect does this produce?

11.3
Symbiosis

The phenomenon of symbiosis is expressed in two basic patterns. In facultative associations, two different organisms
'have the faculty' of entering a more or less intimate symbiotic
relationship. But they need not necessarily do so, being able
to survive as free-living forms. In obligatory associations, on
the other hand, one organism *must* unite symbiotically with
another, usually a specific one, if it is to survive. The ancestors
of obligatory symbionts have invariably been free-living
organisms which in the course of history have lost the power
10 of living on their own. Before becoming obligatory symbionts, they formed facultative associations with organisms
on which they came to depend more and more.

Symbionts affect each other in different ways. Thus,
mutualism describes a relationship in which both associated
partners derive some benefit, often a vital one, from living
together. Commensalism benefits one of the partners, and the
other is neither helped nor harmed by the association. Parasitism is of advantage to the parasite but is detrimental to

the host to greater or lesser extent. These categories intergrade
20 imperceptibly, and in many boundary cases clear-cut distinctions cannot be made.

An example of a loose mutualistic association is the tick-
bird-rhinoceros relationship. The tickbird feeds on skin para-
sites of the rhinoceros, and in return the latter is relieved
of irritation and obtains warning of danger when the sharp-
eyed bird flies off temporarily to the security of the nearest
tree. Another example is the relationship between dairy ants
and aphids, already cited in Chap. 6 in the section on insect
societies. The ant obtains food from the aphid, and the aphid
30 in turn secures protection, food, and care from the ant.
These two examples also illustrate the difference between
facultative and obligatory mutualism. Both tickbird and
rhinoceros can get along without each other if necessary;
but the ant cannot do without its aphids and the aphid cannot
do without its ants.

A somewhat greater degree of physical intimacy is exhibited
in the mutualistic symbiosis of sea anemones and hermit
crabs. Sea anemones attach themselves to empty snail shells,
and hermit crabs use these shells as protective housings. The
40 sea anemone, an exceedingly slow mover by itself, is thus
carried about on the shell of the hermit crab – an obvious
advantage to the anemone in its search for food and in geo-
graphic dispersal. The hermit crab in turn benefits from the
disguise. Moreover, since the anemone is not a dainty eater,
scraps of food become available to the crab when the anemone
catches prey. This is a facultative association; sea anemones
and hermit crabs may and largely do live on their own.

An example of rather more intimate mutualism is provided
by *lichens*, grayish and yellowish incrustations commonly
50 found on rock surfaces and on tree bark. These crusts are
associations of photosynthesising single-celled algae and
saprotrophic threadlike fungi. The meshes of the fungal
threads support the algae, and they also hold rain water like
a sponge. The algae produce food for themselves and for the
fungus. The fungus in turn contributes water, nitrogenous
wastes, and respiratory carbon dioxide, substances which
allow for continued photosynthesis and food production.
Lichens may consequently survive in relatively dry terrestrial
environments. The fungus may live alone in a water-sugar
60 medium, and the alga may persist by itself in mineral-contain-
ing water. Separately, they are merely two types of organisms
not particularly different from many others like them. But

together they become a combination of considerable evolutionary importance. Lichens were among the first organisms capable of eking out a terrestrial existence. Contributing to the crumbling of rock and the formation of soil, they paved the way for a larger-scale colonisation of the land.

from *The Science of Biology*, PAUL B. WEITZ

A: 1 Explain the different ways in which the phenomenon of Symbiosis may be analysed.
2 How have 'obligatory' associations developed from 'facultative' (lines 2–6)?
3 What information as to meaning can be seen in the word Symbiosis and its derivatives?
4 What are the distinctions indicated in the words 'mutualism' (line 14), 'commensalism' (line 16), and 'parasitism' (lines 17–18)?
5 What seems to be indicated by the expression 'boundary cases' (line 20)?
6 Show on what principle the examples in paragraphs 3, 4, and 5 are arranged.
7 Explain in detail the symbiotic association between the algae and the fungi in the growth of lichen?
8 What is the 'evolutionary importance' (lines 63–4) of lichen?

B: 1 How would you define the idea of an 'organism' (line 2) as used in this setting?
2 Which two typographical devices are used to give emphasis in paragraph 1, and what is their relative degree of emphasis?
3 How does the word 'commensalism' (line 16) appear to have been formed?
4 What elements of meaning are conveyed by the word 'mutualistic' (line 22) which are not conveyed by the simpler form – 'mutual'?
5 'The ants obtain food ... the aphid secures protection, food, and care' (lines 33–4). How much detailed observation is conveyed in these words? Would more information have been appropriate in this context?
6 'The anemone is not a dainty eater' (line 44). What is the positive information which the writer aims to convey here?
7 'eking out' (line 65). What impression does this phrase give of the conditions of early life on this planet?

11.4

Magnetohydrodynamics

Magnetohydrodynamics is not an easy word to pronounce, but it seems destined to become familiar in the years ahead, most probably in the form of the abbreviation MHD. In a great many contexts, the word has leapt to prominence in the last few years. It is the name for the important physical processes that go on in the hot atmosphere of the sun and other stars. It also describes some of the things that happen in the pieces of experimental equipment with which people seek to extract useful power from the energy of thermonuclear

10 fusion. More recently, it has become the familiar name for a method by which it may be possible to improve substantially on the performance of existing machines for generating electricity. The complaint, some days ago, of the International Research and Development Company about the difficulty of financing some of its research projects is yet another indication that the word is bound to be freely bandied about.

All these processes have in common the fact that they involve gases in which at least a proportion of the atoms have broken up into separate electrified particles. Inevitably the

20 electrically negative particles are the atomic particles called electrons. Most commonly this separation of atoms into electrical parts is brought about by the influence of high temperature. In all materials, solid, liquid or gaseous, electrons are freed in increasing proportions from the atoms to which they are normally attached as their temperature is increased above 1,000 degrees centigrade. At 10,000 degrees or so a majority of atoms in gases such as hydrogen are electrically ionised in this way. In other materials lower temperatures will do. Everything depends on the structure of the

30 atoms concerned.

Another common characteristic of processes described by the word MHD is that there is a magnetic field to influence the motion of the electrified gas. It is now well known that on the sun the outward movement of incandescent material from the surface is sometimes determined largely by the very large magnetic forces produced by sunspots. In machines like ZETA, intended to see how power may be generated from thermonuclear fusion, magnetic forces are actually used as a means of compressing an ionised gas (or plasma

40 as it is called) into a small volume.

All these things are possible only because the gases concerned are electrified. A pattern of magnetic forces has only a very small influence on the atoms of a gas which is not electrified. But once there are electrons (with negative charges) and other pieces of atoms (carrying positive electricity) moving freely about within a gas, magnetic forces can exert an influence on the body of a gas as a whole. In particular,

158

the two kinds of atomic fragments tend to be moved in opposite directions under the influence of magnetic forces, and
50 this sets up within the body of the gas novel and complicated electrical stresses which are the essence of what is now called plasma physics.

To generate electricity out of M H D, the essential is that a stream of electrified gas can serve as a substitute for the complicated rotating machinery used in conventional power station equipment. An electrified gas will conduct electricity. At sufficiently high temperatures, indeed, gases are far superior to metals in this respect. So, the engineers argue, instead of a copper circuit between the poles of a magnet as in a con-
60 ventional dynamo, should it not be possible to generate electricity by forcing a stream of electrified gas through a pattern of magnetic forces?

This is the essential principle of an M H D electricity generator. Electricity is generated without the intervention of moving mechanical parts. Evidently there is a possibility that such devices could enormously simplify and cheapen the generation of electricity. So much has been recognised for several decades. What is new is that engineers are now able realistically to set about the construction of systems on these
70 lines.

from the *Guardian*, London, 14.4.66 (JOHN MADDOX)

A: 1 Why is the term 'Magnetohydrodynamics' likely to become familiar in the years ahead?
  2 What is the factor common to physical processes in the sun and stars, and some processes carried out under human direction?
  3 What practical consideration has brought M H D to the attention of many people recently?
  4 How could the processes of M H D become of practical advantage?
  5 What happens when atoms are heated?
  6 What part is played in M H D by magnetism?
  7 What do you know of 'plasma physics' (line 52)?
  8 In what ways would M H D be an improvement on existing methods of generating electricity?
  9 What is the recent new factor in the field of M H D?

B: 1 Which elements in this exposition indicate that it is an attempt at popular exposition?
  2 Collect and classify the adjectives used in this passage in the three groups of [a] subjective, [b] descriptive, and [c] technical.
  3 Comment on the use of the word 'conventional' (lines 59–60).

4 What comment do you make on the occurrence of the word 'people' (line 8) in this particular context?

5 Is the word Magnetohydrodynamics in fact difficult to 'pronounce' (line 1)? What features do you observe in it which might reduce the difficulty?

11.5
The Heart-beat

When histologists first discovered nerve cells in the tissues of the heart, some of them held the view that these stimulated the heart muscle to contract at regular intervals. It was found, however, that tissue cultures of bird or mammalian cardiac muscle tissue, although devoid of nerve cells, contracted at regular intervals. The view has therefore become established that the contraction of the heart is *muscular (myogenic) in origin*. Experiments have shown that muscle from different parts of the heart possesses this property of rhythmic contraction,
10 and that the rates of the different parts vary considerably. Thus atrial muscle has a rapid rate of contraction whereas the ventricles have a slow one.

Close to the junction of the superior vena cava with the right atrium is a mass of small, basic-staining and spindle-shaped cells called the *sinoatrial node*. Experiment shows that it is *in these cells that the normal heart-beat originates*. If they send out contraction waves with a slow rhythm the heart-beat is slow. If they send out contraction waves with a fast rhythm the heart-beat is fast. Consequently this node is called the *pace-
20 maker* of the heart.

Having originated in the pace-maker, the contraction wave spreads rapidly in all directions over the atria and so reaches a second node of tissue closely resembling the atrial node. This second node is called the *atrioventricular node*. The cells of the atrioventricular node receive the contraction wave from the atria and pass on the stimulus to the *atrioventricular bundle of His* (Fig. 12). This consists of *Purkinje fibres*, long palely-staining striated fibres, which run parallel with one another. They have a very rapid rate of conduction (about 2·5 m/sec).
30 After a short horizontal course this bundle divides into two limbs. One travels down the *right* side of the septum between the two ventricles lying immediately under the endocardium. It branches repeatedly and conveys the stimulus to numerous

160

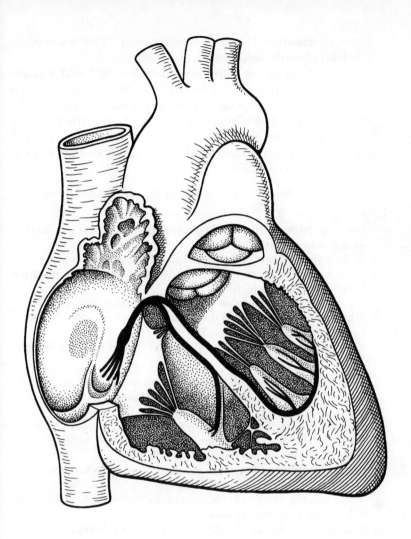

Fig. 12. A schematic representation of the atrioventricular bundle. The course of the bundle is represented by the heavy black lines.

points in the muscle of the right ventricle. The other limb similarly travels down the *left* side of the *interventricular septum*. It likewise branches and thus conveys the stimulus to numerous points in the left ventricle. Experiment shows that the rate of conduction of the stimulus by the atrioventricular bundle is about five times as fast as that of the ventricle itself. The widespread distribution of Purkinje fibres to the muscle of the ventricles ensures that all the muscle fibres are stimu-

40

lated to contract *practically simultaneously*. This ensures an
efficient, co-ordinated, ventricular contraction.

Contraction of the papillary muscles is initiated by contraction of the ventricles. The papillary muscles are attached
to the *chordæ tentinæ* which are inserted on the edges of the
flaps of both atrioventricular valves. Contraction of the
papillary muscles prevents the valve flaps from being everted
into the atria in late systole when the cavity of the ventricle
50 has been reduced in size.

from *Essentials of Physiology*, BAINBRIDGE and MENZIES

A: 1 On what evidence has the theory that the heart-beat was nervous
in origin been confuted?
2 What is the present theory explaining the heart-beat?
3 How is the 'contraction wave' (line 21) passed away from the
'atrioventricular node' (line 24)?
4 What is the most important effect of the 'Purkinje fibres' (line 27)?
5 What is indicated by the fact that Figure 12 is described as a 'schematic representation'?
6 What do you infer to be the specific concern of the histologist
(line 1)?

B: 1 Are there any technical terms which you consider need to be
defined before this passage can be understood? Consider to what
extent their meaning can be inferred from their context.
2 How often do such statements as 'Experiments have shown' (line 8)
occur in this passage? What are their function relative to the
general purpose of the passage?
3 List the specialist nominal groups in this passage. What proportion
of the whole do they account for?
4 'basic-staining' (line 14), 'palely staining' (lines 27–8). What is the
full reference of these epithets?
5 Comment on aspects of cohesion and logical development in this
passage?
6 What is the relationship of the final paragraph with the other
parts of the excerpt?

Section 11 PRACTICAL

C: 1 Study any of the passages 11. 1–5. Then, without referring to the
text, write out what you can remember of the original, or at least
producing a connected account. Then compare your version with
the original and estimate how much of the 'register' in question
you have mastered.

162

2 With any of the passages 11. 1–5, list the words or expressions peculiar to that particular register. Then write a further piece of description or explanation which employs the items you have used, adding any further terms which are necessary and appropriate.

3 Using the register of 'Chemistry', as exemplified in 11.1, write an account of any other chemical phenomenon with which you are familiar, e.g.
    [a] the hardness of water
    [b] the vaporizing of fluids
    [c] the structure of 'plastics'
    [d] metal fatigue, etc. etc.

4 As for a technical publication, write your account (using a diagram if you wish) of any mechanical process or operation you understand clearly, e.g.
    [a] a bicycle 'three-speed'
    [b] a carburettor
    [c] a jet engine, etc. etc.

5 Describe in scientific language any process in the field of biology of which you have knowledge, e.g.
    [a] the growth of a plant
    [b] the life history of a parasite
    [c] the process of grafting
    [d] adaptation of plants or animals to environment, etc.

6 Consulting books of reference as necessary, give a precise account of any of the following:
    [a] X-rays
    [b] sunspots
    [c] low density electrical discharge
    [d] the electron microscope
    [e] an A- or H-bomb
    [f] a cyclotron.
    Observe whether the language you use falls strictly within the register of 'physical science'.

7 Describe the structure and mechanism of any physical organ other than the heart (11.5).

12.1

African Economic Difficulties

The fundamental weakness in African economies, the product of history and physical features, can be summed up in a single phrase – the low development of primary industry, i.e. agri-

culture in all forms,[1] fishing and mining. Africa is not in a position to live by selling skills – i.e. importing raw materials, adding value, and re-exporting; primary production is therefore vital. This is not often so brutally stated, for reasons which will appear. Wherever it is forgotten, the danger of attempting to build an elaborate secondary and tertiary
10 system with no primary base or motive power immediately arises.

Low primary production is associated with low purchasing power and low division of labour: therefore, a small market, low opportunity for investment in secondary industry, and a low level of trade. Even in Zambia or the Congo, where primary mineral resources have been highly developed, the resulting trade in minerals lay to Europe, and the purchasing power generated was largely exported too – the white miners of Northern Rhodesia spent most of their earnings in south-
20 ern Africa,[2] the Congo Belgians in Europe. Certainly, African earnings were remitted to a poverty-stricken subsistence economy in distant rural areas; but they were mainly dissipated in social expenditure there, and little found its way into agricultural improvement. It is where cash-crop agriculture has been strongly developed that the effects on African purchasing power have been felt in a growing local market and in further productive investment.

Low-yield subsistence agriculture – apart from its effect on health and energy – means low division of labour, and a tiny
30 market even for food. Where four families out of five are farming, the market for farm produce, outside the producing family, is 0.25 per cent of a family; it only rises to 1.5 per cent when the proportion of all families in farming has fallen to 40 per cent. It is very largely this low food production which marks the contrast with medieval Europe, where there was usually just enough food to allow division of labour and the development of a market economy.

Subsistence agriculture, a falling death-rate, and scanty employment opportunity outside farming implies huge
40 'underemployment' in crowded rural areas. When widespread education is added to this explosive mixture, concealed underemployment is revealed as overt unemployment, be-

[1]'Agriculture' is used for short to include animal husbandry and forestry.
[2]On holidays, private education of children, and commodities imported from the south or from overseas.

164

cause expectations in a non-hierarchical society have been raised, and because the differential in pay between the modern and the traditional sector is so high. The educated young, in a mobile society, will go where the rewards are greatest; they join the queue seeking wage-paid work in the urban sector.

An additional problem arises from the late entry of Africa
50 into an already developed world economy, with its tendency to produce substitutes for tropical raw materials and with, allegedly, less elasticity of demand for raw materials than for manufactures – though this last point will need more argument. This situation in the outer world is the more serious because the inter-territorial market within Africa has been so hard to develop.

from *The Best of Both Worlds*, GUY HUNTER

A: 1 Explain as simply as possible the 'weakness' (line 1) of African economies?

2 What could be the 'reasons' (line 7) for this not being 'so brutally stated'?

3 Explain the distinction the author suggests between primary, secondary, and tertiary systems of 'production' (lines 9–10). Is there a close parallel with the application of the same three terms to the field of education?

4 Why had the highly developed primary production of the Congo and Zambia not led to a high rate of general development?

5 What is meant by 'social expenditure' (line 23)?

6 Distinguish between 'cash-crop' (line 24) and 'subsistence' (line 28) agriculture.

7 How does 'concealed underemployment' (lines 41–42) becomes 'overt unemployment' (line 42)?

8 What 'additional difficulties' are stressed in the final paragraph?

B: 1 Is there a distinction between 'African economies' (line 1) and African 'countries'?

2 How do you arrive at the general concept of 'primary industry' (line 3)?

3 How clear are the data presented with the help of percentages (lines 30–34)?

4 Discuss the following terms in relation to their degree of abstraction:
history (line 2), agriculture (lines 3–4), value (line 6), and purchasing power (lines 12–13).

5 Which words (if any) convey a moral or emotional attitude towards the evils described in lines 15–20?
Discuss the metaphor of the 'explosive mixture' (line 41).

7 Do you consider that discussion in this kind of language is useful in relation to the poverty of African nations?

12.2

Nouns

Among other English naming devices is the brand name, which has a rather special linguistic status. Etymologically, a brand name may be more or less anything: proper noun (*Morris, Ajax*), possessive proper noun (*Kellogg's*), common noun, count or mass (*Embassy, Surf*), modified common noun (*Double Diamond, Gold Leaf*), or not a noun at all (*Digestive, Startrite*); it may be an existing item of the language, like the foregoing, with or without orthographic innovation, or an invention within the limitations of the phonological system,
10 or anything in between. Syntactically, as pointed out by my colleague Geoffrey Leech, 'there are signs that brandnames have an unstable syntactic function'. The brand name has some of the features of a proper noun – its modifiers are usually descriptive, not defining, for example – but more of those of a common noun: it is assigned count or mass status (*a Morris, some Ajax*; this assignment is independent of the status of the model where this is an existing common noun, cf. *some Tide*), and selects for specific or non-specific determiners *a, the*, etc. The brand name may play a significant role
20 in the search for names for new objects, although there is wide variation here between different language communities. English is particularly prone to accepting brand names into the language; this may in the long term have its effect on the nature and functioning of the English noun, by contributing to a blurring of the distinction between common and proper, the extension of countability to all nouns, and a still greater tendency for interchange of membership between the noun and other word classes. It is possible to construct whole sentences in English in which every lexical item is a
30 brand name, like *the dripolator needs brilloing; let's just have some nescafé in the denby.*

So the simple common noun is certainly outnumbered, in modern English, as a device for naming classes of concrete object. Proper nouns, as in brand names, nominal compounds and modified forms of various kinds (as in *vitreous*

166

enamel, locking nut, tin opener, spirit of salt) are all widely
exploited. What all such forms have in common is that, with
minor exceptions, they take on all the syntactic potentialities
of their parent class the common noun. This means not only
40 the potentiality of entering into further compound forms
and susceptibility to the various choices that are open to the
English nominal group – all forms of determination and
numeration – but also the set of functions which the nominal
group may take on in the clause: subject, direct object, and a
number of others. When function in the clause is taken into
account, however, there turn out to be still further elements
that behave in a noun-like way.

It is for this latter reason that grammarians group together
nouns, nominal groups (noun phrases), and nominalizations.
50 The noun is the class of words (including compounds) that
name classes of things; centrally, concrete objects and
persons, but also abstractions, processes, relations, states,
and attributes: whatever can stand for a pronoun, as Quine
suggests ('Pronouns are the basic media of reference;
nouns might better have been named propronouns').
Nominal groups are nouns plus their determiners and any
other modifiers; while in nominalisations some element other
than a noun, a verb perhaps, or a whole clause, has nominal
status assigned to it. There is no sharp line, in English,
60 dividing compound nouns from nouns plus modifiers, or the
latter from nominalisations. So if scientists or others are
said to write in a 'nominal style' (and nominals are no less
relevant to poetry), this refers to the use of nominals of all
kinds; and criticism of such a style does not necessarily mean
that the critic has found more nouns per sentence than he
likes. Rather otherwise, perhaps; what is objected to is more
likely to be the use of nominalisations, since it is the nominalisation for which alternative devices could be found, whereas
there is ordinarily no alternative to the use of a simple
70 common noun like *cat* or *carburettor*, except not to talk about
cats and carburettors at all.

from *Grammar, Society, and the Noun*. M. A. K. HALLIDAY (Inaugural
Lecture)

A: 1 Show how trade- or brand names create new words in a considerable variety of ways.

    2 Which of the examples given here represent 'orthographic in-
novation' (line 8)?

3 What is the distinction represented by 'Etymologically' (line 2) and 'syntactically' (line 10)?

4 'the simple common noun is outnumbered in modern English' (line 32). By what?

5 Why might 'other language communities' (line 21) follow a different policy in regard to the formation of new words from brand names?

6 Why does the grammarian group together 'nouns, nominal groups and nominalisations' (lines 48–49)?

7 Explain the paradoxical test of a noun given by Quine (line 54).

8 What would be the difference between a 'determiner' and a 'modifier' (lines 56–57)?

9 On what grounds might the use of excessive 'nominalisation' be objected to (lines 66–67)?

B: 1 Why is the subject of the opening sentence placed after the verb? How often does this occur in standard English?

2 Is the complexity of the second sentence (lines 2–10) justified?

3 What kind of information about the occasion of the work from which this is taken can be deduced from the remark 'as pointed out by my colleague Geoffrey Leech' (lines 10–11)?

4 Examine the use of several forms of parenthesis in this excerpt. What is their general effect?

5 Explain the difference between the various 'modified forms' quoted in lines 35–36.

6 'a number of others' (line 45). Why is this left vague? Can you extend the list?

7 Why is it that scientists tend to write in a 'nominal style' (line 62)?

8 'more nouns per sentence than he likes' (line 65). What is the precise meaning of 'per'? Is there a justification for the use of this expression in a learned discourse?

9 Show how, in spite of its technical expressions, the style of this extract is that of an informal talk.

12.3

Owner of Fallen Tree Not Liable to Pay

SIR ROBERT WILLIAMS, BARONET v DEVON COUNTY COUNCIL

Before the Lord Chief Justice, Mr Justice Glyn-Jones *and* Mr Justice Widgery

The Divisional Court dismissed this appeal by the highway authority, Devon County Council, against the successful

appeal of the respondent, Sir Robert Williams, Baronet, of Upcott House, Upcott Hill, Devonshire, to Devon Quarter Sessions against the finding of the Braunton justices, that he was liable to pay the sum of £30 10s. 10d. to the highway authority as costs incurred by them for removing a tree which had fallen from his land across the highway. Under Section 9(1) (c) of the Highways (Miscellaneous Provisions) Act, 1961,
10 a highway authority may recover the cost of removing an obstruction from a highway from the owner of the thing which caused the obstruction but no such cost shall be recoverable from an owner 'who proves that he took reasonable care to secure that the thing in question did not cause or contribute to the obstruction'.

Mr Swinton Thomas appeared for the highway authority; Mr J. H. Inskip, Q.C., for the respondent.

JUDGMENT

The Lord Chief Justice said that during the night of January
20 16–17, 1965, in the course of a high wind, a tree on the respondent's land fell across the highway. It was a matter of urgency that the tree be removed and the highway authority immediately sent a gang of men and equipment to remove it; they removed it by 1.30 p.m. The costs of removal were £30 10s. 10d. In due course they preferred a complaint against the respondent claiming that sum. The justices held that the respondent should pay that sum but the respondent successfully appealed to quarter sessions who dismissed the complaint.
30　It was accepted and quarter sessions found that the respondent had proved that the tree was sound and that he had continuously inspected it and was satisfied that it was neither dangerous nor likely to fall. The inference from these primary facts was that the respondent had taken care that the tree did not fall and cause an obstruction.

The highway authority said that not only had the respondent, under section 9 of the Highways (Miscellaneous Provisions) Act, 1961, to prove that he took reasonable care to secure that the tree did not fall but, once it had fallen, he
40 had taken reasonable care to remove it from the highway.

Section 9 of the Act of 1961 must be read with section 129 of the principal Act, the Highways Act, 1959. It was to be observed that a highway authority was under a duty and, as a matter of urgency, to remove an obstruction on a highway. It would be remarkable if a highway authority who had to

remove the obstruction as a matter of urgency, could recover the expenses of removal from the owner if he did not get in and remove it before them. The words, in section 9(1) (c) of the Highways (Miscellaneous Provisions) Act, 1961, to take
50 'reasonable care to secure that [the tree] did not cause ... the obstruction' were wholly inapt to cover the meaning that the respondent had to take reasonable care to remove the tree.
Mr Justice Glyn-Jones and Mr Justice Widgery agreed.
Solicitors. – Mr H. G. Godsall, Clerk to the Devon County Council; Messrs Vandercom, Stanton & Co. for Messrs Toller, Oerton & Balsdon, Barnstaple.

from *The Times*, London, 9.10.66 (Law Report)

A: 1 Outline clearly the whole sequence of events in which Sir Robert Williams was involved. What was the final outcome?
  2 Explain as simply as possible the issue defined in Section 9(1) (c) of the Highways (Miscellaneous Provisions) Act, 1961.
  3 What degree of responsibility has a property owner in relation to obstruction of the highway?
  4 What was Sir Robert's defence against the 'complaint' (line 25)?
  5 Which words seemed ambiguous enough to lead to the dispute between Sir Robert and the Highway Authority?
  6 What did the Lord Chief Justice rule the meaning of the ambiguous words to be, and how did he introduce fresh evidence enabling the intention of the original law to be ascertained?

B: 1 Why do the proceedings not mention what kind of tree it was that fell across the highway on the night of January 16–17, 1965?
  2 How would the respondent have 'proved' (line 31) that he had discharged his share of responsibility according to the Act?
  3 Discuss the special meaning of the word 'finding' (line 5) in this kind of context?
  4 Select some of the expressions which seem to belong to the characteristic legal 'register', and give their meaning in standard language, e.g.
       costs incurred (line 7)
       no such cost shall be recoverable (line 12)
       Mr Thomas appeared for (line 16)
       preferred a complaint (line 25)
  5 What advantage is gained in situations of this kind by the use of the term 'respondent' (lines 21, 27, etc.)?
  6 Is there a justification for the apparently cumbersome way in which various sections of the Law are referred to (e.g. lines 8–9)?
  7 Under what circumstances might the Highway Authority have successfully claimed the costs from the respondent?

Kachin Society

A male Ego is related to the fellows of his community in three principal ways. Persons of his own local descent group and of other lineages of his own clan are 'brothers' (*hpu-nau*); persons of local descent groups into which he and his male siblings are expected to marry are *mayu*; persons of local descent groups into which his female siblings are expected to marry are *dama*. Most close acquaintances fall into one of these three categories, those who do not do so by strict cognate or affinal relationship are treated much as if they were remote
10 relatives of Ego's own clan. Thus the *mayu* of the *mayu* are classed as 'grandparents'; the *dama* of the *mayu* are classed as 'brothers'; the *dama* of the *dama* are classed as 'grandchildren'. In terms of our diagram Fig. 7 the order of seniority thus runs from left to right, group AA are 'grandchildren', A are *dama*, B are 'brothers', C are *mayu*, CC are 'grandparents'.[1] This suggests that if there is a difference of status between wife giving (*mayu*) and wife taking (*dama*) groups, it is the former and not the latter who are of higher rank. This is in fact the case.
20   The Kachin ideal is that a series of *mayu-dama* lineages should marry in a circle; the explanatory myth specifies five

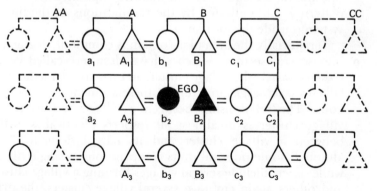

Fig. 7.   Kachin type marriage system (patrilineal). Lines A, B, and C can be thought of as *local lines*. If the whole scheme be considered including lines AA and CC then the vertical lines are *descent lines* (see text).

[1]It should perhaps be stressed that Ego is permitted to marry these classificatory 'grandparents' and 'grandchildren'.

major lineages (clans), but any number greater than two will serve. Circular systems embracing three and occasionally four local descent groups are not uncommon, but, as Lévi-Strauss perceived, the system becomes increasingly unstable as the number of units in a single network of relationship is increased. Lévi-Strauss suggested that the instability will arise from competition to accumulate women for polygynous marriages; the empirical situation is that instability arises
30 from competition for bridewealth.

The empirical Kachin local community has a fairly standardized structural form though its dimensions in terms of geographical area, population and component segments are very variable. The political unit is a single contiguous area ruled over by a chief.[1] This area I shall call the domain (*mung*) of a particular lineage of chiefly rank. The office of chief (*duwa*) will always be held by a member of this lineage, and the title will normally pass from youngest son to youngest son in the male line. The nature of the rights pertaining
40 to this office of chief will be considered presently.

The population of the domain will normally comprise members of many different lineages, some of high rank and some of low rank, but within that domain no other local descent group can rank as high as that of the chief. All the local descent groups within a domain tend to be related to one another in a quite definite manner, explained below. This pattern is little affected by the ramifications of the lineage system outside the local area.

Territorially the area of a domain is commonly segmented
50 into several sections which I have elsewhere called village clusters (*mare*); the village clusters in turn are segmented into villages (*kahtawng*). Structurally these segments are homologous. The relationship between a village and its parent village cluster is in almost all respects identical with that between a village cluster and its parent domain. Thus, although some political units comprise only a single village, while others include several villages forming a village cluster, and others again embrace several village clusters, the principles of organization in each of these political systems is the
60 same.

[1]What follows applies primarily to the Kachin *gumsa* type of political organization. In an alternative type of system known as *gumlao* the structure is somewhat different.

172

To illustrate these principles let us consider a hypothetical domain which consists of a single village cluster comprising four villages. Each of the four villages has an hereditary headman (*salang wa*) whose office is inherited in the same way as that of the chief. One of the four headmen is also chief of the whole domain. The lineage of the chief 'owns' the whole terrritory of the domain. The local descent group of a village headman 'owns' the territory of his village but these two types of ownership are of a different order. The chief's
70 ownership is recognized by the fact that all persons in the domain, who are not of his own lineage, must present him with a hind leg of any animal killed in sacrifice or in the hunt and by recognition that the same persons are under obligation to provide free labour for the chief on certain stated occasions, as at the clearing of the chief's field or the building of the chief's house. The village headman's ownership on the other hand is recognized in the fact that he disposes of the cultivation rights in the village lands among the householders of his village. Neither type of ownership can properly be said to
80 include the right of alienation, though lands can be transferred from one chief to another or from one village to another in certain special circumstances.

The political relationship between chief and village headman – and for that matter between village headman and villager – has considerable resemblances to that of English feudal tenure. If the chief be regarded as Lord of the Manor, then the status of the village headman resembles something between the status of a freeholder, holding his land in fee tail, and the status of a tenant in villeinage holding his
90 land in customary freehold or copyhold. If we accept this analogy, then we might expect to find some clear difference of class status as between chief's local descent groups, village headmen's local descent groups, and commoners' local descent groups. This difference of class status exists, though it is important to emphasize that the class distinctions are defined mainly in terms of rights to non-utilitarian prestige symbols,[1] and the difference in the economic standards of aristocrats and commoners is normally very slight.

from *Rethinking Anthropology*, E. T. LEACH

---

[1]E.g., the right to make a particular kind of sacrifice or to put up a particular kind of housepost.

'The term Kachin applies to a population of about 300,000 scattered over a vast area (some 55,000 square miles) in the Assam-Burma-Yunnan areas' (op. cit. p. 81). For the use of 'Ego', see B (1) below.

A: 1 Explain the terms *Hpu-nau, mayu,* and *dama* (lines 3–7).
   2 How are the terms 'grandparents', 'brothers', and 'grandchildren' applied to Kachin society in a sense different from normal English usage?
   3 How does the institution of 'marriage in a circle' tend to become unstable, and what alternative explanations of this are given?
   4 What could be the 'explanatory myth' (line 21)?
   5 What is the relation between 'structure' and 'dimension' in Kachin society?
   6 How are the two kinds of 'ownership' in paragraph 6 differentiated?
   7 What presumably is the 'right of alienation' (line 80)?
   8 What is the essential difference between 'class distinctions' in Kachin society and in western society?

B: 1 Consider the reasons for the use of the term 'Ego' in this kind of context, using as evidence the following sentence from page 57 of the original work: 'A descent line commonly comprises at least five generations, e.g. grandfather, father, Ego, son, grandson and each of these individuals is given equal weight.'
   2 Why does the author use the expression 'descent group' (line 2) instead of the more familiar 'family'?
   3 Why has the term 'sibling' (line 6) never acquired any strong emotional qualities, as have 'brother', 'sister', etc.?
   4 Justify the algebraic method of representation, e.g. A, B, C, AA, BB, etc. in this discussion.
   5 Compare the uses of the word 'empirical' in line 29 and in line 31. Can they be said to be identical?
   6 Explain the structure of the sentence, lines 55–60. Where does an element of confusion appear?
   7 Why is 'owns' (line 68) in inverted commas?

12.5

Advertising

[a] ## MINISTRY OF TRANSPORT
PUBLICITY SECTION
Assistant
Information Officers

The Ministry of Transport Information Division requires two Assistant Information Officers. Initially, they will work in the Publicity Section which deals with advertising, publications, print, films and T.V. and exhibitions. They will be given training in the various aspects of this work and suitable candidates will have an opportunity later to work on press relations, writing and briefing, and general public relations.

Applicants should have a good standard of education, a lively interest in current affairs, good publicity sense, organising ability and previous experience in some field of publicity or journalism. Candidates in their early twenties would be preferred. There will be opportunities for promotion and establishment.

Salary Scale: £750–£1,684 p.a. according to age and experience. This scale becomes £775–£1,735 p.a. on 1.1.69.

Please write to *Establishment Staffing Division, Room 8/170, Ministry of Transport, St Christopher House, Southwark Street, London, S.E.1* (Telephone: 928-7999, Ext. 3098). Closing date: 25 August, 1968.

Wrinkles should be confined to your face, where they add character.

A shirt that will remain smooth and unruffled the day long, is no longer beyond the wit of man.

Van Heusen have a new Terylene/cotton shirt called Van Heusen 'Evvaset' that does precisely that.

Where a lesser shirt will quickly crumple under the ravages of the day, the 'Evvaset' will keep its shape and its smooth exterior.

For Van Heusen 'Evvaset' is treated with a quite remarkable finish that shrugs off wrinkles in response to body heat.

A self-ironing trick that also gives vastly improved wash and wear performance.

Which should certainly please your lady wife. For they get so terribly upset about wrinkles.

And to cap it all Van Heusen have invented something exceptional in collars called 'Verve'. Verve has the discipline and look of your usual firm collar, but it's absolutely *soft* to the touch and to the neck.

Van Heusen 'Evvaset' shirt, 'Verve' collar.

For character without wrinkles. Price from 55/6

[c]   IT TAKES A LOT TO GET SOMEONE
TO FLY AIR-INDIA

For example: a lot more goodies to eat and drink and generally while away your time to New York than you get on your usual airline.

Who else offers you mango nectar as an alternative to orange and tomato juice?

Who else offers you eighteen different brands of whiskies, gins, liqueurs and brandies?

Who else offers you sizzling hot canapes of whole masala fried shrimp, spicy kebabs, chicken brochettes?

Who else offers you twenty-three different magazines, newspapers and comics?

Who else carries canned French mineral water in case you're partial to it?

Who else carries fans? Or hot water bottles? Or Tabasco sauce?

Who else? Who else indeed.

We do, because when someone like you asks for something on an Air-India flight, we just hate to say no. We're not that sort of airline.

Try us next time. We fly to New York every day at 12.45 p.m.

Come tomorrow.

And find out what a lot you've been missing.

AIR-INDIA

over 36 years of flying experience

[d] TESTING THE CARD

Next time you see some idiot staring at a telly when there's only a test card on, don't laugh.

He may be practising the most sensible way to choose a colour TV.

Over a couple of hours, as the set heats up, a lot of odd things can happen to the pretty picture.

Whites start to go pink.

The little girl turns red-faced.

And the whole scene begins to go fuzzy round the edges.

10   There's a simple explanation for these strange goings-on.

The electricity that runs into the set makes it rather hot. And the heat can upset its sensitive colour circuits.

These are absolutely critical to picture quality.

They make sure each electron beam hits the right colour phosphor dot on the screen. If they even get 1/200 of an inch off the mark your picture will start to look like a badly printed magazine photo.

(Some sets are apparently so prone to this kind of thing that they have to give you a special tint control to help limit

20   their colour drift. We don't.)

All of which means you can spend your evenings fiddling with your set, instead of cosily watching from the fireside.

Now, look at the four photographs of parts of a test card. They were taken from a G.E.C. set, over a period of two hours.

The colour balance has hardly changed.

For three good reasons.

In the first place, there's less electricity running into our sets to get it all hot and bothering. (275 watts, instead of 400 watts in some other sets to get the same picture brightness.)

30   Second, very little of this electricity has to go through our convergence circuit, as we designed it to run on virtually no juice. Which keeps its temperature down.

And third, we've got all our heat sensitive bits tucked away in cool parts of the sets. You'd think this was rather an obvious precaution. But too many people don't bother to take it.

Altogether, we make sure you can leave your set well alone. It doesn't need adjusting every ten minutes.

You might expect to pay extra for this privilege. And if we didn't make 500 or so of the components in each of our

40   sets ourselves, you probably would. As it is, our prices average about £25 to £35 less than anyone else's.

So the only change you'll get from us is in your pocket.

Not on your screen.

Cars, women, drink, yachts ... when I was a young man I was the last of the really big spenders. Then suddenly... **WHAMM.** Nasty. I had no money. My friends all went away. I began reading advertisements about how to get rich again, quick. But after the second Bankruptcy Hearing my financial advisors insisted that I start a _regular_ monthly savings scheme with Abbey Life Assurance. Only 30/- A WEEK could eventually produce results to the tune of £10,000. They said. Investment in the Hambro Abbey Trust, managed by Hambros Bank. Built-in Life Assurance by Abbey Life. So my wife and little ones are protected, (wherever they've got to now).

Also, I'm guaranteed against loss, and at my modest income I can get TAX RELIEF at 16½%. Of course it was boring sending the coupon and filling out the forms. But at least I no longer wake in the night SCREAMING through my clenched teeth . . . .

A: 1 State as concisely and objectively as possible the information given in each of the above advertisements.

B: 1 Discuss the presentation and use of language in each, explaining what assumptions are made about the probable readers, and the kind of appeal which is being made.

2 Consider what information you would require in order to make a rational judgment as to the superiority of each of the items being advertised.

3 What generalizations can be made about possible 'registers' of language encountered in advertising? Bring other examples into discussion if you wish.

FURTHER QUESTIONS ON INDIVIDUAL ITEMS:

[a] Illustrate the difference between vague and exact concepts from these extracts.

[b] (i) To what type of reader does this advertisement seek to appeal?

(ii) Comment on the grammar, and the tone, of the 'sentence' – 'Which should certainly please your lady wife.'

(iii) Account for the pronoun 'they' in the same paragraph.

[c] (i) 'that sort of airline'. What sort of airline is implied? Do such exist?

(ii) Compare the final item of information 'Over 35 years of flying experience' with the others; how relevant does it seem to you?

[d] 'Not on your screen.' How do you discover a meaning for this apparently incomplete expression?

[e] (i) What are the sociological implications of the expression in brackets – '(wherever *they've* got to now)'?

(ii) What is the effect of reproducing this in manuscript?

Section 11 PRACTICAL

C: 1 As with Section 11 Practical (1).

2 As with Section 11 Practical (2).

3 Write an account of the economy of your own town, village, county, or province, as it might be written by the author of 12.1.

4 Describe the features of any novel aspect of language which has recently come to your attention in your own area, e.g. perhaps

the invention of new words, by commerce or technology

the introduction of new 'vogue' words, or slang

the effect of foreign or immigrant elements in the population.

(Cf. 12.2.)

5 Collect accounts of legal proceedings in your own town, or the nearest place where courts are held. If possible attempt to take notes of actual cases yourself. Write out in legal language the report of any case which has aroused your interest, especially in technical 'points of law'.

6 Imagine yourself training as a sociologist or anthropologist.

Describe some aspects of family-relationships, or social structures in an area well known to you as though for an article in a journal devoted to social anthropology. (Cf. 12.4.)

7 Devise a collection of advertisements on commodities or services likely to be in demand in your own area. These may be parodies of those in 12.5, or you may use your ingenuity in new inventions. Then see (8).

8 Make a commentary on the types of appeal and the uses of language you have employed in (7).

PART II

Passages for Comparison

1

Examine the differences in aim and method of the following passages:

[a] ALLAHABAD (alt. 312 ft) 512m. from Calcutta, one of the largest towns in Uttar Pradesh (pop. 332,295), a railway centre and seat of a University and a High Court (est. 1866). It is situated on the left bank of the Jumna, on the wedge of land between it and the Ganges.

The Fort stands near the junction of the two rivers. The Civil Station, Cantonments, and City stretch W and NW 6m. from this point. The present Fort and City were built by Akbar in 1583, but the Aryans possessed a very ancient city here called Prayag, which the Hindus now call Prag (place of sacrifice). It is a very sacred place with them, as they believe that Brahma performed a sacrifice of the horse here, in memory of his recovering the four Vedas. The merit of alms-giving to Brahmans is enhanced a thousand-fold if the gift is made at Prayag.

The Khusru Bagh, close to the railway station on the S side, is entered by an old archway, nearly 60ft high and 46ft deep, overgrown with creepers. Within the garden are three square mausolea. That (domed) to the E is the tomb of Prince Khusru, son of Jehangir. West of it is the grave of a sister of his, and W again that of his mother, a Rajput lady. They are shaded by some fine tamarind trees. The interior of the Mausoleum of Khusru is ornamented with many Persian couplets and with paintings of trees and flowers, which are now faded. The cenotaph of white marble is on a raised platform, without inscription. To the right and left two of Khusru's sons are buried. All three monuments have been put into a thorough state of conservation. East of the Gardens lie the main bazaars.

[b] THE CITY OF CHANDRAPORE: Except for the Marabar Caves-and they are twenty miles off – the city of Chandrapore pre-sents nothing extraordinary. Edged rather than washed by the river Ganges, it trails for a couple of miles along the bank, scarcely distinguishable from the rubbish it deposits so freely. There are no bathing-steps on the river front, as the Ganges happens not to be holy here; indeed there is no river front and bazaars shut out the wide and shifting panorama of the stream. The streets are mean, the temples ineffective, and though a few fine houses exist they are hidden away in gardens or down alleys whose filth deters all but the invited guest.

Inland, the prospect alters. There is an oval Maidan, and a long sallow hospital. Houses belonging to Eurasians stand on the high ground by the railway station. Beyond the railway – which runs parallel to the river – the land sinks, then rises again rather steeply. On the second rise is laid out the little civil station, and viewed hence Chandrapore appears to be a totally different place. It is a city of gardens. It is no city, but a forest sparsely scattered with huts. It is a tropical pleasaunce washed by a noble river. The toddy palms and neem trees and mangoes and pepul that were hidden behind the bazaars now become visible and in their turn hide the bazaars. They rise from the gardens where ancient tanks nourish them, they burst out of stifling purlieus and unconsidered temples. Seeking light and air, and endowed with more strength than man or his works, they soar above the lower deposit to greet one another with branches and beckoning leaves, and to build a city for the birds. Especially after the rains do they screen what passes below, but at all times, even when scorched or leafless, they glorify the city to the English people who inhabit the rise, so that newcomers cannot believe it to be as meagre as it is described, and have to be driven down to acquire disillusionment.

2

Compare the following passages, which are taken from S. I. Hayakawa's 'Language in Thought and Action', pages 97–8. The book referred to is The Frieda Lawrence Collection of D. H. Lawrence Manuscripts: A Descriptive Bibliography, *by E. W. Tedlock, Jr. (University of New Mexico Press, 1948).*

[a] This is a remarkable bibliography. Not only does it examine, with the cool painstaking labor of scholarship, the 193 manuscripts in Mrs Lawrence's collection – and nine others thrown in for good measure – but also, it is informed with warmth, a growing sympathy, admiration, understanding of its subject, never forgetting that that subject was a man, never seeking to claim him as a literary property, as so often tends to be the case when scholars figure they have learned more facts about somebody than anybody else. There is enough material in Professor Tedlock's book to fascinate those with an appetite for such items as that the paper measures eight and a half by ten and five-eights inches, or that the pages are incorrectly

numbered; there is also material for those who want to study how an artist improved, corrected, extended, his initial attempts; beyond all that, the book is interesting to any who care about Lawrence, so that, as Frieda Lawrence says in a brief foreword, the love and truth in him may rouse the love and truth in others. Professor Tedlock's study is a valuable help, and readable.

[*b*] This bibliography examines, with the appalling industriousness of the professional pedant, the 193 manuscripts in Mrs Lawrence's collection – and nine others thrown in for good measure. Professor Tedlock goes completely overboard for his subject. Like other worshippers at the Lawrence shrine, he is almost as much preoccupied with Lawrence the man as with his works – so much so, indeed, that it is surprising he does not take Lawrence over as a literary property, as so often tends to be the case when scholars figure they have learned more facts about somebody than anybody else. There is enough material in Professor Tedlock's book to fascinate those with an appetite for such items as that the paper measures eight and a half by ten and five-eights inches, or that the pages are incorrectly numbered; there is also material for those who, not content with the study of finished works, want to pry into the processes by which an artist improved, corrected, and extended his initial attempts; beyond all that, the book is interesting to any who, in this day and age, still insist on caring about Lawrence, so that what Frieda Lawrence calls, in a brief foreword, the 'love' and 'truth' in him may arouse a similar 'love' and 'truth' in others. To these followers of the Lawrence cult, Professor Tedlock's study is no doubt a valuable help. The style is readable.

3

Consider the differences in thought, feeling, organization and language between these two historically related pieces:

[a] (April) 15th. Thursday (1802). It was a threatening, misty morning, but mild. We set off after dinner from Eusemere. Mrs Clarkson went a short way with us, but turned back. The wind was furious, and we thought we must have returned. We first rested in the large Boat-house, then under a furze bush opposite Mr Clarkson's. Saw the plough going in the field. The wind seized our breath. The Lake was rough. There was a Boat by itself floating in the middle of the bay below Water Millock. We rested again in the Water Millock Lane. The hawthorns are black and green, the birches here and there greenish, but there is yet more of purple to be seen on the twigs. We got over into a field to avoid some cows – people working. A few primroses by the roadside – wood-sorrel flower, the anemone, scentless violets, strawberries, and that starry, yellow flower which Mrs C. calls pile wort. When we were in the woods beyond Gowbarrow park we saw a few daffodils close to the water-side. We fancied that the lake had floated the seeds ashore, and that the little colony had so sprung up. But as we went along there were more and yet more; and at last, under the boughs of the trees, we saw that there was a long belt of them along the shore, about the breadth of a country turnpike road. I never saw daffodils so beautiful. They grew among the mossy stones about and about them; some rested their heads upon these stones as on a pillow for weariness; and the rest tossed and reeled and danced, and seemed as if they verily laughed with the wind, that blew upon them over the lake; they looked so gay, ever glancing, ever changing. This wind blew directly over the lake to them. There was here and there a little knot, and a few stragglers a few yards higher up; but they were so few as not to disturb the simplicity, unity, and life of that one busy highway.

WRITTEN 1802

I wandered lonely as a cloud
That floats on high o'er vales and hills,
When all at once I saw a crowd,
A host, of golden daffodils;
Beside the lake, beneath the trees,
Fluttering and dancing in the breeze.

Continuous as the stars that shine
And twinkle on the milky way,
They stretched in never-ending line
Along the margin of a bay:
Ten thousand saw I at a glance,
Tossing their heads in sprightly dance.

The waves beside them danced; but they
Out-did the sparkling waves in glee:
A poet could not but be gay,
In such a jocund company:
I gazed – and gazed – but little thought
What wealth the show to me had brought:

For oft, when on my couch I lie
In vacant or in pensive mood,
They flash upon that inward eye
Which is the bliss of solitude;
And then my heart with pleasure fills,
And dances with the daffodils.

4

Compare the following:

[a]   LOVE SONG

You lime of the forest, honey among the rocks,
Lemon of the cloister, grape in the savannah.
A hip to be enclosed by one hand;
A thigh round like a piston.
Your back – a manuscript to read hymns from.
Your eye triggerhappy, shoots heroes.
Your gown cobweb-tender,
Your shirt like soothing balm.
Soap? O no, you wash in Arabian scent,
Your calf painted with silver lines.
I dare not touch you!
Hardly dare to look back.
You mistress of my body:
More precious to me than my hand or my foot.
Like the fruit of the valley, the water of paradise.
Flower of the sky; wrought by divine craftsmen;
With muscular thigh she stepped on my heart
Her eternal heel trod me down.
But have no compassion with me:
Her breast resembles the finest gold;
When she opens her heart –
The Saviour image!
And Jerusalem herself, sacred city,
Shouts 'holy, holy!'

Ask me no more, where Jove bestows,
When June is past, the fading rose?
For in your Beauties orient deep
These flowers, as in their causes, sleep.

Ask me no more, whither do stray
The golden atoms of the day?
For in pure love heaven did prepare
Those powders to inrich your hair.

Ask me no more, whither doth haste
The Nightingale, when May is past?
For in your sweet dividing throat
She winters, and keeps warm her note.

Ask me no more, where those stars light,
That downwards fall in dead of night?
For in your eyes they sit, and there
Fixed become as in their sphere.

Ask me no more, if east or west
The Phœnix builds her spicy nest?
For unto you at last she flies,
And in your fragrant bosom dies.

5

Compare the following passages, two taken from twentieth-century novels, the third from an autobiography.

[a] A PORTRAIT OF THE ARTIST

He was alone. He was unheeded, happy and near to the wild heart of life. He was alone and young and wilful and wild-hearted, alone amid a waste of wild air and brackish waters and the seaharvest of shells and tangle and veiled grey sunlight and gayclad lightclad figures of children and girls and voices childish and girlish in the air.

A girl stood before him in midstream, alone and still, gazing out to sea. She seemed like one whom magic had changed into the likeness of a strange and beautiful seabird. Her long slender bare legs were delicate as a crane's and pure save where an emerald trail of seaweed had fashioned itself as a sign upon the flesh. Her thighs, fuller and softhued as ivory, were bared almost to the hips where the white fringes of her drawers were like feathering of soft white down. Her slateblue skirts were kilted boldly about her waist and dovetailed behind her. Her bosom was as a bird's, soft and slight and soft as the breast of some darkplumaged dove. But her long fair hair was girlish: and girlish, and touched with the wonder of mortal beauty, her face.

She was alone and still, gazing out to sea; and when she felt his presence and the worship of his eyes her eyes turned to him in quiet sufferance of his gaze, without shame or wantonness. Long, long she suffered his gaze and then quietly withdrew her eyes from his and bent them towards the stream, gently stirring the water with her foot hither and thither. The first faint noise of gently moving water broke the silence, low and faint and whispering, faint as the bells of sleep, hither and thither, hither and thither; and a faint flame trembled on her cheek. – Heavenly God! cried Stephen's soul, in an outburst of profane joy.

He turned away from her suddenly and set off across the strand. His cheeks were aflame; his body was aglow; his limbs were trembling. On and on and on and on he strode, far out over the sands, singing wildly to the sea, crying to greet the advent of the life that had cried to him.

We are grateful to The Viking Press Inc. for permission to reproduce this extract from *A Portrait of the Artist as a Young Man* by James Joyce.

For now the rain streamed down in a curtain of endless, slanting grey between the tossing launch to whose rail I clung and the little group waving farewell at the top of the wharf steps. The mooring ropes were cast off and the gap widened quickly, until the outlines of glistening umbrellas and raincoats blurred and dissolved. As we passed close to a waterside backyard, a young girl of about my age was taking advantage of the rainfall, as I had so often done, to take a bath out of doors with no more elaborate equipment than a piece of soap. Her face radiant with the vast enjoyment she was deriving form her simple toilet, she threw her head back, shut her eyes and laughed out her happiness as she worked the soap up into thick lather all over her skin. The string of red beads round her waist disappeared momentarily beneath the lather, to re-emerge a moment later as a shower of rain water swept the lather down her legs in a rush. On a sudden impulse I waved to her and so received my final farewell from my homeland. She waved back vigorously, still laughing, her white teeth flashing, and an instant later was lost to my sight.

Africans are very conscious of the importance of symbolism in life; and that happy, bathing girl has always summed up for me all that has been worth returning to Africa for. My last farewell was also, for me, my most meaningful. I have never, so far as I know, set eyes on this particular girl again; but neither have I ever forgotten the intensity of her happiness or the utter purity and innocence of its source. I did not need to be a hedonist to perceive that she had obtained the highest good man can hope for on earth, and had done so without sacrificing anything of any consequence to herself or anyone else. To be completely happy, and yet not to have to pay too much for it in any way, physical or spiritual – this is perhaps what we all live for ultimately. And yet the capacity to do this would become increasingly lost to the peoples of Africa, as I could have told even then from my own limited experience. But to have glimpsed the ideal was enough to impress indelibly on my mind that all would in the end be lost if, in gaining the world, we were to lose our souls.

[c] The following morning I packed my few possessions into the canoe which was to take me across the Ankodera river on the first stage of my journey to Takoradi. As I looked up the river where the swirling muddy waters disappeared among a mass of jungly growth, I saw the men and women of the village standing knee-deep in the water unconcernedly bathing or washing clothes. At this peaceful picture of African rural life, I felt my first pang of homesickness. I took a deep breath and forced myself to smile as I came back up the bank to say a final goodbye to my mother. Then I saw that she was in tears. In spite of trying so hard to hide her feelings, this final parting proved to be too much. With tears in my own eyes, I told her that if she would rather I stayed behind she had only to say so. She stood and looked at me for a few minutes; 'It cannot be helped,' she said, 'may God and your ancestors guide you.'

And so, with very heavy hearts, we waved goodbye, little knowing that it would be twelve years before we saw each other again.

6

Compare the two following approaches to the same topic.

[a]   LONDON: THE SWINGING CITY

In this century, every decade has had its city. The *fin de siècle* belonged to the dreamlike round of Vienna, capital of the inbred Habsburgs and the waltz. In the changing '20s, Paris provided a movable feast for Hemingway, Picasso, Fitzgerald and Joyce, while in the chaos after the Great Crash, Berlin briefly erupted with the savage iconoclasm of Brecht and the Bauhaus. During the shell-shocked 1940s, thrusting New York led the way, and in the uneasy 1950s it was the easy Rome of *la dolce vita*. Today, it is London, a city steeped in tradition, seized by change, liberated by affluence, graced by daffodils and anemones; so green with parks and squares that, as the saying goes, you can walk across it on the grass. In a decade dominated by youth, London has burst into bloom. It swings; it is the scene.

This spring, as never before in modern times, London is switched on. Ancient elegance and new opulence are all tangled up in a dazzling blur of op and pop. The city is alive with birds (girls) and beatles, buzzing with minicars and telly stars, pulsing with half a dozen separate veins of excitement. The guards now change at Buckingham Palace to a Lennon and McCartney tune, and Prince Charles is firmly in the long hair set. In Harold Wilson, Downing Street sports a Yorkshire accent, a working-class attitude and a tolerance toward the young that includes Pop Singer 'Screaming' Lord Sutch, who ran against him on the Teen-Age Party ticket in the last election. Mary Quant, who designs those clothes, Vidal Sassoon, the man with the magic comb, and the Rolling Stones, whose music is most In right now, reign as a new breed of royalty. Discs by the thousands spin in a widening orbit of discotheques, and elegant saloons have become gambling parlours. In a once sedate world of faded splendour, everything new, uninhibited and kinky is blooming at the top of London life.

London is not keeping the good news to itself. From Carnaby Street, the new, way-out fashion in young men's clothes is spreading around the globe, and so are the hairdos, the hairdon'ts and the sound of beat; in Czechoslovakia alone, there are 500 beat groups, all with English names. London is exporting its plays, its films, its fads, its styles, its people. It is also the place to go. It has become the latest mecca for Parisians who are tired of Paris, where the stern and newly puritanical domain of Charles de Gaulle holds sway. From the jets that land at its doors pour a swelling cargo of the international set, businessmen, tourists – and just plain scene-makers.

The new vitality of the city amazes both its visitors and inhabitants. 'The planet which was English,' confided Paris' *Candide* recently, 'has given birth to a new art of living – eccentric, bohemian, simple and gay'. Says Robert Fraser, owner of London's most pioneering art gallery: 'Right now, London has something that New York used to have: everybody wants to be there. There's no place else. Paris is calcified. There's an indefinable thing about London that makes people want to go there.'

Not everyone looks upon London's new swing as a blessing. For many who treasure an older, quieter London, the haystack hair, the suspiciously brilliant clothes, the chatter about sex and the cheery vulgarity strike an ugly contrast with the stately London that still persists in the quieter squares of Belgravia or in such peaceful suburbs as Richmond. They argue that credulity and immorality, together with a sophisticated taste for the primitive, are symptoms of decadence. The *Daily Telegraph's* Anthony Lejeune two weeks ago decried 'aspects of the contemporary British scene which have not merely surprised the outside world but which increasingly provoke its contempt and derision. To call them symptoms of decadence may be facile as an explanation, but it has a disturbing ring of truth.' Tradition-loving Londoners like to cite John Ruskin's eloquent description of 16th and 17th century Venice, another ageing empire built on maritime power. 'In the ingenuity of indulgence, in the varieties of vanity, Venice surpassed the cities of Christendom, as of old she had surpassed them in fortitude and devotion.'

The comparison is fair, if not perfectly apt. Britain has lost an empire and lightened a pound. In the process, it has also recovered a lightness of heart lost during the weighty centuries of world leadership. Much of the world still thinks of Britain as the land of Victorianism, but Victorianism was only a temporary aberration in the British character, which is basically less inhibited than most. London today is in many ways like the cheerful, violent, lusty town of William Shakespeare, one of whose happiest songs is about 'a lover and his lass, that o'er the green cornfield did pass'. It is no coincidence that critics describe London's vibrant theatre as being in the midst of a second Elizabethan era, that one number on the Rolling Stones' newest LP is a mock-Elizabethan ballad with a harpsichord and dulcimer for accompaniment, or that Italian Novelist Alberto Moravia describes the British cinema today as 'undergoing a renaissance'.

[b] London Airport last Thursday was a good place to read, by courtesy of *Time*, that London is the world's swingingest city, the place everyone wants to live. Looking around me, I reflected that an awful lot of Londoners appeared very anxious to leave it, and were quite failing in the attempt. Outside, a feeble blizzard provided a gratefully-snatched excuse for chaos. Inside, people struggled to get at the few telephones, queued for tea or just searched unsuccessfully for a place to sit down. The only thing in plentiful supply appeared to be inaccurate information. The speed with which London can re-create the conditions of the Blitz, down to the last 'Don't you know there's a war on?' is a national miracle. Speaking personally, I would gladly swop Carnaby Street, Mary Quant, the pop-industry, switched-on chicks, with-it dolly girls, Mick Jagger, Princess Margaret and everybody else on *Times's* roll call for three simple, square things: a telephone service that works, a transport system that doesn't collapse at the first hint of bad weather, and an airline that tells passengers the truth, the whole truth and nothing but the truth.

When *Time* magazine rejoices, careful men beware, looking uneasily around for the tripwire. When *Time* salutes a cause one values, or as in this case a place one inhabits, the reflex action is to wonder where one has slipped up. To be at one with Mr Luce is a vaguely disturbing experience, like receiving a smile from Lord Salisbury.

Now *Time* has given its imprimatur to London, and bestowed on our town its own Order of Newthink in the form of a cover-story of a lavish effusiveness it has rarely evinced for anything since the late John Foster Dulles. The previous cover which demanded in menacing type: 'Is God Dead?' is replaced by one affirming that London is Alive, with a startling collage of pop-art symbolism depicting the city of Dr Johnson as something between Walpurgisnacht and Mardi Gras in Martinique.

I reflected then, not for the first time, that the only moment really to worry is when *Time* is on one's side. I am nevertheless a constant reader. It is the handicap of an insecure and uncertain nature like mine frequently to doubt the correctness of my attitudes or the value of my opinions. On such occasions it has long been my custom to consult the pages of *Time*, in the fair assurance that any point of view that won its approval was to be avoided at all costs, and that anything denounced by *Time* must at least have merit of some kind.

If all this sounds an ungracious response to a eulogy, then I can only repeat the warning that anything flattered by *Time* should take a solemn reappraisal of itself to determine wherein it has erred. And in truth this sudden and glowing journalistic accolade is more than a characteristic piece of *Time-centricity*; it is a grim example of the new American Patronage and an alarming glimpse of the imbecile values by which prosperity is now judged.

7

Compare the three following translations of the same poem.

FLUTE PLAYERS

[a] Your flute,
    Cut from the thighbone of a mighty bull,
    Polished on the bleak hillsides
    Scourged by the sun.
    Her flute,
    Cut from the reed that quivers in the wind
    Pierced on the banks of running water
    Drunken with moonlight dreams.

In the deeps of evening, play them together
As if to right the sphered canoe
Capsizing by the shores of sky
And keep it
From its doom.
But your plaintive incantations
Do they reach the wind-gods
And the earth-gods and the wood-gods
And the gods of sand?

Your flute
Draws out a note where the ear can catch the tread of
    a maddened bull
Pounding toward the desert
And pounding back
Burnt by thirst and hunger
Felled by fatigue
At the foot of the tree without shadow
Without fruit, without leaves.

Her flute
Is like a reed that bends beneath the weight of a
    passing bird –
Not a bird trapped by a child
Ruffling its feathers
But a bird lost from the flock
Looking at his reflection in running water
For comfort.

Your flute
And hers –
Longing for their past
In the songs of your grief.

[b]   Your flute,
           you fashioned from the shin of a mighty bull
           and you polished it on the arid hillsides
           scourged by the sun;
           his flute,
           he fashioned from a quivering reed in the breeze
           and he pierced it at the brink of running waters
           drunk with the dreams of the moon.

    You play your flutes together in the depths of the evening,
           as if to hold back the spherical canoe
           which capsizes at the banks of the heavens;
           as if to deliver it
           from its fate:
           but your plaintive songs
           are they heard by the gods of the winds,
           of the earth and of the forest,
           and of the sand?

    Your flute
           draws out a note charged with the stamp of a raging
                  bull
           which runs to the waste-lands
           and returns at a run,
           scorched by thirst and hunger,
           but felled with fatigue
           at the foot of a tree that is shadeless,
           fruitless, leafless.
           His flute
           is like a pliant reed
           bending 'neath the weight of a bird of passage –
           not a bird caught by a child
           with ruffled feathers,
           but a bird far from his own kin
           watching his shadow, to seek consolation,
           on the running water.

    Your flute
           and his –
           mourn for their origins
           in the songs of your sorrows.

[c] Your flute
        you carved from the shinbone of a strong bull
        and polished it on barren hills beaten by sun.

    His flute
        he carved from a reed trembling in the breeze
        and cut its little holes beside a flowing brook
        drunk on dreams of moonlight.

    Together
        you made music in the late afternoon
        as if to hold back the round boat
        sinking on the shores of the sky
        to save it from its fate:
        but are your plaintive incantations
        heard by the gods of the wind,
        of the earth, of the forest, and the sand?

    Your flute
        throws out a beat like the march of an angry bull
        towards the desert –
        but who comes back running,
        burned by thirst and hunger and defeated by weariness
        at the foot of a shadeless tree
        with neither leaves nor fruit.

    His flute
        is like a reed that bends
        beneath the weight of a bird in flight –
        but not a bird captured by a child
        whose feathers are caressed,
        but a bird lost from other birds
        who looks at his own shadow for solace
        in the flowing water.

    Your flute and his
        regret their beginnings
        in the songs of your sorrow.

8

Discuss the following types of historical writing:

[a] This is the history of the lords of this country called Kano. Barbushe, once its chief, was of the stock of Dala, a black man of great stature and might, a hunter, who slew elephants with his stick and carried them on his head about nine miles. Dala was of unknown race, but came to this land, and built a house on Dala hill. There he lived – he and his wives. He had seven children – four boys and three girls – of whom the eldest was Garageje. This Garageje was the grandfather of Buzame, who was the father of Barbushe. Barbushe succeeded his forefathers in the knowledge of the lore of Dala, for he was skilled in the various pagan rites. By his wonders and sorceries and the power he gained over his brethren he became chief and lord over them. Among the lesser chiefs with him were Gunzago, whose house was at the foot of Gorondutse to the east. After him came Gagiwa, father of Rubu, who was so strong that he caught elephants with rope. These were next to Barbushe in rank. Tsanburo lived at Jigiria, and Jandamisa at Magum. The last named was the progenitor of the Rumawa. From Gogau to Salamta the people traced their descent from Ruma, and were called Rumawa because they became a great people. Hambaro's house was at Tanagar. Gambarjado, who lived at Fanisau, was the son of Nisau. All these and many more there were – pagans. From Toda to Dan Bakoshi and from Doji to Dankwoi all the people flocked to Barbushe on the two nights of Idi – for he was all-powerful at the sacrifical rites.

[b] And while these ragged hosts of enthusiasts were chanting the Marseillaise and fighting for *la France*, manifestly never quite clear in their minds whether they were looting or liberating the countries into which they poured, the republican enthusiasm in Paris was spending itself in a far less glorious fashion. The revolution was now under the sway of a fanatical leader, Robespierre. This man is difficult to judge; he was a man of poor physique, naturally timid, and a prig. But he had that most necessary gift for power, faith. He set himself to save the Republic as he conceived it, and he imagined it could be saved by no other man than he. So that to keep in power was to save the Republic. The living spirit of the Republic, it seemed, had sprung from a slaughter of royalists

and the execution of the King. There were insurrections; one in the west, in the district of La Vendée, where the people rose against the conscription and against the dispossession of the orthodox clergy, and were led by noblemen and priests; one in the south, where Lyons and Marseilles had risen and the royalists of Toulon had admitted an English and Spanish garrison. To which there seemed no more effectual reply than to go on killing royalists.

The Revolutionary Tribunal went to work, and a steady slaughtering began. The invention of the guillotine was opportune to this mood. The Queen was guillotined, most of Robespierre's antagonists were guillotined, atheists who argued that there was no Supreme Being were guillotined; day by day, week by week this infernal new machine chopped off heads and more heads and more. The reign of Robespierre lived, it seemed, on blood; and needed more and more, as an opium-taker needs more and more opium.

[c] One weakness which runs through most of these European contributions – Barth is the outstanding exception – is the lack of a sense of history. The myth that Africans are 'people without a history', although it can be traced back at least as far as Hegel, was probably not a conscious European presupposition until the end of the nineteenth century. The fact was rather that most Europeans who visited West Africa were not competent, nor expected, to do more than report on the contemporary state of the societies which they encountered: they combined, in varying proportions, the qualities of journalists and amateur sociologists. Probably they assumed that these were – from a technological and institutional point of view – somewhat static societies; but then, until the end of the eighteenth century, their own societies changed relatively slowly too. Moreover, European historical thinking, as contrasted with the recording of past events, was itself largely a product of the nineteenth century. In these extracts changes in kings, or dynasties, or the power-relationships between states, wars, and revolutions – disturbances of the political surface – are recorded where they are observed. But the approach is, in general, photographic. Writers describe what has occurred within their span of observation. They may even refer back to previous travellers, and note ways in which the present state of affairs differs from the recorded past: mention that the city of Benin has declined since Dapper's day; or that Bonny has now established itself as the main

centre of the slave-trade. But, before Barth, there is little attempt to discuss the direction of change, or explain the deeper cause of change.

[d] Kano was the delivery point of the first airmail service from Europe in 1936, and almost immediately an emergency flight was necessary to bring in Bank of England currency notes flown out to meet the shortage caused by the purchase of a record tonnage of ground-nuts. Kano had indeed now consummated the reorientation of her trade outlook away from being the southern focus of camel-borne goods across the Sahara towards her new status of being the northern end of the Nigerian ground-nut trade. The year is also remembered in Kano for the fact that the Governor rode through the streets on horseback in splendid procession with the Emir, a spectacle that could be recalled only as a memory. On the death of Waziri Alhaji Gidado (he was the father of a later Waziri, Alhaji Abubakar) in 1937, the office, which as we have seen was not indigenous to Kano, temporarily lapsed. He was a great old man, who had been appointed Chief Alkali in 1903 and then Waziri in 1909. The new adviser on legal affairs was turbanned as Wali, and the Ciroma was appointed to the Council with responsibility for financial supervision.

In 1951 the Emir Abdullahi Bayero, whose name is still so well respected in Kano, made his second pilgrimage to Mecca, and on his return he officially opened the beautiful new mosque. The year, however, was saddened by the terrible El Dunia cinema fire, and it is in respect of the dead that the site has since been turned into a memorial garden. Sadness, indeed, seemed the lot of Kano for a while, for the following year brought the death of the venerable Arabic scholar, the Wali, and in December 1953 the Emir died, at the age of seventy. He was succeeded by his eldest son, Alhaji Muhammadu Sanusi, who in a broadcast speech promised a number of administrative reforms such as public sessions of his own court, limitation of the high offices to be held by his own family, retrenchment of his personal household, and land registration and reform in Kano City. The new Emir was also instrumental in forcing through subsidiary legislation to curb the hounding activities of Kano's notorious beggar minstrels. Formerly anyone of rank or wealth had been at the mercy of these minstrels who levied a perennial blackmail: 'There was the choice,' noted an official report, 'between paying for their worthless praise or being held up to hatred, ridicule and contempt in an endless calypso in which personal character, domestic difficulties and private affairs were reeled out with pitiless comment for the edification of the vulgar and to the delight of enemies.'

[e] The National government now had their mandate for rearmament. They also still had the Abyssinian affair on their hands. Economic sanctions had been intended as a bluff, a solemn warning to Mussolini. The bluff had not worked. Now more would have to be done against Italy, or a way out would have to be found. It was generally held that stopping oil supplies to Italy – the 'oil sanction' – would do the trick. The government hesitated. Mussolini, it was alleged, would answer the oil sanction by war – the spook which had formerly been raised in regard to Japan. France would not support Great Britain. The British navy would have to fight alone, and it was apprehensive of the Italian air force. It was maybe a little unreasonable for the British to claim the mastery of the Mediterranean and then to complain that fighting there would fall on them. Such is the price of Empire. These were not much more than rationalisations. The government, and the British people, had said: all sanctions short of war. Therefore any sanctions which raised the shadow of war were automatically ruled out. Besides, the British government had no wish to topple Mussolini. On the contrary, the foreign office wanted to enlist him as an ally against Hitler. Compromise on the Manchurian model was the only alternative – some settlement favourable enough to persuade Mussolini to stop the war.

Hoare dug out the offer which had been made to Mussolini before the war; improved it to Italy's advantage; and on 7 December crossed to Paris with Baldwin's blessing. Laval made the offer still more favourable to Italy. She would receive the fertile plains. The emperor of Abyssinia would keep his old kingdom in the mountains. The two men endorsed the 'Hoare-Laval plan'. The British cabinet approved it. Mussolini was ready to agree. The next step was to present it at Geneva. Then the emperor would have to accept it or could be abandoned to his fate. Hoare departed cheerfully for a holiday in Switzerland, confident that he had pulled off a great stroke. Things went wrong. Someone leaked the plan to the Paris press. In England the storm blew. The high minded supporters of the League had just helped to return the National government. They felt cheated and indignant. The League of Nations Union, the two archbishops, *The Times* newspaper, Sir Austen Chamberlain, and many younger Conservatives protested. The government tried to brazen things out; then put the blame on Hoare, who had been 'tired', 'a sick man'. Halifax, formerly Irwin, who had just joined the cabinet as lord privy seal, devised this let-out. Hoare returned from Switzerland, sobbed, resigned. Eden took his place as foreign secretary. The Hoare-Laval plan was dead. The League died with it.

9

Explain the aim of each of the following passage as exactly as possible. Discuss and compare the methods of expression employed:

[a] Ladi Mamman is a lively and intelligent girl who would like to enjoy life with other children of her age. But for over six months she has been confined to her home, becoming progressively weaker, and experiencing great difficulty in breathing.

About a fortnight ago the girl, who is of the Bima tribe, was sent from her home at Gowl, near Gombe, to a doctor in Jos, where an examination revealed a large mediastinal tumour within her chest, compressing her windpipe over about four inches.

The position was desperate and in view of the difficulties of anaesthesia created by the tracheal compression and the extensive nature of the surgery that would be required, it was the collective opinion of doctors in Jos that she should go to London for an operation.

Authorities at the Brompton Chest Hospital, London, which is one of the leading hospitals of its kind in the world, have been contacted and have agreed to perform what, by any standards, is a major operation.

But one big problem remains. A problem that must be solved if Ladi is to be given a chance to fight for her life. Cash must be raised to pay for the trip and the necessary hospital fees. Already the Amalgamated Tin Miners of Nigeria of Jos has donated £50, a further £75 has been collected and the Red Cross has promised £100.

Still needed is about £300.

The *New Nigerian*, which has promised to help with meeting the cost of the air fare, appeals for donations to help raise the balance. Any individual or firm prepared to help is to contact the Managing Director, Northern Nigerian Newspapers, Kaduna, immediately.

This girl needs this operation if she is to stand a chance of recovery. Are YOU prepared to help?

[b] At noon the fever reached its climax. A visceral cough racked the sick man's body and he now was spitting blood. The glands had ceased swelling, but they were still there, like lumps of iron embedded in the joints. Rieux decided that lancing them was impracticable. Now and again, in the intervals between bouts of fever and coughing fits, Tarrou still gazed at his friends. But soon his eyes opened less and less often and the glow that shone out from the ravaged face in the brief moments of recognition grew steadily fainter. The storm, lashing his body into convulsive movement, lit it up with ever rarer flashes, and in the heart of the tempest he was slowly drifting, derelict. And now Rieux had before him only a mask-like face, inert, from which the smile had gone for ever. This human form, his friend's, lacerated by the spear-thrusts of the plague, consumed by searing superhuman fires, buffeted by all the ravaging winds of heaven, was foundering under his eyes in the dark flood of the pestilence, and he could do nothing to avert the wreck. He could only stand, unavailing, on the shore, empty-handed and sick at heart, unarmed and helpless yet again under the onset of calamity. And thus, when the end came, the tears that blinded Rieux's eyes were tears of impotence; and he did not see Tarrou roll over, face to the wall, and die with a short, hollow groan as if somewhere within him an essential chord had snapped . . .

[c]   A slumber did my spirit seal;
         I had no human fears:
         She seemed a thing that could not feel
         The touch of earthly years.

         No motion has she now, no force;
         She neither hears nor sees;
         Rolled round in earth's diurnal course,
         With rocks, and stones, and trees.

10

The three following passages were all evoked by the Galapagos or Encantadas, a group of islands off the coast of South America. Compare their treatment of the subject:

[a] Take five-and-twenty heaps of cinders dumped here and there in an outside city lot; imagine some of them magnified into mountains, and the vacant lot the sea; and you will have a fit idea of the general aspect of the Encantadas, or Enchanted Isles. A group rather of extinct volcanoes than of isles; looking much as the world at large might, after a penal conflagaration.

It is to be doubted whether any spot of earth can, in desolateness, furnish a parallel to this group. Abandoned cemeteries of long ago, old cities by piecemeal tumbling to their ruin, these are melancholy enough; but, like all else which but once been associated with humanity, they still awaken in us some thoughts of sympathy, however sad. Hence, even the Dead Sea, along with whatever other emotions it may at times inspire, does not fail to touch in the pilgrim some of his less unpleasurable feelings.

But the special curse, as one may call it, of the Encantadas, that which exalts them in desolation above Idumea and the Pole, is, that to them change never comes; neither the change of seasons nor of sorrows. Cut by the Equator, they know not autumn, and they know not spring; while already reduced to the lees of fire, ruin itself can work little more upon them. The showers refresh the deserts; but in these isles, rain never falls. Like split Syrian gourds left withering in the sun, they are cracked by an everlasting drought beneath a torrid sky. 'Have mercy on me,' the wailing spirit of the Encantadas seems to cry, 'and send Lazarus that he may dip the tip of his finger in water and cool my tongue, for I am tormented in this flame.'

Another feature in these isles is their emphatic uninhabitableness. It is deemed a fit type of all-forsaken overthrow, that the jackal should den in the wastes of weedy Babylon; but the Encantadas refuse to harbour even the outcasts of the beasts. Man and wolf alike disown them. Little but reptile life is here found: tortoises, lizards, immense spiders, snakes, and that strangest anomaly of outlandish nature, the *iguana*. No voice, no low, no howl is heard; the chief sound of life here is a hiss.

On most of the isles where vegetation is found at all, it is more ungrateful than the blankness of Atacama. Tangled thickets of wiry bushes, without fruit and without a name, springing up among deep fissures of calcined rock, and treacherously masking them; or a parched growth of distorted cactus trees.

In many places the coast is rock-bound, or, more properly, clinker-bound; tumbled masses of blackish or greenish stuff like the dross of an iron-furnace, forming dark clefts and caves here and there, into which a ceaseless sea pours a fury of foam; overhanging them with a swirl of grey, haggard mist, amidst which sail screaming flights of unearthly birds heightening the dismal din. However calm the sea without, there is no rest for these swells and those rocks; they lash and are lashed, even when the outer ocean is most at peace with itself. On the oppressive, clouded days, such as are peculiar to this part of the watery Equator, the dark, vitrified masses, many of which raise themselves among white whirlpools and breakers in detached and perilous places off the shore, present a most Plutonian sight. In no world but a fallen one could such lands exist.

[b] September 15th – This archipelago consists of ten principal islands, of which five exceed the others in size. They are situated under the Equator, and between five and six hundred miles westward of the coast of America. They are all formed of volcanic rocks; a few fragments of granite curiously glazed and altered by the heat, can hardly be considered as an exception. Some of the craters, surmounting the larger islands, are of immense size, and they rise to a height of between three and four thousand feet. Their flanks are studded by innumerable smaller orifices. I scarcely hesitate to affirm, that there must be in the whole archipelago at least two thousand craters. These consist either of lava and scoriæ, or of finely-stratified, sandstone-like tuff. Most of the latter are beautifully symmetrical; they owe their origin to eruptions of volcanic mud without any lava: it is a remarkable circumstance that every one of the twenty-eight tuff-craters which were examined, had their southern sides either much lower than the other sides, or quite broken down and removed. As all these craters have apparently been formed when standing in the sea, and as the waves from the trade-wind and the swell from the open Pacific here unite their forces on the southern coasts of all the islands, this singular uniformity in the broken state

of the craters, composed of the soft and yielding tuff, is easily explained.

Considering that these islands are placed directly under the Equator, the climate is far from being excessively hot; this seems chiefly caused by the singularly low temperature of the surrounding water, brought here by the great southern Polar current. Excepting during one short season, very little rain falls, and even then it is irregular; but the clouds generally hang low. Hence, whilst the lower parts of the island are very sterile, the upper parts, at a height of a thousand feet and upwards, possess a damp climate and a tolerably luxuriant vegetation. This is especially the case on the windward sides of the islands, which first receive and condense the moisture from the atmosphere.

In the morning (17th) we landed on Chatham Island, which, like the others, rises with a tame and rounded outline, broken here and there by scattered hillocks, the remains of former craters. Nothing could be less inviting than the first appearance. A broken field of black basaltic lava, thrown into the most rugged waves, and crossed by great fissures, is everywhere covered by stunted, sunburnt brushwood, which shows little signs of life. The dry and parched surface, being heated by the noonday sun, gave to the air a close and sultry feeling, like that from a stove: we fancied even that the bushes smelt unpleasantly. Although I diligently tried to collect as many plants as possible, I succeeded in getting very few; and such wretched-looking little weeds would have better become an arctic than an equatorial Flora. The brushwood appears, from a short distance, as leafless as our trees during winter; and it was some time before I discovered that not only almost every plant was now in full leaf, but that the greater number were in flower. The commonest bush is one of the Euphorbiaceæ: an acacia and a great odd-looking cactus are the only trees which afford any shade. After the season of heavy rains, the islands are said to appear for a short time partially green. The volcanic island of Fernando Noronha, placed in many respects under nearly similar conditions, is the only other country where I have seen a vegetation at all like this of the Galapagos Islands.

The *Beagle* sailed round Chatham Island, and anchored in several bays. One night I slept on shore on a part of the island, where black truncated cones were extraordinarily numerous: from one small eminence I counted sixty of them, all surmounted by craters more or less perfect. The greater number consisted merely of a ring of red scoriæ or slags, cemented together: and their height above the plane of lava was not more than from fifty to a hundred feet: none had been very lately active. The entire surface of this part of the island seems to have been permeated, like a sieve, by the subterranean vapours: here and there the lava, whilst soft, has been blown into great bubbles; and in other parts, the tops of caverns similarly formed have fallen in, leaving circular pits with steep sides. From the regular form of the many craters, they gave to the country an artificial appearance, which vividly reminded me of those parts of Staffordshire, where the great iron-foundries are most numerous. The day was glowing hot, and the scrambling over the rough surface and through the intricate thickets, was very fatiguing; but I was well repaid by the strange Cyclopean scene. As I was walking along I met two large tortoises, each of which must have weighed at least two hundred pounds: one was eating a piece of cactus, and as I approached, it stared at me and slowly stalked away; the other gave a deep hiss, and drew in its head. These huge reptiles, surrounded by the black lava, the leafless shrubs, and large cacti, seemed to my fancy like some antediluvian animals. The few dull-coloured birds cared no more for me, than they did for the great tortoises.

[c] Two of the unique species on the Galapagos Isles, which gave Charles Darwin the key to 'that mystery of mysteries – the first appearance of new beings on this earth,' have recently become extinct.

At least two other species are in immediate peril of being wiped out by human intervention in the delicate balance of natural life on the 13 islands – and more are threatened in the near future by tourism from Ecuador, 600 miles away.

Alan and Joan Root, of Anglia Television's 'Survival Unit,' who spent three months shooting the film with the Darwin Foundation Research Station, said this yesterday after seeing the finished version of their film, 'The Enchanted Isles.'

Last night, at the National Film Theatre, it became the first television documentary to have a royal première. It will be shown on all networks on December 5.

The Roots said the Narborough Island tortoise and the Pinta Island tortoise had been wiped out by rats, introduced either by early buccaneers or by the 2,000 Ecuadorian colonists, who had brought with them cats, dogs, pigs, and other predators. Tortoises on Hook Island were down to 'about five,' and there were only about 40 or 50 adult tortoises on Duncan Island.

It was the versatile, physical adaptation of tortoises, finches, iguanas, and other species to different conditions on different islands where they had few natural enemies, which in 1835 gave Darwin the first stirrings of his theory that 'no living thing was created ready made' – the Theory of Evolution.

But now, the Roots said yesterday, Galapagos faces the prospect of 20 tourists a month from Ecuador a number that is expected to increase.

The Darwin Foundation, they said, lacked the staff and money to ensure that tourists did not disturb the uniquely tame birds and mammals, or to find efficient ways of reducing the predators, which had already 'ruined' several islands.

None of these fears is mentioned in the film – which was was seen last night by the Queen, the Duke of Edinburgh (president of the World Wildlife Fund), and Miss Jennie Lee, Minister responsible for the Arts – although the aim of the première was to raise money to replace the Foundation's defunct research ship Beagle II.

11

Compare the three following treatments of a similar theme:

[a]   Beneath those rugged elms, that yew-tree's shade,
      Where heaves the turf in many a mould'ring heap,
    Each in his narrow cell for ever laid,
      The rude Forefathers of the hamlet sleep.

The breezy call of incense-breathing morn,
    The swallow twittering from the straw-built shed,
The cock's shrill clarion, or the echoing horn,
    No more shall rouse them from their lowly bed.

For them no more the blazing hearth shall burn,
    Or busy housewife ply her evening care:
No children run to lisp their sire's return,
    Or climb his knee the envied kiss to share.

Oft did the harvest to their sickle yield,
    Their furrow oft the stubborn glebe has broke:
How jocund did they drive their team afield!
    How bow'd the woods beneath their mighty stroke!

Let not Ambition mock their useful toil,
    Their homely joys, their destiny obscure;
Nor Grandeur hear with a disdainful smile
    The short and simple annals of the poor.

The boast of heraldry, the pomp of power,
    And all that beauty, all that wealth e'er gave,
Awaits alike the inevitable hour.
    The paths of glory lead but to the grave.

[b]   Only a man harrowing clods
          In a slow silent walk
       With an old horse that stumbles and nods
          Half asleep as they stalk.

       Only thin smoke without flame
          From the heaps of couch-grass;
       Yet this will go onward the same
          Though Dynasties pass.

       Yonder a maid and her wight
          Come whispering by:
       War's annals will cloud into night
          Ere their story die.

[c]   Iago Prytherch his name, though, be it allowed,
      Just an ordinary man of the bald Welsh hills,
      Who pens a few sheep in a gap of cloud.
      Docking mangels, chipping the green skin
      From the yellow bone with a half-witted grin
      Of satisfaction, or churning the crude earth
      To a stiff sea of clods that glint in the wind –
      So are his days spent, his spittled mirth
      Rarer than the sun that cracks the cheeks
      Of the gaunt sky perhaps once in a week.
      And then at night see him fixed in his chair
      Motionless, except when he leans to gob in the fire.
      There is something frightening in the vacancy of his mind.
      His clothes, sour with years of sweat
      And animal contact, shock the refined,
      But affected, sense with their stark naturalness.
      Yet this is your prototype, who, season by season
      Against siege of rain and the wind's attrition,
      Preserves his stock, an impregnable fortress
      Not to be stormed even in death's confusion.
      Remember him then, for he, too, is a winner of wars,
      Enduring like a tree under the curious stars.

12

Compare the two following responses to a great cathedral:

[a] When I was in Paris preparing these lectures I went one
Sunday afternoon to the cathedral of Notre-Dame. As I looked up at the tremendous vertical lines of the nave I found that
there were tears in my eyes. Why is it that one is sometimes
moved in this way by a great church? When I left Notre-Dame
I walked around the outside and looked at the mountain of
stone, supported by its flying buttresses. Then, sitting in
the sun, I speculated on this extraordinary human habit of
making great buildings. As a biologist I naturally considered,
first, what may be its significance for human survival, and,
secondly, why do such works move us in this way?

I have been maintaining in earlier lectures that a special
characteristic of modern man is the faculty of communication between individuals. I believe that it is possible to show
that the symbols of society, such as churches, form a link
in the process of ensuring communication. They play an
essential part in establishing the rules of brain action that
make co-operation possible. Our emotion when faced with
them confirms the importance of communication in our lives.
The symbol gives a sudden powerful reminder of our depen-
dence upon others and elicits one of our earliest responses –
crying. I want now to try to use these ideas to help in tracing
the development of communication, both in the history of the
race and in each individual person. In doing so I shall suggest
one of the main reasons why these symbols of religion become
the most important features of our lives.

The great new societies that grew up with the development
of irrigation and other special forms of agriculture came to
use some striking new means for keeping individuals together.
By study of the remains left by these early civilisations, and
by comparison with modern man, we can make a plausible re-
construction of how this came about. The methods that
emerged were based on a continuation of the ways of brain
action used by mammals for millions of years already. To
find out what these methods were let us look at two of the
characteristic actions of social man.

First, there is a tendency for large numbers to assemble
together at one place. There is evidence of this from earliest
times to the great crowds that gather today for rallies, con-
gresses, processions, football matches, and many other

events. Secondly, much effort is spent in building great structures within or around which these assemblies take place. The largest and most durable buildings that men make are not generally used mainly for the daily business of life, but are symbolic or religious. It is curious that biologists have paid so little attention to these two peculiar human characteristics. In no other animal is the habit of assembly quite so well developed as it is in man. The biological significance of the habit is that by it the brain associations necessary for communication are formed. Some of the earliest of these assemblies occurred at prominent hills of suitable shape, on and around which large numbers of people came together. One of the clearest pieces of evidence that we have about early social man is that he soon began to build large artificial hills. Objects nearly as big as anything that we build now were the product of some of the early agricultural communities, nearly 10,000 years ago. Such huge objects are found all over the world – an English example is Silbury Hill in Wiltshire.

I suggest that the value of building these objects was that they and their names were the signs by which men were trained to react to each other in such a way as to make society possible. At first, this must have been learned by all coming together at one place. Ritual feasting at such assemblies would indicate the satisfaction to be derived from association. Perhaps sacrificial ceremonies indicated the dangers of separation from the community – for this purpose, human sacrifice is no doubt best of all. Such ceremonies are occasions of training of the brains of the members of the community, so that they shall continue to react correctly, and hence get a living by co-operation and communication. Mankind has gone on assembling and building assembly places ever since. It is assuredly one of those features that the biologist should notice about him, that he tends to come together at intervals in huge swarms. Generally he puts on his finest clothes for the occasion and watches some display, whose symbolism often involves a struggle in which someone is victorious over someone else.

[b] When he saw the cathedral in the distance, dark blue lifted watchful in the sky, his heart leapt. It was the sign in heaven, it was the Spirit hovering like a dove, like an eagle over the earth. He turned his glowing ecstatic face to her, his mouth opened with a strange, ecstatic grin.

'There she is,' he said.

The 'she' irritated her. Why 'she'? It was 'it'. What was the cathedral, a big building, a thing of the past, obsolete, to excite him to such a pitch? She began to stir herself to readiness.

They passed up the steep hill, he eager as a pilgrim arriving at the shrine. As they came near the precincts, with castle on one side and cathedral on the other, his veins seemed to break into a fiery blossom, he was transported.

They had passed through the gate, and the great west front was before them, with all its breadth and ornament.

'It is a false front,' he said, looking at the golden stone and the twin towers, and loving them just the same. In a little ecstasy he found himself in the porch, on the brink of the unrevealed. He looked up to the lovely unfolding of the stone. He was to pass within to the perfect womb.

Then he pushed open the door, and the great pillared gloom was before him, in which his soul shuddered and rose from her nest. His soul leapt, soared up into the great church. His body stood still, absorbed by the height. His soul leapt up into the gloom, into possession, it reeled, it swooned with a great escape, it quivered in the womb, in the hush and the gloom of fecundity, like seed of procreation in ecstasy.

She too was overcome with wonder and awe. She followed him in his progress. Here, the twilight was the very essence of life, the coloured darkness was the embryo of all light, and the day. Here, the very first dawn was breaking, the very last sunset sinking, and the immemorial darkness, whereof life's day would blossom and fall away again, re-echoed peace and profound immemorial silence.

Away from time, always outside of time! Between east and west, between dawn and sunset, the church lay like a seed in silence, dark before germination, silenced after death. Containing birth and death, potential with all the noise and transition of life, the cathedral remained hushed, a great involved seed, whereof the flower would be radiant life inconceivable, but whose beginning and whose end were the circle of silence. Spanned round with the rainbow, the jewelled gloom folded music upon silence, light upon darkness, fecundity upon death, as a seed folds leaf upon leaf and silence upon the root and flower, hushing up the secret of all between its parts, the death out of which it fell, the life into which it has dropped, the immortality it involves, and the death it will embrace again.

13

Compare:

[a]   THE AGE (View I)

For fifteen years I have lived in the flats, rooms, and garrets of
this city, the drawers of the human filing-cabinets that stand in
blank rows down the streets of Kensington and Notting Hill.
Yet when I talk of my home I still think of that damp, green
valley near Painswick where I was brought up. The boys I went to
school with have long since grown and fattened, got married and
gone bald, and they would probably have to give me a very long
look before they recognised me if I turned up there again. But
that is my home, and the image of it the day I left it is still more
real to me that fifteen years of this crowded capital city.

There is one great virtue in size, and, of course, London *is* the
greatest show on earth, for never have so many human characters
been gathered together at one place. Here, in a day, you can see
the world. Stand at the entrance to a mainline railway station,
during the rush-hour, and you see every possible human species
scurrying past. One becomes amazed and transported by the
multiplicity of the human face, by its infinite differences, by its
almost prismatic graduations from ugliness to beauty, evil to
good. And you cannot get this concentrated view anywhere but
London. The sad, noisy clamour of life lived at close quarters;
lovers in doorways, children in back-streets, singing on bus-tops
on Saturday nights, whelk stalls, fish shops, cinemas, fairs,
chimneys on fire, and the warmth in the winter streets generated
by a million fires and a million bodies – it is this mass gregariousness, this feeling that one is at a non-stop party, that I like best
of all.

Yet even this makes me long more for home. For this very
gregariousness whets the appetite to know more of the human
story, and in the country personal histories are everybody's
property, but in London, man is the most secret animal on earth.
And his translation seems to me to be a symbol of the change
which everything undergoes on its way from country to city.

[b]   THE AGE (View II)

To look back on the first fifty years of this century is, for one who
has lived through them, a terrifying experience. We have meant
well. It is hard to see what we have done to land us in this age of
unparalleled oppression and cruelty and haunting dread. We are

not a harsh and inhuman generation; on the contrary, in the western world at least, we have been constantly carrying further our old practice of making our laws more merciful, our customs and institutions more sympathetic to the unfortunate. We are not a decadent age. On the contrary, in athletic contests this century is surpassing all previous records; in war and in exploration it has shown itself an age of heroes. We are not stationary and unprogressive. Quite the reverse; the advances made in every kind of science, from astronomy and physics to medicine and even sociology, have been greater than in any other half-century of human history.

Besides, man has much greater power over his whole environment. The improved methods of communication and locomotion have turned distant nations into neighbours, and made the world smaller and more manageable. International co-operation, once so difficult, has become an easy thing. Why is it that all the increased powers of improving the general life of mankind have somehow gone wrong?

Our time of hardship and discomfort will last, and may become worse, but who is afraid of hardship and discomfort for the sake of freedom? Have we the men and women who are capable both of meeting the danger and suffering that may well lie before us, and capable also of the more difficult but inevitable task, not merely of resisting evil but in the end of overcoming evil with good? Here I am hopeful. In every country of the west we have abundant records of heroism and endurance. In every centre of suffering and danger there has been a rush of voluntary workers eager to help – and, which is sometimes harder – even to forgive. They are a dauntless band, not in this country only, but in almost every country of western Europe. I have seen enough of the ordinary unsensational relief to children, to refugees and displaced persons, to feel quite clear that if we do fail in our combat with evil things, it will at any rate not be from lack of charity. Psychologically speaking, I suspect that the frightful harvest of hate over the world has generated in the heart of man its own antidote.

[c]   THE AGE (View III)

Somebody said – what was it – we get our cooking from Paris (that's a laugh), our politics from Moscow, and our morals from Port Said. Something like that, anyway. Who was it? (*Pause.*) Well, you wouldn't know anyway. I hate to admit it, but I think I can understand how her Daddy must have felt when he came back from India, after all those years away. The old Edwardian brigade do make their brief little world look pretty tempting. All home-made cakes and croquet, bright ideas, bright uniforms. Always the same picture: high summer, the long days in the sun, slim volumes of verse, crisp linen, the smell of starch. What a romantic picture. Phoney too, of course. It must have rained sometimes. Still, even I regret it somehow, phoney or not. If you've no world of your own, it's rather pleasant to regret the passing of someone else's. I must be getting sentimental. But I must say it's pretty dreary living in the American Age – unless you're an American of course.

I suppose people of our generation aren't able to die for good causes any longer. We had all that done for us, in the thirties and the forties, when we were still kids. (*In his familiar, semi-serious mood.*) There aren't any good, brave causes left. If the big bang does come, and we all get killed off, it won't be in aid of the old-fashioned, grand design. It'll just be for the Brave New-nothing-very-much-thank-you. About as pointless and inglorious as stepping in front of a bus. No, there's nothing left for it, me boy, but to let yourself be butchered by the women.

14
THE ENGLISH

Compare the following:

[a]   Shall I compare thee to a summer's day?
        Thou art more lovely and more temperate.

To describe his beloved, Shakespeare referred typically to the weather, for the English are moulded by the elements – first by the limitless salt waters that surround them, and secondly by the sweet waters which bring gentle and subtle life to their green homelands. Only secondarily are they conditioned by men.

One of England's greatest virtues is her cultivated instinct for living time – that fluid organic time of plants, animals and children – heard in the music of Dowland, Orlando Gibbons, or Purcell, or in the spoken word in prose or poetry.

The Teuton-American's arbitrariness, the Gallic cleverness are both equally alien to the English spirit. 'Not competitive but superior' should be his motto – as the Rolls Royce car which does not on principle participate in motor tournaments. Passionate and sensitive, yet avoiding all obvious emotional display, slow to rise to anger, patient in compromise, original and eccentric, yet a responsible subject, citizen or companion, reliable member of a community or team, an Englishman none the less has a reserve of creative and vital power, a capacity for adaptation and tolerance, a decorum together with an all-pervading good humour, a courtesy combined with firmness, which are unique qualities and about which he must now, against his inclination, become supremely aware, so that in our inimical age he may cultivate and protect them for the good of a humanity for which they are daily becoming more rare and more precious.

Faced with a world increasingly technocratic and less organic, obliged to compete on mainly alien ground where once she enjoyed vast home territories, England has to adjust herself to a way of life which she may find hard. One fervently hopes that in this adaptation she will not jettison those sovereign qualities for which she has for so long been trusted, respected and loved.

[b] What I like most about England is the civilised quality of living there. Some of the things that go to produce it are material, like the comfort and convenience of your public transport, and English pubs, where a stranger can find people to talk to and get advice on anything at all, from where to buy a dog to which is the nearest pleasant park for the children to play in. And the milk and the newspapers are delivered to your door, and the quality of the better Sunday newspapers is a very high average, and the best of your food is splendid. I still remember steak and oyster pudding, and roast Angus beef, and a wine bar in the Strand where we used to go every Wednesday to eat Stilton that had been delivered on Monday and had port poured into it. It was perfect by Wednesday.

Some of them come from the fact that there is not in your country an inordinate lust for individual power, and so there is less ambition and intriguing, more kindness and less elbow play. You achieve efficiency without standardisation. Life seems leisurely, but your top research and technology ranks high in Europe. The scope and objectivity of the BBC's foreign news is acknowledged everywhere. Your hospitals have great technical efficiency but they have kept their humanity. One of my children was born in the Westminster. Since my wife still had difficulties with the English language,

I wondered how she, as a foreigner, would be treated there. What we found was sympathy and special kindness and attention from every member of the staff involved.

These are values which must be preserved if England becomes continental.

[c] Divested of empire and reduced by circumstance from its former global primacy, Great Britain is passing through one of those difficult historical transitions that tax to the utmost the moral resources of a great people. Friends and admirers of Britain all over the world are observing the change with sympathy and apprehension; for my own part I observe it with a good deal of hope and confidence as well.

The loss which Britain has suffered, I firmly believe, is more one of sentiment than of substance. There will be no more Kiplingesque poetry about valorous deeds in India and the Sudan, no more Palmerstonian rhetoric about Englishmen striding the world like Roman citizens of antiquity. The romance of world empire and of the Grand Fleet is at an end. It is understandable, probably inevitable, that the loss is saddening and disruptive. That it is deeply damaging as well, condemning the British people to neurotic despondency or mediocrity, I very much doubt.

I doubt it because the passing of imperial primacy is a liberation as well as a loss. It is first of all a liberation from onerous expense, the expense of vast armaments, of gun-boat diplomacy and dubious expeditions for the purpose of of punishing trivial wrongs or intruding where one has no business. Empires, no doubt, are exciting for buccaneers and enriching for a few business men. But for ordinary people the only reward is pride – not the self-respecting kind of pride of a man who had really accomplished something, but the hollow and vicarious pridefulness of those who lacking or deprived of genuine personal satisfactions, find solace in the romantic adventures of others.

It is this dream that is lost when empire passes. But is it really a loss or is it, as I strongly suspect, more of a liberation – a liberation from the extravagant waste of resources, a liberation from psychic illusion, a liberation from the arrogance and egotism to which power, inevitably, gives rise?

Deprived of empire but not of the soil in which British greatness took root and grew, Britain is free, as she has not been for centuries, to devote her major energies to the recultivation of that fertile soil. The source of British greatness is and always has been in Britain. It was not in the Empire or even on the seas, but rather in the life and history of the United Kingdom that British people created a great literature, spawned the industrial revolution, and developed their *extraordinary* talent for government.

Britain has bequeathed a great legacy to much of the world, the legacy of her own experience in constitutional government, peaceful evolution, and the orderly accommodation of diverse interests within a society. Many nations, including my own, have emulated the British example. Some have failed and others have succeeded but none to a degree exceeding the model itself.

[d]   NOTES ON THE ENGLISH CHARACTER
(1936)

Just as the heart of England is the middle classes, so the heart of the middle classes is the public-school system. This extraordinary institution is local. It does not even exist all over the British Isles. It is unknown in Ireland, almost unknown in Scotland (countries excluded from my survey), and though it may inspire other great institutions – Aligarh, for example, and some of the schools in the United States – it remains unique, because it was created by the Anglo-Saxon middle classes, and can flourish only where they flourish. How perfectly it expresses their character – far better, for instance, than does the university, into which social and spiritual complexities have already entered. With its boarding-houses, its compulsory games, its system of prefects and fagging, its insistence on good form and on *esprit de corps*, it produces a type whose weight is out of all proportion to its numbers.

On leaving his school, the boy either sets to work at once – goes into the army or into business, or emigrates – or else proceeds to the university and after three or four years there enters some other profession – becomes a barrister, doctor, civil servant, schoolmaster, or journalist. (If through some mishap he does not become a manual worker or an artist.) In all these careers his education, or the absence of it, influences him. Its memories influence him also. Many men look back on their school days as the happiest of their lives. They remember with regret that golden time when life, though hard, was not yet complex; when they all worked together and played together and thought together, so far as they thought at all: when they were taught that school is the world in miniature and believed that no one can love his country who does not love his school. And they prolong that time as best they can by joining their Old Boys' society; indeed, some of them remain Old Boys and nothing else for the rest of their lives. They attribute all good to the school. They worship it. They quote the remark that 'the battle of Waterloo was won on the playing-fields of Eton.' It is nothing to them that the remark is inapplicable historically and was never made by the Duke of Wellington, and that the Duke of Wellington was an Irishman. They go on quoting it because it expresses their sentiments; they feel that if the Duke of Wellington didn't make it he ought to have, and if he wasn't an Englishman he ought to have been. And they go forth into a world that is not entirely composed of public-school men or even of Anglo-Saxons, but of men who are as various as the sands of the sea; into a world of whose richness and subtlety they have no conception. They go forth into it with well-developed bodies, fairly developed minds, and undeveloped hearts. And it is this undeveloped heart that is largely responsible for the difficulties of Englishmen abroad. An undeveloped heart – not a cold one. The difference is important, and on it my next note will be based.

For it is not that the Englishman can't feel – it is that he is afraid to feel. He has been taught at his public-school that feeling is bad form. He must not express great joy or sorrow, or even open his mouth too wide when he talks – his pipe might fall out if he did. He must bottle up his emotions, or let them out only on a very special occasion.

Sources of Passages in Part II

11 *a* THOMAS GRAY, *Elegy Written in a Country Churchyard* (extract)
   b THOMAS HARDY, *In time of the Breaking of Nations*
   c R. S. THOMAS, *A Peasant*

12 *a* J. Z. YOUNG, *Doubt and Certainty in Science*
   b D. H. LAWRENCE, *The Rainbow*

13 *a* LAURIE LEE (from the Listener)
   b GILBERT MURRAY (from the Listener)
   c JOHN OSBORNE, *Look Back in Anger*

14 *a* YEHUDI MENUHIN
   b PAUL BORCIER
   c WILLIAM FULBRIGHT
   d E. M. FORSTER, *Abinger Harvest* (Notes on the English Character)

Extracts 14 *a*, *b* and *c* were taken from a series AS OTHERS SEE US published in the *Guardian* (London) during March 1968.

Appendix

SUGGESTIONS FOR READING

1 Some notable books in the modern study of Language:
   EDWARD SAPIR *Language*, Milford, 1922
   LEONARD BLOOMFIELD *Language*, Allen and Unwin, 1935
   B. L. WHORF *Language, Thought and Reality*, Chapman, 1956
   J. R. FIRTH *Papers in Linguistics*, O.U.P., 1957
   I. A. RICHARDS *Interpretation in Teaching*, Kegan Paul, 1937

2 Some books with closer reference to classroom activities:
   I. A. RICHARDS *How to Read a Page*, Routledge, 1943.
   R. QUIRK *The Use of English*, Longman, 1962
   JOHN WILSON *Language and the Pursuit of Truth*, C.U.P. 1956
   S. HAYAKAWA *Language in Thought and Action*, G. Allen & Unwin, 1952
   J. PRESS (*ed.*) *The Teaching of Literature Overseas*, Methuen 1962